"If you're on the lookout for the rare and elusive combination of a commentary that can explain the basics of what the text means and provide practical help in preaching it, then you need look no further. Shaddix and Akin explain the text, illustrate and apply it, and provide clear sermon outlines to boot. If I were preaching 2 Peter or Jude, I would utilize this volume."

David Allen, dean of the School of Preaching, Southwestern Baptist Theological Seminary

"I love the pastoral usefulness of these commentaries. The explanations are theologically rich and accurate—never abstract or merely academic. There is additionally a serious intent to serve pastors who must connect with the lives and struggles of God's people through thoughtful illustration and meaningful application. But nothing is as impactful or as intentional as the consistent Christ-focused content, relating our responses to the grace of God that pervades Scripture for those with the eyes to see and the heart to share."

Bryan Chapell, senior pastor, Grace Presbyterian Church, Peoria, Illinois

"Every devoted student and faithful teacher of God's Word looks for commentaries that provide sound textual insights while also being both readable and relevant. This is precisely why Akin and Shaddix's volume on 2 Peter and Jude is such an invaluable resource for anyone who is studying or preparing to expound these important, though often neglected, epistles. The work of these two renowned scholars and practitioners epitomizes the Christ-centered, text-driven distinction that has become synonymous with this series!"

Scott Pace, associate professor of Preaching and Pastoral Ministry, Southeastern Baptist Theological Seminary

"Sometimes it seems that scholars write commentaries primarily for other scholars. Though their commentaries are erudite and comprehensive, the busy pastor cannot possibly wade through their lengthy and complex discussions of various views in his weekly task of sermon preparation. *Exalting Jesus in 2 Peter and Jude* digests the discussions in the best commentaries for the busy pastor. Shaddix and Akin offer sound exegesis, faithful theological reflection, and fresh and timely illustrations, and they constantly show how these neglected New Testament books exalt our Savior and edify the saints. A great resource for the biblical expositor!"

Chuck Quarles, professor of New Testament and Biblical Theology, Southeastern Baptist Theological Seminary

"Unfortunately, 2 Peter and Jude are often ignored in churches today, but they have a vital message for today's church. Thankfully, Shaddix and Akin have written commentaries to help fill the gap. Here we have faithful exposition and powerful application so that we see how the message of 2 Peter and Jude apply today. Pastors, teachers, and all who want to learn from the Scriptures will be encouraged and strengthened in reading this work."

Tom Schreiner, associate dean of Theology, The Southern Baptist Seminary

"Dr. Akin and Dr. Shaddix have created a commentary that will actually help real preachers preach real sermons in real churches. This is practical scholarship at it's finest."

Jimmy Scroggins, lead pastor, Family Church, West Palm Beach, Florida

"Jim Shaddix and Danny Akin have crafted a marvelous tool for generations of pastors, preachers, and Bible students. With careful attention to the detail of the text, yet equal devotion to the grand sweep of Scripture's focus on Christ, they have produced a beautifully balanced commentary on 2 Peter and Jude. Their thoughtful exegesis is punctuated with insightful illustration and organized into outlines that reflect the natural structure and seams of the apostolic authors and allow these ancient letters their full power to speak into life today. Their scholarship and clarity make this satisfying to the seminary professor and the novice alike."

Hershael York, Victor and Louise Lester Professor of Preaching, The Southern Baptist Theological Seminary

CHRIST-CENTERED

Exposition

NT / COMMENTARY

FEATURING

AUTHORS **Jim Shaddix and Daniel L. Akin**
SERIES EDITORS **David Platt, Daniel L. Akin, and Tony Merida**

CHRIST-CENTERED

Exposition

EXALTING JESUS IN

2 PETER AND JUDE

REFERENCE

NASHVILLE, TENNESSEE

SERIES DEDICATION

Dedicated to Adrian Rogers and John Piper. They have taught us to love the gospel of Jesus Christ, to preach the Bible as the inerrant Word of God, to pastor the church for which our Savior died, and to have a passion to see all nations gladly worship the Lamb.

—David Platt, Tony Merida, and Danny Akin
March 2013

AUTHOR'S DEDICATION

To Dad and Mom,
who taught me to long for our Lord's coming
and to let that longing inform the way I live.

—Jim Shaddix

TABLE OF CONTENTS

SERIES INTRODUCTION

Augustine said, "Where Scripture speaks, God speaks." The editors of the Christ-Centered Exposition Commentary series believe that where God speaks, the pastor must speak. God speaks through His written Word. We must speak from that Word. We believe the Bible is God breathed, authoritative, inerrant, sufficient, understandable, necessary, and timeless. We also affirm that the Bible is a Christ-centered book; that is, it contains a unified story of redemptive history of which Jesus is the hero. Because of this Christ-centered trajectory that runs from Genesis 1 through Revelation 22, we believe the Bible has a corresponding global-missions thrust. From beginning to end, we see God's mission as one of making worshipers of Christ from every tribe and tongue worked out through this redemptive drama in Scripture. To that end we must preach the Word.

In addition to these distinct convictions, the Christ-Centered Exposition Commentary series has some distinguishing characteristics. First, this series seeks to display exegetical accuracy. What the Bible says is what we want to say. While not every volume in the series will be a verse-by-verse commentary, we nevertheless desire to handle the text carefully and explain it rightly. Those who teach and preach bear the heavy responsibility of saying what God has said in his Word and declaring what God has done in Christ. We desire to handle God's Word faithfully, knowing that we must give an account for how we have fulfilled this holy calling (Jas 3:1).

Second, the Christ-Centered Exposition Commentary series has pastors in view. While we hope others will read this series, such as parents, teachers, small-group leaders, and student ministers, we desire to provide a commentary busy pastors will use for weekly preparation of biblically faithful and gospel-saturated sermons. This series is not academic in nature. Our aim is to present a readable and pastoral style of commentaries. We believe this aim will serve the church of the Lord Jesus Christ.

Third, we want the Christ-Centered Exposition Commentary series to be known for the inclusion of helpful illustrations and theologically driven applications. Many commentaries offer no help in illustrations, and few offer any kind of help in application. Often those that do offer illustrative material and application unfortunately give little serious attention to the text. While giving ourselves primarily to explanation, we also hope to serve readers by providing inspiring and illuminating illustrations coupled with timely and timeless application.

Finally, as the name suggests, the editors seek to exalt Jesus from every book of the Bible. In saying this, we are not commending wild allegory or fanciful typology. We certainly believe we must be constrained to the meaning intended by the divine Author himself, the Holy Spirit of God. However, we also believe the Bible has a messianic focus, and our hope is that the individual authors will exalt Christ from particular texts. Luke 24:25-27,44-47 and John 5:39,46 inform both our hermeneutics and our homiletics. Not every author will do this the same way or have the same degree of Christ-centered emphasis. That is fine with us. We believe faithful exposition that is Christ centered is not monolithic. We do believe, however, that we must read the whole Bible as Christian Scripture. Therefore, our aim is both to honor the historical particularity of each biblical passage and to highlight its intrinsic connection to the Redeemer.

The editors are indebted to the contributors of each volume. The reader will detect a unique style from each writer, and we celebrate these unique gifts and traits. While distinctive in their approaches, the authors share a common characteristic in that they are pastoral theologians. They love the church, and they regularly preach and teach God's Word to God's people. Further, many of these contributors are younger voices. We think these new, fresh voices can serve the church well, especially among a rising generation that has the task of proclaiming the Word of Christ and the Christ of the Word to the lost world.

We hope and pray this series will serve the body of Christ well in these ways until our Savior returns in glory. If it does, we will have succeeded in our assignment.

David Platt
Daniel L. Akin
Tony Merida
Series Editors
February 2013

2 Peter

Remember Christ's Provision

2 PETER 1:1-4

Main Idea: Jesus has provided everything we need to grow in his likeness as we wait for his return.

I. **The Background (1:1)**
    A. The writer of the letter
    B. The origin of the letter
    C. The recipients of the letter
    D. The reason for the letter
II. **The Blessing (1:2)**
    A. The blessing of knowing Jesus
    B. The blessing of being reminded
III. **The Big Idea (1:3-4)**
    A. The power to be like Christ (1:3)
    B. The process of becoming like Christ (1:3)
    C. The promise of being like Christ (1:4)

Every self-respecting sports fan knows the story of how Vince Lombardi, the legendary coach of the Green Bay Packers, started every season. He gathered his players together and gave them what became one of his most famous speeches. With a football in hand, the feared and revered coach would walk to the front of the meeting room, take a moment to gaze over the group of assembled players, hold out the pigskin in front of him, and say, "Gentlemen, this is a football." After describing the importance of the football as if no one on his team had ever seen one, he then would lead the team outside and show them the field. He would explain the out-of-bounds lines and the end zones and then remind the players that the football was intended to go across the end-zone line. Lombardi knew the importance of reminding his players about fundamentals . . . even the seasoned athletes. No doubt that emphasis played a huge role in his winning five NFL Championships—including Super Bowls I and II—during his tenure with the Packers.

Peter apparently also knew something about the importance of reminding people about fundamental truths. He wrote his second letter to equip the members of his flock to face and overcome the subtle spiritual deception of false teachers who were assaulting the church. But instead of giving them new information to mount their defense, the apostle simply wanted to remind his readers about the truth of the gospel they had already been taught (see 1:12-15; 3:1-2). He wanted to bring some things to their remembrance that were sufficient to protect and preserve them after his life was over.

The importance of remembering makes 2 Peter a timely and critical word for today's Christian. The explosion of television, radio, publications, the Internet, social media, websites, blogs, podcasts, and other forms of mass media makes heretical teaching easily accessible and widely received. Our rock star Christian culture provides false teachers with coliseum-size audiences who are eager to hear some new thing or have some new spiritual experience. And lack of discernment, fear of rejection, and misunderstanding of love leads the church to be reluctant to expose contemporary heretics. Instead of countering them, we welcome them into our fold, or at the very least just ignore them in the name of politically correct tolerance (MacArthur, *2 Peter*, 2). Numerous Christians today are doing nothing short of exchanging the truth for lies (cf. 1 Tim 1:19; 2 Tim 2:16-18). Consequently, we are in desperate need of being reminded about gospel truth to help us wage this war.

That's why it's so surprising that the book of 2 Peter had to fight its way into the canon of Scripture. Some books of the Bible have had to work harder than others to gain entrance into the canonical kingdom. They've had a little harder road to travel to make it into the catalog of Holy Scripture. Second Peter is one of those books; it's taken some hits along the way. Not a few Christian leaders have questioned its inclusion in the canon. "At the Reformation it was regarded as second-class Scripture by Luther, rejected by Erasmus, and regarded with hesitancy by Calvin" (M. Green, *2 Peter*, 19). But in the end the letter made the cut, and the church recognized its apostolic authorship, authoritative content, crucial role in the canon of inspired Scripture, and relevance for the church in every age.

Second Peter opens with the commonly used letter form of New Testament times. It included a reference to the writer and the recipients and then a greeting in the form of a blessing. Like other New Testament authors, Peter extended a theological description of the writer and the recipients as well as a specifically Christian wish for those receiving the correspondence (Vaughan and Lea, *1, 2 Peter*, 142).

The Background
2 PETER 1:1

The Writer of the Letter

This letter begins in a similar fashion to most first-century epistles: "Simeon Peter, a servant and an apostle of Jesus Christ." The apostle Peter is the stated author of the book in verse 1, and there's no good reason for us to think otherwise. In light of the numerous internal references (1:1,14,16-18; 3:1,15), it would be difficult to see how another author could have avoided ethical compromise with any Christian conviction at all. Additionally, there are some striking similarities in both vocabulary and doctrine between 1 and 2 Peter, as well as with Peter's speeches and sermons in Acts (M. Green, *2 Peter*, 47–48).

However, many have argued against Petrine authorship through the centuries. Opposing views have included: (1) the claim that the letter is pseudepigraphical, a writing published after Peter's death to honor him and to say what he might have said in a difficult situation; (2) its unpopular status among the church fathers; (3) the author's perceived dependence on Jude; and (4) the suggestion that Peter's reference to Paul in 3:15 indicates a time when a collection of Paul's writings had been made, which certainly would have been after Peter's lifetime. But none of these arguments have been able to overshadow the more natural and literal understanding that the apostle Peter is the one who penned the letter.

Peter introduces himself as "Simeon," a designation rarely used in the New Testament for the apostle (see Acts 15:14). The term is the Hebrew spelling for the name *Simon* and a possible indication of the authenticity of the letter (Vaughn and Lea, *1, 2 Peter*, 142). Peter also calls himself "a servant and an apostle of Jesus Christ." The word *servant* is *doulos* in Greek, which means "slave" or "bondservant." Peter, no doubt, is tempering the authority of his apostolic office with the personal humility that he learned through his own denial of Christ Jesus. Now he confidently can present himself as both the servant and the ambassador (*apostolos*) of his Lord.

A related issue to the authorship of 2 Peter is its source, specifically the close relationship between Peter's letter and the letter of Jude. Vaughan and Lea say, "There is such extensive agreement between Jude and 2 Peter that some common linkage is almost certain" (*1, 2 Peter*,

138). There are three primary views regarding the specific nature of this relationship. First is the proposal that Peter copied Jude. Proponents of this view cite Jude's fresh writing style and the probability that the longer letter would have taken its cue from the shorter one. Second, perhaps Jude copied Peter. This perspective leans on Peter's use of the future tense in forecasting the work of false teachers (cf. 2 Pet 2) in contrast to Jude's use of the present tense. Advocates of this view also say that someone with the status of an apostle wouldn't likely draw from a less prominent source like Jude. Third, some propose that both writers drew from a common source. This case is rooted in the differences in language, ideas, and order between the two letters. Such a common source could have been a document that condemned heretical doctrines that promoted antinomian ideas and prophesied the fate of their false heralds (M. Green, *2 Peter*, 72).

Regardless of who drew from what source, the similarities between the two letters are notable. Both letters provide similar descriptions of false teachers (see 2 Pet 2; Jude 4-19), although they develop their treatments differently. Peter gradually ramps up to addressing the issue of false teaching, while Jude comes out of the gate hammering on the heretics. But they basically address many of the same things that characterized the false teachers. First, false teachers denied the lordship of Christ (2 Pet 2:1; Jude 4). Second, they defiled the Christian love feast, practiced immorality, and influenced others to do the same (2 Pet 2:10,12-14; Jude 16). Third, they manipulated people with their speech to the end of financial gain (2 Pet 2:3,14; Jude 16). Fourth, they masqueraded as either visionaries or prophets to support their contentions (2 Pet 2:1; Jude 8). Fifth, they were headstrong and caused divisions that reflected their feelings of superiority (2 Pet 2:2,10,18; Jude 19). While I lean toward believing that Jude copied Peter, I think these similarities are the details that are most notable for us, simply because they help us better understand the issues being addressed in both letters (M. Green, *2 Peter*, 51-52).

The Origin of the Letter

Just like the uncertainty of the original source of 2 Peter, we really don't have any indication of its specific time and place of writing. While Peter chose not to mention these details, it likely was written from Rome shortly after his first letter and shortly before his death (see 1:14-15). That would put the date sometime prior to AD 68. More than for the specifics of this bibliographic information, Peter's greater concern obviously was for the believers to whom he was writing and the grave danger they were facing.

The Recipients of the Letter

Like the place and time of writing, there's no solid evidence to identify clearly Peter's recipients. They're just referred to as "those who have received a faith equal to ours through the righteousness of our God and Savior Jesus Christ." His seemingly intimate address, however, indicates that he wrote the letter to a specific group of people as opposed to a general audience (e.g., 1:10,12-15; 3:1,14). While it's possible that he was writing to Christians in the same provinces as he did in 1 Peter (see 1 Pet 1:1), this second letter seems to have a more Gentile flavor. It doesn't have any specific quotations from the Old Testament like the first letter, although it does have several references to Old Testament events (2:5,6,7,15).

What we do know about the people receiving this letter is how Peter felt about them. They were a people who had "received a faith equal to" the apostles, a faith that was just as precious as the salvation Jesus had given to his earliest and closest followers. The word "received" comes from *langchanō*, which means "to obtain by lot." Peter reminded his readers that their faith that was equal to that of the apostles was a gift of God's grace (Vaughn and Lea, *1, 2 Peter*, 142).

This glorious, exalted, and unmerited standing is theirs—and ours—"through the righteousness of our God and Savior Jesus Christ." It could not have come in any other way. Helm rightly says,

> Our ability to stand before God someday as rescued and
> reclaimed persons depends entirely on the righteousness of
> Jesus Christ. He alone has flown through this world without
> falling. He alone can and did make atonement for sin. Thus
> he alone can bring us home. (*1 & 2 Peter*, 187)

The equal privilege between apostles and all of us who have followed them is only due to the work of Christ on the cross.

Peter calls Jesus both "God" and "Savior." Scholars have debated whether he's drawing a distinction between God and Christ or if he's saying that Jesus is God. Some have suggested the former, citing the supposed distinction in 1:2 as support, as well as the close conjunction between "God" and "Savior." But the absence of the Greek article before "Savior" suggests that both terms refer to Jesus (see also John 1:1; 20:28; Heb 1:8). "Peter is taking the term 'Savior,' an Old Testament name for Jehovah, and is boldly applying it to Jesus" (Vaughn and Lea, *1, 2 Peter*, 143). It is the God of the universe who has made believers righteous, and his name is Jesus!

The Reason for the Letter

The absence of the specific identity of the readers doesn't in any way cloud the clarity of Peter's reason for writing. A key idea introduced in this salutation shows us where Peter is headed in his letter. First, the idea in 1:1 of his readers receiving an equally strong faith provides a foretaste of the themes of *falling* and *strengthening* that unfold in the words that follow. Peter will exhort his readers to "make every effort to confirm your calling and election, because if you do these things you will never stumble" (1:10). Peter was familiar with what it meant to fall. On that dark night before Jesus's crucifixion, he told his disciples, "Tonight all of you will fall away because of me, for it is written: I will strike the shepherd, and the sheep of the flock will be scattered" (Matt 26:31). To that pronouncement Peter immediately retorted, "Even if everyone falls away because of you, I will never fall away" (Matt 26:33). Do you remember Jesus's response to Peter's confident claim? "Truly I tell you, tonight, before the rooster crows, you will deny me three times" (Matt 26:34). And so Peter did. He knew what it meant to fall.

However, Peter also knew what it meant to get up again after you fall. In Luke's account of that same conversation, we find Jesus telling Peter, "Simon, Simon, look out. Satan has asked to sift you like wheat. But I have prayed for you that your faith may not fail. And you, when you have turned back, strengthen your brothers" (Luke 22:31-32). The word "strengthen" is *sterizō*, which means "to stand," "to set fast," or "to fix firmly." And so Peter did. In 1:12 of this current letter, he will say, "Therefore I will always remind you about these things, even though you know them and are established in the truth you now have." The word "established" here is *sterizō*, the same word as "strengthen" in Luke 22:32. And a negative form of this same word (*asteriktos*) will show up again in 2:14 where he warns that false teachers will "seduce unstable people." Then to top it all off, Peter will close his letter by using another form of the same word (*sterigmos*) to exhort his readers to "be on your guard, so that you are not led away by the error of lawless people and fall from your own stable position" (3:17). So three times we'll find variations on the same word—translated "established," "unstable," and "stable"—that Jesus used in Luke 22:32 to set the course of the remainder of Peter's ministry. "In this little letter, the term is leveraged afresh, along with the word *fall*, to capture Peter's intention in writing" (Helm, *1 & 2 Peter*, 186).

What is that intention? Peter obviously wanted to make sure his readers—and all of us who have followed them—would stand fast and be fixed firmly in the faith. So the one who fell, who—by the grace of Christ—was then strengthened to get back up, who was charged to then do the same for others, we now find obediently carrying out his assignment.

The Blessing
2 PETER 1:2

Similar to his first letter, Peter blesses his current readers in verse 2 by wishing "grace and peace" to them. Grace is the resource God gives to undeserving sinners for both conversion and sanctification. Peace is that blissful joy and contentment we have as a result of being made right with him. Together they describe the blessed condition of being right with God and growing into Christ's image (see also Rom 5:1-5). This blessed condition, however, doesn't exist in a vacuum. Peter will close his letter with the same ideas, emphasizing the proactive and dynamic nature of these conditions as they are lived out in the Christian life. So his desire here is for grace and peace to be multiplied in the lives of his readers "through the knowledge of God and of Jesus our Lord" (1:2). Grace and peace are increased by knowing God through Jesus Christ, a knowledge about which believers constantly need to be reminded.

The Blessing of Knowing Jesus

Peter implies that this blessed condition of grace and peace is brought about and fleshed out in its fullness only in the gospel. Specifically, he says it's found "through the knowledge of God and of Jesus our Lord," a construction that indicates that the object of this "knowledge" is both God and Jesus. And this knowledge is no mere intellectual exercise but instead is a genuine personal experience with the Lord Jesus, who is the only way for anyone to truly know God. "In a true sense it is Jesus alone who is the object of the knowledge of the Christian" (Vaughn and Lea, *1, 2 Peter*, 144). In short, grace and peace can only be found and experienced when one knows God, and one can only know God in relationship with Jesus Christ. This, beloved, is at the heart of the gospel!

It's incredibly important for us to consider the huge role *knowledge* plays in Peter's letter. Peter uses two different words in Greek that are both translated by our English word *knowledge*. The word used here in 1:2 as well as in 1:3; 1:8; and 2:20 is *epignōsis*, which is a reference to full knowledge, the most intimate kind of knowledge possible. But Peter also uses *gnōsis* in 1:5-6 and 3:18, which indicates good sense, understanding, and practical wisdom. It is often used to communicate the idea of knowing by experience.

Peter bookends his letter with this emphasis, opening here in 1:2 with a prayer for his readers to know God in Christ intimately and closing in 3:18 with an exhortation for them to know Christ experientially. In between he tells his readers that both the full knowledge of God and the experiential knowledge of God are necessary for them to stand fast and be fixed firmly in the faith as they wait for Jesus's return. Such a decisively anchored faith will be especially crucial if they are to be unwavering against the assault of heretical teachers whose doctrine is contrary to gospel truth (e.g., 1:16; 2:1; 3:3).

The importance of this charge can't be overestimated for the contemporary pilgrimage of believers in Christ. In the midst of a culture that champions truth as being relative, Christians need a strong foundation of objective reality to navigate their journey home. When I open the GPS app on my phone and plug in my destination, I expect the lady's voice coming out of the speaker to give me clear and accurate directions that are based on someone's real knowledge. And while there may be several alternate routes, they all are based on objective realities. The only chance I have to reach my destination is to get real knowledge that is based on what is true and right.

If this is true for something as trivial as getting me from my house to the closest Starbucks for a cup of coffee, how much weightier is having accurate knowledge about matters of life and death, eternity and entrance into God's kingdom! Certainly we need clear directions that are rooted in real knowledge for these things (Helm, *1 & 2 Peter*, 177). That's why Peter will say, "For in this way, entry into the eternal kingdom of our Lord and Savior Jesus Christ will be richly provided for you" (2 Pet 1:11). He wants his readers to make it, and the only chance we have is to have real knowledge that only comes through knowing Jesus!

The Blessing of Being Reminded

There's an implicit relationship between knowledge and the need to be reminded that I mentioned earlier. We can know something and yet from time to time push it into the shadows of our forgetfulness. And if that knowledge is crucial for our well-being, then we welcome someone who will remind us of it. That's what Peter does for his readers. Second Peter 1:12-15 serves as somewhat of a hinge paragraph for the letter. Three times in four verses Peter emphasizes his intention to remind his readers of needed spiritual truth. He says, "I will always remind you" (v. 12). He says, "I think it is right . . . to wake you up with a reminder" (v. 13). And he says, "I will also make every effort so that you are able to recall these things at any time after my departure" (v. 15). His words here appear to point backward to the truths he unfolds in 1:3-11, as well as forward to those he proposes in 1:16–3:18. And in the middle of that latter section, he will again emphasize his desire to remind his readers of things they can't afford to forget (3:1-2).

There's nothing new under the sun, and that includes in the realm of spiritual truth. People today don't need new truth but only to gain a clearer understanding of the eternal truth God has already revealed in his Word (Isa 40:8; 1 Pet 1:23-25; cf. Matt 5:18). Peter's opening line in the body of this letter asserts that we have been granted "everything required for life and godliness through the knowledge of him" (1:3). Peter—along with every preacher and teacher of the Word who has followed him—sees himself as responsible for reminding people of what God has said in his Word so that his truth will stick (MacArthur, *2 Peter*, 49).

Such repetition obviously is part of God's economy. In his inspired Word, Deuteronomy 5:1-22 is a restatement of the giving of the law at Sinai (Exod 20). The people were being reminded of what God said as part of their preparation to enter the promised land. Chronicles reviews much of the same material that we find in 1 and 2 Samuel and 1 and 2 Kings. The psalms echo the attributes and works of God. The Old Testament prophets were in sync with their common themes of law, judgment, and forgiveness.

The practice of repetition continues in the New Testament. All four Gospels recount many of the same aspects of Jesus's life, ministry, and teaching. And the Synoptics actually tell the same story from three different perspectives. Jesus often repeated his sermons, parables, and object lessons, which solidified their truth in the minds of his followers.

And the epistles largely are an explanation and application of the same gospel truth as it relates to the church and the Christian life.

So Peter's approach is consistent with the Bible's emphasis on the need for us to be reminded about truth by hearing it over and over again. The apostle Paul, like Peter, was a big fan of repeating truth for his followers: "To write to you again about this is no trouble for me and is a safeguard for you" (Phil 3:1). To the Romans he said, "I have written to remind you more boldly on some points" (Rom 15:15). To the Thessalonians he asked, "Don't you remember that when I was still with you I used to tell you about this?" (2 Thess 2:5). Jude took the same approach: "Now I want to remind you, although you came to know all these things once and for all" (Jude 5). These are just a few examples that illustrate the principle of divine repetition in Scripture.

The Big Idea
2 PETER 1:3-4

I love working with my hands—construction, remodeling, and even putting things together. Like many people, I order items off Amazon that sometimes require assembly. When I open the instructions, they usually tell me what I need to put the item together. Some instructions even show pictures of a drill, a tape measure, a level, and other items under a heading that says something like, "Items Needed for Assembly." At other times, however, the instructions pleasantly surprise me and say something like, "All items necessary for assembly are included." And underneath will be a picture of an Allen wrench, a template, or some other small item that's included in the box. How convenient! I don't even have to make the trip out to my shop and haul in a bunch of tools.

That's the kind of package God delivers when he saves someone: "All items necessary for assembly are included." The knowledge of God in Christ referenced in verse 2 lays the foundation for the big idea of Peter's letter in verses 3-4. Basically, these verses contain his proposition for everything else he'll say. In these verses Peter tells his readers that God has provided everything we need to grow in Christlikeness as we wait for his return, even in the face of false teaching. How? "Through the knowledge of him" (v. 3), a knowledge that includes his "very great and precious promises" (v. 4). Not the least of these promises is the assurance that he will come back for his people and bring to completion our journey toward sharing in "the divine nature" (v. 4), which arguably is the pressing issue in 2 Peter (1:11,16-21; 3:1-18). In verses 3-4 we find the assurance of Christ's *power* to be like Jesus, the *process* he's ordained to get us there, and the *promise* that we'll arrive safely and securely in his likeness.

The Power to Be like Christ (1:3)

What God ultimately desires for his children is that they look like his Son, Jesus Christ. The apostle Paul says that before time began God delighted in and marked out a group of people "to be conformed to the image of his Son, so that he would be the firstborn among many brothers and sisters" (Rom 8:29). Then when time did begin in Genesis 1, "God created man in his own image; he created him in the image of God; he created them male and female" (Gen 1:27). In Genesis 3 sin messed up that image. He said, "Since the man has become like one of us, knowing good and evil, he must not reach out, take from the tree of life, eat, and live forever" (Gen 3:22). Mankind had been created in the image of God, but that image had been perverted. God can know good and evil, and he can always choose good. Human beings can't. So God banished Adam and Eve from the garden so they wouldn't eat from the tree of life and remain in that wretched condition forever. And from that point the rest of the Bible is the story of God's activity in Christ to recover his image and restore the purpose he intended for mankind.

That's why Peter says Christ has given us everything we need that pertains to "life and godliness" (v. 3). That's just another way of describing the image of God for which we were created. The "life" here is true life, the life of God believers were created to have. The word "godliness" is a reference to practical conduct more than it is to mere devotional service. Jesus has provided everything that's needed for Christians to "flesh out" his life in everyday living so as to reflect his image. He's made it possible for us to grow and mature in the life we were created to have—life that we lost because of sin but that was restored to us through his resurrection. And this God-life is supposed to be expressed in practical ways through our daily conduct. The progressive maturity and practical godliness intended for the Christian will be unpacked more in verses 5-11.

So Peter begins by describing the resource necessary for living out the Christian's calling to be like Jesus. He describes it as "his divine power," obviously reaching back to the antecedent "of God and of Jesus our Lord" at the end of verse 2. This is God's power in Christ that we're talking about. The word for "power" is *dunamis*, from which we get our word *dynamite*. But this dynamite is different from our dynamite. The dynamite we know about has an initial loud explosion that wreaks havoc all around it, but then it's over. The dust settles, and we pick up the pieces. But the dynamite Peter uses is different. It's more like the gasoline you put in your car. It's not flashy and has no big bang. In fact, you really don't even see it. It's just a dependable, ongoing source of power that gets you where you're going.

Paul used *dunamis* in Ephesians 1:19-20 to describe this same resource that God—in Christ—has given to believers. Grasping for adequate descriptors, he said he wanted us to know "what is the immeasurable greatness of his power toward us who believe, according to the mighty working of his strength" (Eph 1:19). And if that were not enough, what he says next is absolutely astounding! Paul says that God "exercised this power in Christ by raising him from the dead and seating him at his right hand in the heavens" (Eph 1:20). In other words, the power that's been given to believers to live out their calling faithfully is the same power that it took to raise Jesus from the dead and seat him at God's right hand!

So when Peter said that "his divine power has given us" everything we need to look like Jesus, he could've just dropped the mic and walked off the stage! Enough said. All bets are off, and all excuses are rendered null and void. When the power of God through Christ is at play in the Christian life, the believer has absolutely everything he or she needs to be true to the calling of spiritual maturity and growth in Christlikeness. No exceptions and no excuses. God wants us to know that he didn't save us and then say, "Now, knock yourself out!" or "Good luck out there!" He didn't do the work of redeeming us and then leave us on our own as far as surviving and growing in our faith. "His divine power has given us everything required for life and godliness." There isn't anything outside of *everything*! In Christ, God has provided everything we need to mature in our faith and be faithful to the calling that he's exercised in our lives.

The Process of Becoming like Christ (1:3)

But exactly how does this progressive transformation take place? To answer that question, Peter makes an early installment in one of the key themes of his letter—knowing God through Christ. He says that growth in godliness comes by way of "the knowledge of him" (v. 3). Peter uses *epignōsis* here, which is full and intimate knowledge. Distinguished from *gnōsis*—good sense, understanding, and practical wisdom—this word conveys the idea that the one gaining the knowledge is playing a more comprehensive role in its acquisition. In the New Testament it frequently speaks of a knowledge that affects spiritual life in a profound way.

So Peter basically says that the believer's re-creation into the image of Christ comes about by way of active participation in the pursuit of knowing him more and more. Many believers limit their knowledge of God to their conversion. "I came to know Christ" or "I believed on Christ" are frequent confessions, as if knowing him was a one-time deal tied to conversion. But knowing God, Peter says, is a lifetime pursuit. And it's the avenue through which God's children access all the powerful resources he's provided to make them look more like Jesus. And remember—to know God is to know Jesus. Knowing Jesus is the way to know God.

In knowing Jesus, believers are called "by his own glory and goodness" (v. 3), indicating the agency of Christ's calling. In this context the word "glory" is a reference to Christ's splendor and majesty as a divine being, not his renown. The word "goodness" refers to his moral excellence, an idea that Peter will begin to unpack in verse 5 as having practical implications for believers. When combined together, these two words describe the divine moral excellence of Christ, focusing especially on the beauty of his goodness (Starr, *Sharers*, 42–44). We can actually experience true life and godly living through knowing Christ. That's why Paul says you "have put on the new self. You are being renewed in knowledge according to the image of your Creator" (Col 3:10). As we grow in this knowledge of Christ, we "are being transformed into the same image from glory to glory" (2 Cor 3:18). As we journey through this world, God intends for us to be growing to look more and more like Jesus.

The Promise of Being like Christ (1:4)

Finally, the end awaiting believers for such a journey is described in verse 4. While at conversion we begin to experience God's glorious radiance and moral excellence, that's not all he has in store for us. We are assured that we ultimately will look like him in the way God fully intended. Believers in Christ inherit "very great and precious promises" that have been given to God's people through the gospel. Specifically, the promises Peter has in mind are those involved in sharing "in the divine nature," which will happen fully when the Lord returns. This phrase has some similarities to Greek philosophical and religious thought but is couched in distinctively Christian terms.

Peter wasn't suggesting that Christians will actually *become* gods, be absorbed into deity, or even share in the divine nature in every way. He was simply saying they will be morally perfected by sharing in God's moral excellence. He's speaking of that real union with Christ Jesus that begins at conversion (cf. John 1:12; Rom 8:9; Gal 2:20) but won't ultimately be realized until he comes again. The apostle John articulated this "now but not yet" understanding well when he said, "Dear friends, we are God's children now, and what we will be has not yet been revealed. We know that when he appears, we will be like him because we will see him as he is" (1 John 3:2).

Peter apparently is tipping his hat here to what he will address later concerning the Lord's coming (1:11,16-21; 3:1-18). There he will counter head-on the false teachers' denial of Christ's future coming when they mockingly ask, "Where is his 'coming' that he promised?" (3:4). Peter understood that to deny the return of the Lord was to undercut the gospel, which promises the believer's moral perfection when Christ comes back. "If there is no future coming of Christ, their salvation does not include the promise of likeness to God, and the gospel is a sham" (Schreiner, *1 and 2 Peter*, 294).

The final phrase in verse 4—"escaping the corruption that is in the world because of evil desire"—describes the ultimate freedom Christians will experience as part of their reward when they finally participate in the divine nature. The aorist participle indicates a definitive act, one that will be realized when believers finally are released from the war with sinful flesh that characterizes their journey in this world. I can't wait for this glorious reward! Paul said, "We groan in this tent, desiring to put on our heavenly dwelling. . . . Indeed, we groan while we are in this tent, burdened as we are, because we do not want to be unclothed but clothed, so that mortality may be swallowed up by life" (2 Cor 5:2,4; cf. Rom 7:1-25). That's when our precious Lord "will wipe away every tear from their eyes. Death will be no more; grief, crying, and pain will be no more, because the previous things have passed away" (Rev 21:4). O, come quickly, Lord Jesus!

Conclusion

Most dads and granddads have had the same embarrassing experience at least once on Christmas morning. Here's how it looked at our house on more than one occasion. The kids wake up all excited, storm into our bedroom, and stir me and my wife out of bed. Then they hurry into the living room to get ready to open presents. After stumbling to the kitchen and putting the coffee on, we make our way into the living room and collapse sleepily into our chairs. After we read the Christmas story from the Bible and pray together, my daughter begins to hand out the gifts. And then inevitably one of the kids opens a gift that has the words "Batteries not included" printed on the box. Immediately my wife looks at me with panic in her voice and says, "Did you get the batteries?" My wide-eyed silence incriminates me. In that moment my kid slumps in disappointment and the joyful air escapes from the room like someone letting the air out of a tire. Cool present, but no batteries.

That never happens with the heavenly Father and his children. When he adopts us into his family, he does it with batteries included. He provides everything that's needed for us to experience true life, to live our lives in a way that reflects his character on the road of sanctification and to arrive safely at our glorification where we look fully like his Son, Jesus. None of us can ever say that we don't have what it takes to live the Christian life and grow in God's grace. He's provided everything we need in our knowledge of him through Jesus Christ.

No doubt Peter's readers had an intimate knowledge of God in Christ, and they had been given additional deposits of knowledge about him during their Christian journeys. That was knowledge they would need to remember. So Peter provides clear and right direction for them to remember, as well as for all who have come after Jesus's apostles passed off the scene. He knew that after his death people would push back against the gospel, and some would even abandon it. Believers would need to remember the answers to great gospel questions about final judgment, Christ's future coming, and life in light of these realities. And those answers would need to conform to real knowledge (Helm, *1 & 2 Peter*, 177). So they needed to be reminded—and we need to be reminded—about the differences between a true knowledge of God found only in Jesus Christ and the ideas being served up by false teachers today. This letter, then, is meant to remind us that the content of the gospel message as proclaimed by the apostles tells us what it really means to *know God*, and that knowledge fully equips us to live for him. That is truth we need to remember.

Reflect and Discuss

1. Is it important to affirm the apostle Peter as the author of this letter? If so, why?

2. In verse 1, how else could "servant" be translated? Why is this significant? Are all believers servants, or is this title unique to Peter and the other apostles?

3. Do believers today have "a faith equal to" the apostles? On what basis?

4. Because of a commonly used Greek construction, we can be confident that Peter describes Jesus as "our God and Savior." Why is affirming the deity of Jesus important?

5. What is significant about Peter's word choice of *epignōsis* in reference to knowing God? What does it mean to grow in/have "the knowledge of God and of Jesus our Lord"?

6. Why is there continual repetition throughout the Scriptures? How should we apply that principle in our lives and ministries?

7. We have been given everything we need to live godly lives. What keeps us from doing that sometimes? What stumbling blocks to Christ living through us need to be identified and removed?

8. What dangers arise when salvation (knowing Christ) is understood merely as a one-time, past event?

9. What does it mean to "share in the divine nature"?

10. In what ways do the hope and promise of eternal perfection with Jesus spur you on to live a godly life?

Remember Your Calling

2 PETER 1:5-11

Main Idea: Because of God's grace, believers must demonstrate and confirm their calling by reflecting Christ's character in daily living.

I. **Your Obligation to His Calling (1:5-9)**
    A. The appeal: Be progressing in your faith (1:5-7)!
    B. The aim: Be productive in your faith (1:8-9)!
II. **Your Validation of His Calling (1:10-11)**
    A. The plea: Be sure of your salvation (1:10)!
    B. The promise: Be steadfast in your salvation (1:10-11)!

In my estimation, one of the most astounding statements Jesus ever made came after a long day of healing and casting out demons among the citizens of Capernaum. The following morning his disciples pleaded with him to give the crowd an encore. And to be sure, there were still many cancers to heal, limbs to repair, and demons to cast out. But in response to their urging, our Lord spoke these words: "Let's go on to the neighboring villages so that I may preach there too. This is why I have come" (Mark 1:38). Wow! Jesus not only walked away from the opportunity to be hailed as a hero and carried around on everybody's shoulders, but he seemingly turned his back on some hurting people who hadn't made it to the front of the line during his previous day's ministry. Why? Because he knew his calling, and he unapologetically allowed that calling to order his priorities and dictate everything he did.

God wants us to know the calling he's placed on our lives. And he wants us to let that calling determine how we live. In verses 3-11 Peter appears to use numerous terms to refer to and describe the believer's calling. The words "faith" (v. 5), "the knowledge of our Lord Jesus Christ" (v. 8), "cleansing from his past sins" (v. 9), and "entry into the eternal kingdom of our Lord and Savior Jesus Christ" (v. 11) all refer to our position of being in right relationship to God through Jesus Christ. But probably the verb "called" (*kaleō*) in verse 3 and the noun "calling" (*kalēsis*) in verse 10 provide us with the best references to this sovereign work of God in salvation. They frame up this paragraph and remind us that without any help or initiative from us, God has *called* us to himself in Jesus Christ. Consequently, our lives are to be defined by this gracious *calling.* So under the inspiration of the Holy Spirit, Peter exhorts us on how to steward this glorious calling.

Your Obligation to His Calling
2 PETER 1:5-9

The phrase "skin in the game" has been attributed to the American business magnate Warren Buffett. Supposedly the first fund the great investor and philanthropist ever raised was in the amount of $105,000 that he secured from eleven doctors, but only after he personally invested a token sum of $100. The meager C-note supposedly came to be known as Buffett's "skin in the game."

The glorious calling given to believers doesn't come without responsibility. If we are granted the power of God to embark on a journey of knowing God in order that we might be re-created into the image of God and one day share fully in the nature of God, then Peter says we have some skin in the game. But our "skin" in our calling is not something we invest in order to reap these benefits but an obligation we have as a result of already receiving them. And that obligation is to make sure our calling matures and doesn't remain stagnant. Peter unpacks this obligation with an *appeal* for his readers to progress in their faith with the *aim* of their being productive in their faith.

The Appeal: Be Progressing in Your Faith (1:5-7)!

Peter first issues his appeal to his readers for them to make progress in their calling. Specifically, this plea is to add certain moral traits to the believer's life as a result of having received God's call. The NEB translators insightfully capture Peter's heartbeat by rendering the first part of verse 5 as, "With all this in view, you should try your hardest to supplement your faith." In view of everything delineated in verses 3-4, believers are obligated to increase in some things that grow out of their call to faith! The believer's initial faith is merely the foundation on which God intends to build a full-orbed calling to re-creation into his image. And every believer has the responsibility of being a bricklayer in this divine construction project, adding bricks of increasing influence!

Here again we find the beautiful tension in Scripture between divine sovereignty and human responsibility. Verses 3-4 radiate with the undeniable declaration that this calling is the work of God alone. But then—with what appears to be striking contrast—verse 5 leaps off the pages of the Bible screaming about the liability we have in doing something with this calling. Oh, that Christians today would become comfortable with resting in this mysterious tension!

Spurgeon is said to have been asked how he reconciled God's sovereignty with human responsibility. His response: I never try to reconcile friends! And neither should we. One of the many distinguishing factors between us and God is manifested in the numerous passages in the Bible that can only be reconciled in his mind, not ours. Maybe that's why Peter is pleading with his readers here. He knows that the glory of God's sovereignty has a tendency to lull his children into passivity. And believers can't afford to be passive about their stewardship of God's call.

Peter's appeal is followed by a list of certain attributes necessary for the believer's calling to mature. He lists seven of them in verses 5-7. The structure of these verses indicates that each attribute is connected to its predecessor by the verb "supplement" (*epichorēgeō*) found in verse 5. This word indicates generous and costly participation. The idea was drawn from Athenian drama festivals. A rich but generous donor, called the *chorēgos*, would help fund a production along with the writer and the state. He would try to outdo other donors by paying the expenses of the chorus, including lavish equipment and training. So the word came to represent generous and costly cooperation (M. Green, *2 Peter*, 86).

What an awesome concept! In light of God's generous and costly calling that he's given to us in Christ Jesus, we're compelled to do the same thing in cooperating with him in the work of maturing that calling. And when we do, he gets glory for it because it highlights his work! We would never want to cheapen the gospel by suggesting that it's anything less than the ultimate expression of God's generosity and sacrifice. One of the primary ways believers maintain the integrity of this gospel, then, is by generously and sacrificially building on their faith.

Peter suggests that all these attributes are qualities to be added generously and sacrificially to "your faith" (v. 5). As we previously noted, *faith* is one of many ideas in this paragraph that are synonymous with the believer's calling. Here it represents the believer's initial acceptance of the gospel, which is the basis for the entire Christian life. By identifying faith as the root of all the other virtues on the list, Peter illustrates what he's already said in verse 3: "His divine power has given us everything required for life and godliness through the knowledge of him." Again, that "knowledge" is the knowledge of Christ, and the believer receives that knowledge by faith (Bauckham, *2 Peter*, 185). Peter is providing a list of attributes that grow out of our initial faith in Christ.

So what bricks ought to be laid on the foundation of our faith in Christ? In progressive fashion Peter lists the seven additional qualities of Christian character in verses 5-7. The first five appear to be characteristics that grow out of one's relationship with God, while the last two represent one's relationship to his or her fellow man.

Goodness (v. 5). "Supplement your faith with goodness," Peter writes. He's talking here about raw goodness, or "moral excellence" as the NASB translates it. Vaughan and Lea say, "By this trait good habits are established, and fleshly desires are dissipated" (*1, 2 Peter*, 149). Nobody is born good or virtuous (see Rom 3:10-12,23). But believers in Christ can live out his goodness by his grace.

Knowledge (v. 5). Next, Peter makes another deposit in the "knowledge" conversation. Knowledge should be added to goodness. This word is *gnōsis*, which is practical wisdom, distinguishing it from the full and intimate knowledge used in verses 2 and 3. In context it's the wisdom and discernment that every Christian needs in order to live a virtuous life (Bauckham, *2 Peter*, 186).

Self-control (v. 6). This wisdom and discernment is to be followed by "self-control." To the Greeks this word carried the idea of controlling the passions instead of being controlled by them. But believers understand that controlling passions is only possible as one submits to the control of the indwelling Christ (M. Green, *2 Peter*, 88). Peter's readers needed reminding of this because the false teachers believed that following their own lusts and showing no restraint were signs of maturity (2:2; 3:3).

Endurance (v. 6). Peter's readers certainly would need this attribute. To self-control they must add "endurance" in order to persevere under the persecution coming their way. Michael M. Green describes this quality as "the temper of mind which is unmoved by difficulty and distress, and which can withstand the two Satanic agencies of opposition from the world without an enticement from the flesh within" (*2 Peter*, 88).

Godliness (v. 6). To perseverance should be added "godliness," the piety and devotion to God that is manifested in both right feeling and right behavior toward him. Believers should demonstrate appropriate respect and reverence toward their God, a posture that should then be expressed in relationships he has sanctioned as reflected in the two remaining qualities in verse 7 (Davids, *Letters*, 181).

Brotherly affection (v. 7). Peter turns his attention now toward the horizontal relationships informed by the first five attributes. To godliness, he says, should be added "brotherly affection." This affection is one that's to be shared between brothers and sisters in Christ and is manifested in expressions of things like kindness, generosity, and courtesy.

Love (v. 7). The pinnacle of Peter's list of attributes for Christian maturity is "love." This is the *agapē* love that God demonstrated to us and desires us to demonstrate to him and to others. This love has its origin in the agent—God—not in the object—us—which is the case with the other kinds of love described in the New Testament (*philia*, *eros*). It desires the highest good for the one being loved and demonstrates itself in sacrificial actions on behalf of that one (Vaughn and Lea, *1, 2 Peter*, 150).

Let's make three particular applications from Peter's list before moving on. One is a **reminder**: This list of qualities is driven by the divine nature in verses 3-4. Christians are able to live out this virtuous life not because of our efforts alone but because of Christ's life within us. As we know him more and more, our love and commitment are expressed through these attributes flowing from what God has done in us through Christ. As believers we must never allow ourselves to begin thinking that godly character is the result of our efforts.

A second application is a **challenge**: Nurture these qualities in your life. Peter isn't suggesting that Christians only possess faith at conversion and that they need to add to their faith these other virtues. Remember verse 3? God's power has already provided us with *everything* that pertains to life and godliness. And Peter will go on to imply in verse 8 that we already possess *all* of the qualities he's just listed (many of which actually are fruits of the Spirit!). The issue isn't whether the believer has them or not; the issue is that the believer needs to grow in the degree he or she is demonstrating them (Moo, *2 Peter*, 47). These qualities are to be ever increasing in their influence in our lives as disciples. So nurture them and turn them loose!

A third application is a **caution**: Don't be legalistic and limiting with this list! Outside of the bookend characteristics—faith and love—Peter likely has chosen familiar qualities from the Stoic and philosophical ethics of the Hellenistic world as representative examples of the kind of virtuous life the Christian faith should inspire (Bauckham, *2 Peter*, 185). Surely other fruits of the Spirit like joy, peace, and patience (Gal 5:22) are worthy attributes manifested in Christian maturity. So we shouldn't limit the measurement of our Christian growth by these seven qualities alone. Nor should we think something is amiss in our progress toward Christlikeness if one of these qualities doesn't follow in the order noted. The point is that authentic faith in Christ ought to ever be progressing in our lives by manifesting attributes like the ones on Peter's list.

The Aim: Be Productive in Your Faith (1:8-9)!

After his appeal and corresponding attributes, Peter then identifies, in verses 8-9, his aim in wanting believers to be productive in their faith. Notice how this aim is fleshed out with a positive (v. 8) and a negative (v. 9). Contrast the phrase "For if you possess these qualities" at the beginning of verse 8 with "The person who lacks these things" at the beginning of verse 9. It's one or the other—either you're progressing in the influence of godly character, or you're not!

The positive in verse 8 indicates that progressive growth in the influence of godly character will enable the believer to stand strong against impending assaults of false teaching. The condition for such perseverance is described in the clause, "For if you possess these qualities in increasing measure" (v. 8). As we've already alluded to, Peter assumes his readers possess the attributes listed in verses 5-7. The participle "increasing" (*pleonazonta*) now adds to the stakes. In this context the word is best understood to mean "abound" or "overflow" (Schreiner, *1 and 2 Peter*, 302). The virtues listed in verses 5-7 are not only existent and discernible in a disciple's life, but they are to be overflowing and progressively more prominent in their demonstration and influence. Individually and collectively they are to escalate as forces with which to be reckoned.

The result of these dynamic and ever-expanding character qualities is that they will "keep you from being useless or unfruitful in the knowledge of our Lord Jesus Christ" (v. 8). The two adjectives—"useless" (*argos*) and "unfruitful" (*akarpos*)—are almost synonymous in this context. The difference is that the former describes the faith without works spoken of by James in James 2:20, and the latter represents the failure to do good works as ethical traits spoken of by Paul in Titus 3:14.

Recently I've seen a number of athletes on television—after making a good play—cup one of their hands and repeatedly move it toward their mouth as if it were a spoon. The idea they're trying to convey is, "Keep feeding me the ball, and I'll keep producing!" By implication, if you don't give the athlete the ball, then he won't be able to keep making good plays. In the same way, Peter is suggesting that if we don't unleash these qualities in our Christian lives, then ineffectiveness and unfruitfulness will be the result.

Both of the negative traits in verse 8 qualify "the knowledge of our Lord Jesus Christ" (v. 8), one of the dominant themes of Peter's letter. Once again the word here is *epignōsis*, referring to that full and intimate knowledge of Christ secured at conversion. The idea is not that having the virtues listed in verses 5-7 leads to a greater knowledge of Christ but that the knowledge of Christ provides everything the believer needs for godly living (Vaughn and Lea, *1, 2 Peter*, 152). Repeating the same idea found in verse 3, Peter reiterates that knowing Christ provides everything that's needed for the believer to live an effective, fruitful life. And a failure to unleash these godly characteristics will produce an impotent knowledge of Christ!

By way of contrast, Peter strengthens his aim in verse 9 by showing the result of disobeying his appeal. He says, "The person who lacks these things is blind and shortsighted" (v. 9). Most translations place the rare word "nearsighted (*myōpazō*) before the term "blind" and convey the two as parallel terms. However, the language of the New Testament is actually in reverse order—blind and then nearsighted. But that seems strange. How can someone be both blind and nearsighted? The resolution is likely found in the fact that the word *nearsighted* is a participle that qualifies the state of blindness. So a better reading is that "they are blind, being nearsighted." An even more colloquial expression would be that these people are "so short-sighted that [they] cannot see" (GNB).

The point is that such a person is focused on his or her present desires (Davids, *Letters*, 186). He is blind to how the gospel of God's forgiveness affects everything in his life and instead is engrossed in earthly pursuits. He can't see the big picture but only what is close at hand. This understanding is consistent with the immorality and earthliness of the false teachers that Peter is soon to describe (M. Green, *2 Peter*, 92).

This spiritual blindness is a result of such a person's having "forgotten the cleansing from his past sins" (v. 9). The Bible frequently uses the idea of "forgetting" to convey not a mental process but a practical failure to take into account something's true meaning and significance. So there's an intentionality involved in basically "ignoring" the fact that Christ has died for one's sins and rendered them forgiven. While many think the phrase "cleansing from his past sins" refers to baptism as the ceremonial expression of this forgiveness, Peter is likely just using the frequent biblical metaphor of "washing" or "cleansing" as a way of portraying the forgiveness of sins (Moo, *2 Peter*, 48).

By way of application, there are two ways to look at the condition being described here. One is to see this as a description of the beginning of what eventually manifests itself as apostasy, or a denial of the faith. This is a subject Peter will pursue in more detail in the next chapter (cf. 2:20-22). Moo sees the people being described here as "fake Christians . . . who at least claim to have had their sins forgiven by Christ but who are not now living as if that makes any difference to them" (Moo, *2 Peter*, 48). This is a reality for "professing" believers who never grow in Christian virtues, whose lives really don't look any different than they did before their profession. Their lives have no fruit.

A second way to understand Peter's description is to hear him describing people who are truly saved but whose sin is clouding their testimony. And no doubt their "gospel amnesia" is also undermining their assurance of salvation. Believers who forget the cross and begin to dabble in the sin that characterized their former lives can never be confident that they were ever cleansed and rescued in the first place. If we don't see an increasing effect of godly character in our lives, we can't be sure that we've ever truly been saved. "Assurance of salvation is directly related to present spiritual service and obedience, not merely to a past salvation event made dim in the disobedient believer's memory" (MacArthur, *2 Peter*, 44).

We don't have to know which of these two conditions Peter had it mind. In fact, it's safe to say that Peter didn't know. All he knew was that there were some professing Christians who were ineffective and unfruitful when it came to the godly traits he listed in verses 5-7. It's still that way today. Our faith in Christ was never intended to be limited to our initial conversion experience. Faith was and is intended to mature. Many people have professed faith in Christ for decades, but their faith looks exactly like it did when they first confessed it. So the jury is still out on whether their "calling" (cf. vv. 3,10) is legitimate. That's why Peter goes on to compel his readers—then and now—to remove any shadow of doubt.

Your Validation of His Calling
2 PETER 1:10-11

Periodically I take my wife to a nice restaurant where they have valet parking. In those situations I usually need to tip the valet for taking care of my car while we're eating. But I've been to other restaurants that share parking spaces with other vendors; and, therefore, they simply "validate" parking instead of providing a valet. In those situations I park my own car but then get my parking ticket validated in the restaurant. When I exit the parking lot after dinner, I don't have to pay for parking because the restaurant validated the fact that I ate there. The validation isn't necessary for me to get my food, but it is necessary to prove that I had some!

Paying for parking is one thing, but being sure about whether you'll spend eternity in heaven or hell is on a whole different level. The stakes are much higher, so God wants us to be sure about this issue. Therefore he inspired Peter to strongly encourage us to nail that down, to "validate" that we are true disciples of Christ and legitimate citizens of his kingdom. He doesn't ask us to earn our salvation, but he does require that we demonstrate that we have it. That's what's happening in verses 10-11, where Peter offers a sobering *plea* and a stirring *promise*.

The Plea: Be Sure of Your Salvation (1:10)!

Based on the sobering realities of verses 3-9—God's gracious provision, our responsibility to bear his fruit, the risk of having to wonder if we're really saved—Peter pleads for his beloved readers to "make every effort to confirm your calling and election" (v. 10). The imperative *make every effort* is the main verb in the sentence and speaks of zeal, diligence, and expending energy. Peter has already used it in verse 5, so obviously he is unapologetic in his conviction that believers have some responsibility in their salvation journey. The term indicates making something a high priority by exerting both physical and moral effort (Davids, *Letters*, 187). And because it's in the present tense, whatever it is that Peter is talking about is to be an ongoing activity for the believer.

What is that activity? This expenditure of effort is to be offered in relation to one's "calling and election." These words obviously are synonymous in concept, both referencing the glorious, gracious, and sovereign work of God in our salvation. God's salvation is both elective and effective. It's elective in verses 3-5 of this text—creating faith, resourcing us for the God-life, giving us the divine nature, and freeing us from sin. It's effective when at some point in history the gospel is preached, we respond, and all of the above are applied to our lives (Schreiner, *1 and 2 Peter*, 304). Praise be to his glorious name for his gracious calling and election!

But hold the phone for a moment! Many have erred at this point by settling in on this gracious work of God as if it were the main thrust of these verses. It's not what God has done that Peter is emphasizing here but what man needs to do! We are to "confirm" (*bebaian*)—or ratify—our callings as believers in Christ. The verb is in the emphatic position. So Peter is underlining, putting in bold, and highlighting this activity and thus calling attention to its importance. The Christian is responsible for doing this, and it's of utmost importance.

How do we do this? The context indicates that we ratify our callings by growing in the virtues discussed in verses 5-7. What Peter is describing is the active involvement of the Christian in confirming his or her salvation. As believers, we aren't assured of our salvation because we pray a prayer, respond to an altar call, go through a class, memorize verses like 1 John 5:13, or even get baptized. We're assured of our salvation as we progressively grow in our likeness to Christ and in the influence of his character to the culture around us. If that's not happening, the authenticity of the believer's salvation is suspect at best. As Bauckham says, "The ethical fruits of Christian faith are objectively necessary for the attainment of final salvation" (Bauckham, *2 Peter*, 190).

This truth flies in the face of some believers who attempt to take Reformed theology to a place it was never intended to go. They highlight God's role in salvation while neglecting—and even ignoring—man's responsibility. Michael Green is helpful at this point:

> *Make your calling and election sure* is an appeal that goes to
> the heart of the paradox of election and free will. The New
> Testament characteristically makes room for both without
> attempting to resolve the apparent antinomy. So here; election
> comes from God alone—but man's behaviour is the proof or
> disproof of it. Though "good works" (gratuitously read here
> by some mss) are possible only through the appropriation of
> God's gracious aid, they are absolutely necessary, and fairly
> and squarely our responsibility. . . . Christian calling and
> Christian living go together. (*2 Peter*, 93; emphasis original)

Apparently, the false teachers were boasting about their divine calling and election, and they were using that glorious truth as a license to sin with abandon because they claimed to be predestined to righteousness. Many professing believers today toy with this heresy, believing their salvation is secure enough without them progressing in the qualities of

Christlikeness. Peter—under the inspiration of the Spirit—emphatically denies such a contradiction in the lives of Christ's disciples.

So the concern here is nurturing assurance of salvation, not earning it. Peter isn't suggesting that we must add Christlike qualities in order to be elected. He is suggesting that doing so is the verification of whether we've truly been elected. This tension is at "the heart of the paradox of election and free will" (M. Green, *2 Peter*, 93). Our calling and election are secure in the mind of God, but our calling and election are insecure if they aren't validated by growth in Christ's character.

Beloved, this is a serious and urgent matter! Peter's plea must be heard and heeded by church members today. In the language of the New Testament, the infinitive *to confirm* highlights the necessity of the professing Christian to exercise his or her will to get this done. Nothing is more deceptive than the lie that going through some religious motion or exercise secures eternity and that such an effort excuses stagnant and even rebellious Christian living. At the same time, the true believer whose life isn't bearing fruit will constantly wrestle with wondering whether he or she is really saved. Only progressive growth in Christlikeness clearly demonstrates genuine salvation that gives assurance to the child of God and brings delight to the heart of God (cf. Phil 2:12-13).

The Promise: Be Steadfast in Your Salvation (1:10-11)!

Peter wants his readers to be sure of their salvation so they won't cave in under the onslaught of false teaching. He wants them to be steadfast as they face the invasion of error. The last part of verse 10 and all of verse 11 contain a wonderful, twofold promise to the Christians who ratify their calling and election with progressive growth in Christlikeness that leads to confidence in their salvation. The two ideas have to be seen together in order to get the meaning. When Peter says, "Because if you do these things you will never stumble" (v. 10), he no doubt is thinking ahead to his reference to "entry into the eternal kingdom" (v. 11). The stumbling referred to in verse 10 is of a final nature and stands in contrast to receiving entrance into the kingdom. The general idea in this context is that the individual who progressively displays godly virtues won't stumble and fall on the pathway to God's kingdom and thus fail to arrive (cf. Jude 24; Bauckham, *2 Peter*, 191).

Let's back up and unpack this truth in more detail. The first part of the promise is that a person who demonstrates what's described in verses 5-7 will never "stumble" (v. 10). The imagery here is taken from the sure-footedness of a horse. If an individual is making steady progress in manifesting Christian virtues, then his or her life will be the tacit evidence of God's calling and election (M. Green, *2 Peter*, 94). And that person won't stumble along the way by demonstrating unregenerate qualities. Instead he will travel the path to heaven with a surefooted confidence and the assurance that he will never commit apostasy.

The second part of the promise is that such a person will gain "entry" (*eisodos*), which is the focal point in verse 11 and stands over against the stumbling in the previous verse. The *entry* image is common in the New Testament, especially in Jesus's teaching (Matt 5:20; 7:21; 18:3; 19:23; Mark 10:23-25; Luke 18:17,24-25; John 3:5; Acts 14:22). So Peter picks up that gospel theme here and answers the question, "Who will enter, and what will enable that person to enter?" (Davids, *Letters*, 189–90). His answer is the person whose life is characterized by the progressive demonstration of Christlike character. Peter isn't describing salvation *by* works; he's describing salvation *with* works (Schreiner, *1 and 2 Peter*, 306).

This entrance into Christ's eternal kingdom won't be any routine or mundane affair. It will be "richly provided" (v. 11) for the one who lives in a godly way. The main verb in verse 11 is the same as the main verb in verse 5, making an obvious unit. The divine wealth expressed in the phrase *richly provided* serves as the reward for the temporal exertion expressed in the phrase *supplement your faith* (v. 5). The picture here is of someone extravagantly welcoming a friend who has arrived at his home, or of the citizens of a city celebrating the hometown hero who is returning from his triumph at the Olympic Games. This lavish welcome no doubt results from the richness of divine generosity (Rom 10:12; Eph 1:7; 1 Tim 6:17; Titus 3:6), and it reciprocates what the believer has provided for himself by growing in godly virtue (Davids, *Letters*, 189).

Conclusion

Many different views exist about God's activity in salvation. One of the realities that clouds the discussion is that there's often no uniform view even among those in the same camp. While I certainly don't claim to have solved all the disputes, I have my opinions. My personal conviction is that God sovereignly and graciously calls some people to be saved, woos them by his grace into his salvation, and ultimately makes sure they safely arrive in his eternal kingdom. I can't explain all of that, but I believe the Bible says it. I do know, however, that it's easy to overemphasize these truths to the point that we overlook what God says about human responsibility in passages like 2 Peter 1:3-11 (see Rom 6:15-23). When we do that, we end up manipulating the truth to fit our theology.

For example, some have suggested that Peter is calling on the elect simply to make their election sure in their own minds. In other words, they see "confirm" as referring to a person's subjective *awareness* of his or her election, not that person's actual objective *status*. But the language in this text won't let us go there. It demands that we accept this as an "antinomy," a truth that is not contradictory but that we can't neatly reconcile in our minds. What is this antinomy? We have to respond to God's grace in our lives if we're going to confirm his calling and election of our lives and make it into his heaven. "God chooses us and ensures that we get to heaven. We need to choose God and live godly lives so that we can reach heaven" (Moo, *2 Peter*, 60).

I love antinomies! Why? Well, partly because the word is just fun to say! But mostly because antinomies in the Bible remind me of the difference between me and God. There are some seeming contradictions in the Bible that the human mind can't reconcile, but they can easily be reconciled in the mind of a sovereign and almighty God. The truth in this paragraph is one of them. How can it be that God already "has given us everything required for life and godliness" (v. 3), and yet we have to "confirm [our] calling and election" (v. 10)? Only God knows. What we know is that this text begins with what we already are in Christ, as ones possessing the divine nature, but then it moves to what we are to become, as ones who are compelled to live accordingly (M. Green, *2 Peter*, 96). Beloved, remember your calling as a steward of the divine nature and live to confirm its validity by looking more and more like Jesus every day.

Reflect and Discuss

1. Why is it dangerous to allow the pendulum of God's sovereignty and man's responsibility to swing too far in one direction?
2. What makes Peter's list of godly characteristics possible? Why is this important?
3. How do we keep from being "useless" or "unfruitful" in our Christian walk?
4. Why is a fruitless Christian walk both problematic and dangerous?
5. Is the gospel opposed to effort and/or energy? Why or why not?

6. Based on this text, how would you encourage a brother or sister who is struggling with assurance of salvation?
7. How/where do we find that assurance of salvation? In our efforts? In God's promises?
8. At what point is it appropriate to judge whether someone else is saved? Is it an appropriate action for a believer to confront a person with what they believe to be a false salvation?
9. For a believer, entrance into the kingdom will be richly provided. How should this truth spur believers on toward godliness?
10. Is it possible for human beings to accept or even embrace divine antinomies? How can they actually lead us to worship God?

Remember Christ's Coming

2 PETER 1:12-21

Main Idea: Believers must be reminded often of the certainty of Christ's return in order to live godly lives.

I. **The Significance of Remembering (1:12-15)**
   A. Remembering sustains our godliness (1:12).
   B. Remembering stimulates our passion (1:13-14).
   C. Remembering strengthens our readiness (1:15).

II. **The Sources for Remembering (1:16-21)**
   A. The apostolic witness (1:16-18)
   B. The prophetic word (1:19-21)

I've frequently recounted the story about how a colleague and I used to meet every morning to jog around our seventy-five-acre campus when I was teaching at New Orleans Seminary. Because the street that borders the campus wasn't a formal track or workout area, there were always people moving around it in both directions. The toughest part of that daily routine for me wasn't the discipline of doing it, or having the stamina to complete the laps, or even the frustration of wondering whether it was doing any good. The toughest part for me was trying to figure out creative ways to greet the same people moving in the opposite direction every time you passed them! I mean, seriously, there are only so many ways to sincerely greet the same people within a ten- to twenty-minute time period!

I noticed that people responded to that awkwardness in one of three ways. Some of these serious health nuts never acknowledged that anyone else was on the planet! They just kept their eyes focused straight ahead like they were on some kind of special ops mission. Others, who are more recreational in their journey, would say a hearty "Good morning" on the first encounter and then would wave or nod at the subsequent encounters. But the social exercisers were the funniest. After their initial greeting of "Good morning" or "Hello" or "Hi," their courteous demeanor forced them to feel like they had to engage in small talk on the second and third laps. So they would offer comments like "Beautiful weather today, huh?" "Nice shorts!" or "How 'bout those New

Orleans Saints?" All three of these responses were simple attempts by human beings to overcome the awkwardness of repetition.

Not only is repetition awkward; it's often frustrating. Whether it's having to tell our kids the same thing over and over again or having to listen to the same recorded "options" menu every time we call our cable company, we have a tendency to grow weary of repetition. But even though repetition can be awkward and frustrating, it is helpful, especially if what's being repeated is something we need. Each time our kids hear our repeated instructions, they probably hear some detail they didn't hear the first few times. And every time we listen to menu options, we become a little more familiar with them to the point we can navigate them more quickly the next time we call. So repetition helps us remember important things. Consequently, repetition of important lessons isn't something that should bore or frustrate but something we should welcome.

While trying to be creative about how to greet people when you're doing laps can be a little stressful, figuring out how to respond to the awkwardness of repeating gospel truth in our lives and churches is a much bigger task. But Peter was up for the challenge. He knew something his readers couldn't afford to forget. This important truth surfaces in the relationship between two ideas in this passage. In 1:12 Peter says, "I will always remind you about these things," referring back to the reality that the gospel life implied progressive maturity in Christlikeness (see 1:3-11). In 1:16 he says, "For we did not follow cleverly contrived myths when we made known to you the power and coming of our Lord Jesus Christ," obviously referencing our Lord's second coming. Peter wanted his readers to remember that Jesus is coming again, not just as an entry in their systematic theology but as a motivation for their holiness.

The false teachers of the day mocked the idea that there was a powerful, heavenly Christ who could resource them to live godly lives (2:1-2); and they denied the literal nature of gospel miracles, including a future physical return of Christ (3:3-4). This eschatological skepticism gave them a license for immoral living, something they undoubtedly used to lure Peter's readers. "With no prospect of future judgment, one did not have to worry much about living a righteous life" (Moo, *2 Peter*, 70). So Peter shows us the significance of remembering the second coming for our daily lives and then the credible sources available to us to jog our memories about that glorious event.

The Significance of Remembering
2 PETER 1:12-15

The approach Peter takes to addressing the issue of the second coming is somewhat indirect. His initial concern is the effect that denying the Lord's return will have on the way believers live their lives. So he determines that before he dies he will do everything in his power to remind Christians of the need to live godly lives if they're going to be sure of their salvation and confidently enter the eternal kingdom when Jesus comes back (see 1:5-11). As we've already noted in the introduction, three times in four verses he stresses his deliberate plan to remind them of this spiritual reality. The first time he says, "I will always remind you" (v. 12). Then he says, "I think it is right . . . to wake you up with a reminder" (v. 13). And finally he says, "I will also make every effort so that you are able to recall these things at any time after my departure" (v. 15). Peter obviously felt his readers needed this spiritual truth repeated to them!

The words "therefore" and "these things" at the beginning of verse 12 refer back to the pathway that leads to entrance into Christ's eternal kingdom referenced in verses 4-8. The believer's future hope will be fully realized as godly character is nurtured through strenuous moral effort and built upon God's glorious promises. Peter's readers needed this reminder because in their day—as in ours—the "grace card" was being played as an excuse for immoral living (see 2:19; cf. Rom 6:1) and the "knowledge-of-God card" for lack of obedience (cf. 1 John 2:4). Peter wanted to make sure his readers didn't buy into those deceptive heresies that lured many into a false sense of security. He wanted them to remember the *true* gospel, one that included progressive spiritual maturity as a validation of true salvation.

However, there's more at play here than just a reminder about the need to mature in Christ. If—as false teachers maintain—there is no eternal kingdom ushered in by Christ's return, then Peter's claim about godly living is bankrupt. If Christ is coming back, however, then failing to progress in spiritual growth will most certainly lead to shipwrecked faith. So Peter suggests three important reasons remembering the nature of the true gospel is so crucial for our growth in Christ and as a defense against false teaching. He proposes that remembering this truth will *sustain* godliness, *stimulate* passion, and *strengthen* readiness in the lives of true disciples of Christ.

Remembering Sustains Our Godliness (1:12)

Peter appears to be paying his readers a compliment when he says about their grasp of the truth, "You know them and are established in the truth you now have" (1:12). The participle "established" (*stērizō*) means "to firmly establish" or "to strengthen." The construction indicates a settled condition. Peter's readers were genuine, maturing believers. Bauckham describes them as "well-grounded in the Christian faith, instructed in it, firmly committed to it, and therefore not likely to be easily misled by false teaching" (*2 Peter*, 197). These believers were like the Colossians, whom Paul said had

> *already heard about this hope in the word of truth, the gospel that has come to you. It is bearing fruit and growing all over the world, just as it has among you since the day you heard it and came to truly appreciate God's grace.* (Col 1:5b-6)

They had received the gospel, and it had taken root in their lives.

Some Bible scholars believe Peter was just being polite here and acting according to the guidelines of classical rhetoric. I'm not sure Peter was that refined. It's more likely that he truly saw his readers as being grounded in the truth. But he also knew that just because someone was grounded in the truth didn't guarantee he or she would remain so. And that's something Peter knew from experience. As previously mentioned, he likely was remembering that infamous occasion when he so passionately claimed to be established in the truth and yet in such a short time he turned around and denied his Lord (Luke 22:33-34). Jesus used a form of this same word to instruct Peter on what to do for others once he himself had regained his spiritual footing: "When you have turned back, strengthen [*stērizō*] your brothers" (Luke 22:32). Peter knew how easy it was to be spiritually strong at one point and then to crash and burn at another. But he also knew what it meant to rise again to a solid footing.

The lesson here is that being reminded of spiritual truth sustains the godliness that's already present in our lives. That's why Peter says, "I will always remind you about these things, even though you know them and are established in the truth you now have" (1:12). Being reminded builds godliness up so that it continues to grow and not wither. Yesterday's godliness won't suffice for today if left unattended and undernourished. It has to be fed every day. The tendency of the human heart is to be forgetful. So we all need the truth of the gospel to be rehearsed in our hearts and minds. It's all too easy for seasoned Christians to lapse into serious sin and doctrinal error (M. Green, *2 Peter*, 98). Believers are prone "to lose the fine edge of their zeal for godliness, for the world tries to 'squeeze us into its mold' (cf. Rom 12:2), and false Christians arise to propagate their own brand of faith without fervor" (Moo, *2 Peter*, 62). True godliness will only be sustained when we remember gospel truth, or else it will falter and fade under the assault of false teaching.

Remembering Stimulates Our Passion (1:13-14)

The idea that "a picture paints a thousand words" was used by Frederick R. Barnard in *Printer's Ink* in 1921 to contend that graphics can tell a story as effectively as a large amount of descriptive text. But the opposite is true as well—a word can paint a thousand pictures. In these verses Peter picks up his literary paintbrush to describe the transitory nature of his life. In the language of the New Testament, Peter uses the word for "tent" to describe his body (v. 13), a clear indication that he recognized that his human body was a temporary dwelling place that one day would be folded up. The fleeting nature of life is emphasized again in his reference to "[laying] aside my tent" (v. 14), a clear image of removing a piece of clothing.

So to say "as long as I am in this bodily tent" (v. 13) and "I know that I will soon lay aside my tent" (v. 14) are just the apostle's way of saying "I don't have much time left." And he had arrived at such a conclusion based on a credible source: ". . . as our Lord Jesus Christ has indeed made clear to me" (v. 14). Whether this is a reference to his breakfast conversation with Christ on the shores of Galilee (John 21:18-19) or to some special revelation from Christ on another occasion, Peter was convinced that he only had a short time to exercise his ministry of reminding. He communicated this conviction in vivid language that conveyed an utter sense of urgency.

However, we have to be careful not to let Peter's picturesque language in verses 13-14 distract us from his main point. The focus here is not so much the brevity of time but the function of Peter's reminders to his readers in that small window. Even though they were already firmly established in the truth, Peter said, "I think it is right . . . to wake you up" (v. 13). The word translated "wake you up" (*diegeirein*) means to be "stirred" or "provoked." It's a strong word intended to convey the idea of persuasively stimulating the believers to prize the gospel in a fresh way. That was the function of Peter's reminders! He "hoped that his words would stab the believers awake so they would reject what the opponents taught" (Schreiner, *1 and 2 Peter*, 309). Even when we know the gospel, our passion for it needs to be stimulated afresh every day if we're to continue in godliness and deflect the fiery darts of falsehood. God wants us to treasure the gospel and rehearse it in our hearts and minds on a regular basis.

Remembering Strengthens Our Readiness (1:15)

For the second time Peter references his impending death ("departure"). This time he intensifies his desire to remind his readers of gospel truth before he's gone. He says, "I will also make every effort" (v. 15) to make sure you don't forget. The verb here (*spoudazō*) indicates more than a casual desire but instead an earnest, intense effort (Vaughn and Lea, *1, 2 Peter*, 158). Peter also uses the future tense, which is a bit awkward. Consequently, Bible scholars have speculated on the specific subject of Peter's reminder. Was he referring to some future document, like Mark's Gospel, or another letter from him that hasn't been preserved? While arguments for such sources are interesting, it's far more likely that Peter is simply referencing his current letter and either the fact that it wouldn't arrive to his readers until sometime in the future (Davids, *Letters*, 197) or to his desire that it continue to be present as a source of authority in the church (G. L. Green, *Jude*, 213).

However, a debate over the specific source Peter has in mind once again risks missing the point. We know that his concern is for the memory of gospel truth consistent with that contained in the current letter. Greater emphasis in this verse, however, should be put on the new slant to Peter's mission of reminding his readers about that gospel truth. He says he wants them to be able "to recall these things at any time" (v. 15). The emphasis here is on the *scope* of the reader's remembrance. Here Peter alters the language of memory a bit by using a word that's fairly common in the Septuagint but found nowhere else in the New Testament. While the construction can simply mean "to call to mind" or just "to make mention of a thing," it also carries the more solemn idea of "holding things in remembrance" (G. L. Green, *Jude*, 214). This seems to best capture the spirit of the context. Peter wanted his readers to hold the gospel in remembrance. He was burdened that they would be ready at all times, not simply to "call up" truth that is needed in the heat of the moment but constantly to live with a gospel consciousness so they always are ready to deflect the assault of false teachers.

Peter's purpose here has an earthy implication. He doesn't want Christians to have a mere intellectual recollection of gospel truths. He's concerned—along with other biblical writers (see comments on 1:1-2)—that believers can *functionally* forget even the most basic truths of the gospel even though they can recite them in their minds. In other words, believers can experience functional amnesia when it comes to living out the gospel. Gospel truth might be remembered mentally yet never become a vital part of a Christian's life. It's possible to remember that Jesus died for your sins but never to embrace that truth in such a way that it overcomes your feeling of guilt over the past or dread of the future. It's possible to remember that Jesus calls you to holy living but never to allow holiness to grip your conscience or inspire your hands and feet. We are called to remember the gospel in a tangible and practical sense, and the repetition of its truths—in both word and ritual (e.g., baptism, communion)—is a necessary component of our readiness for vibrant Christian living (Moo, *2 Peter*, 66).

The Sources for Remembering
2 PETER 1:16-21

In verses 16-21 Peter raises the stakes on the importance of godly living by unpacking for his readers the certainty of "the eternal kingdom of our Lord and Savior Jesus Christ" (1:11). The doctrinal issue of Christ's return in glory and judgment at the end of history was the most important gospel truth his readers needed to remember under their circumstances. He felt it was so important that he somewhat bookends his letter with the subject (1:16-21; 3:1-18). Maybe above all other gospel truths, Christ's return provides the greatest motivation and highest accountability for growing in spiritual maturity and living a godly life (1:3-11). "Living a godly life is optional, to say the least, if one's heavenly destiny is not involved" (Schreiner, *1 and 2 Peter*, 312). But because heaven is a reality for every true believer in Christ, godly living is the only option.

After underscoring the importance of recounting the truths regarding the relationship between godly living and entrance into Christ's kingdom, Peter turns his attention to establishing the veracity of Christ's coming. Peter chose this doctrinal issue over all others simply because the false teachers were attacking his readers at precisely this point (see 3:3-4; Moo, *2 Peter*, 69). So he identifies two sources his readers have available to them to spiritually jog their memories about the certainty of

Christ's coming, all to the end that they would pursue godliness as they wait for him. The two sources are the *apostolic witness* and the *prophetic word*. Together they provide a solid footing—the eyewitness accounts of Jesus's apostles combined with the messianic foretelling of the Old Testament prophets. These two sources also countered the accusations of the false teachers against the teaching of Peter and the other apostles.

The Apostolic Witness (1:16-18)

The transfiguration of Christ (Matt 17:1-8; Mark 9:2-8; Luke 9:28-36) serves as the backdrop of 2 Peter 1:16-18. On that mountain God the Father gave divine witness to the glory and majesty of God the Son, including his fulfillment of and superiority over both the law (Moses) and the prophets (Elijah). The event also foreshadowed the revelation of that same glory and majesty in Christ's return. It's no accident that the transfiguration accounts in all three Synoptic Gospels are prefaced by Jesus's declaration that some of his apostles were about to witness a preview of his second coming (see Matt 16:28; Mark 9:1; Luke 9:27). The theophany that took place at the transfiguration no doubt was an advanced screening of our Lord's return and God's coming kingdom. Here Peter recalls the event because it represented and anticipated Christ's powerful coming (Schreiner, *1 and 2 Peter*, 316).

That's exactly where the rub had come with Peter's opponents. This cosmic testimony of Christ's return flew in the face of the false teachers who derided "his 'coming' that he promised" (3:4). They held fast to the stability of the world, the impossibility of sudden interventions, and the constancy of the natural order (Schreiner, *1 and 2 Peter*, 313). But in Peter's mind there was no doubt that "one historical event calls for another" (Vaughn and Lea, *1, 2 Peter*, 159). Consequently, he wanted his readers to know they could be confident of the gospel truth that one day Jesus would return with the same "honor and glory" (v. 17) that he had received from God the Father on that holy mountain.

To strengthen the faith of his readers, Peter uses the transfiguration as one example of the validity and credibility of the apostolic witness to the gospel as well as to one of its crucial components. While his reminder about the apostolic proclamation of Christ's return is grammatically at the center of verse 16, Peter's major point is the contrasting qualifications at play. He and the other apostles made known the return of Christ by being "eyewitnesses," something the false teachers couldn't put on their resumes (Moo, *2 Peter*, 71). He denies the accusation of his critics that he and the other apostles were simply blind followers of "cleverly contrived myths" (v. 16), or fictitious stories, when it came to their gospel. Instead, he counters that they actually "heard this voice when it came from heaven while we were with him on the holy mountain" (v. 18). The apostles had been there; they had seen it with their own eyes and heard it with their own ears.

These verses are radiant with at least three magnificent descriptions of the awesome display of Christ's greatness that the apostles saw and heard that day. First, Peter identifies the nature of the event—it was "the power and coming" of "his majesty" (v. 16). The terms "power" (*dunamis*) and "coming" (*parousia*) are best interpreted together (Bauckham, *2 Peter*, 215). While *parousia* usually refers to the future return of Christ, here—combined with the divine *dunamis* that Jesus has as the resurrected Lord—it's best translated and understood as the "powerful coming" exhibited on this occasion as well as the one to come. Peter saw Jesus's powerful coming at the transfiguration as a precursor to the ultimate demonstration at his second coming. The word *majesty* (*megaleiotēs*) is most often used in reference to God (e.g., Luke 9:43). But here—in the context of Christ's "powerful coming"—it has to be understood as a reference to Jesus's deity (Schreiner, *1 and 2 Peter*, 314; cf. 1:1).

Second, Peter describes what happened at the transfiguration— Christ "received honor and glory" from "the Majestic Glory" (v. 17). The word "honor" denotes the exalted status being bestowed on Jesus, while "glory" indicates the heavenly radiance most often seen in the Bible as belonging to God (cf. John 1:14; 1 Pet 1:7; Jude 25). The title "the Majestic Glory" is likely a circumlocution used to refer to the Divine Being without mentioning him by name. But here it seems to be more than a roundabout way of showing reverence for God. In fact, the title seems to connect verses 16 and 17 together. While the word for "Majestic" in Greek is different from the one used for Christ in verse 16, the idea is the same. The "Majestic Glory"—the one to whom all majesty and glory belongs—is here bestowing "majesty" (v. 16) and "honor and glory" (v. 17) on Christ Jesus! Could there be any stronger statement of the deity of our Lord and its place in the gospel (cf. John 1:1,14; Col 1:15-20)?

Third, Peter reports what God said about Jesus—"This is my beloved Son, with whom I am well-pleased" (v. 17). The first part of this sentence is probably best understood as reading, "This is my Son, my Beloved." It serves as a heavenly expression of the deep and abiding love the Father has for the Son. The latter part of the sentence indicates the good pleasure the Father has in the Son (Vaughn and Lea, *1, 2 Peter*, 161). Together, the pronouncement attested to God's affirmation and affection for Jesus Christ in both his person and his work.

This text is a reminder that our faith isn't rooted in fairy tales and fiction. While the source of most world religions can't be traced to historical facts, Christianity is lashed to the eyewitness testimony of those who had a complete knowledge of the historical Jesus (cf. John 15:26-27; Acts 1:21-22; 2:42). Peter and the other apostles didn't have to fabricate stories about Jesus; they had actually seen him and done life with him. Having such a knowledge passed along by firsthand account ought to edify us as Christ's disciples. And Peter's reminder of Jesus's glory and majesty should compel us to godly living and sustain us in the face of falsehood and worldliness until we see him face-to-face (Titus 2:11-14; 1 John 3:1-3).

The Prophetic Word (1:19-21)

True to his promise to "make every effort" (v. 15) to remind his readers about the validity of Christ's return, Peter offers them two verifications of that claim. He's already reminded them about his own eyewitness account of the transfiguration. Now he puts a second credible source of authority on the table—the Old Testament Scriptures. In these verses Peter refers to the Scriptures variously as "the prophetic word" (v. 19), "prophecy of Scripture" (v. 20), and "prophecy" (v. 21). When we come to 2 Peter 1:19-21, we find ourselves at one of the most potent places in all of the Bible regarding the inspiration of Scripture. Few passages magnify the supernatural origin and nature of God's Word as clearly and succinctly as this one.

As we unpack what Peter says about the Old Testament Scriptures, let's keep in mind that the truth found here is equally applicable to all of Scripture, both the Old and New Testaments. It's true that Peter was referring in this letter to the Old Testament Scriptures, but God—at the same time Peter was writing—was sovereignly in the process of using him and other godly men to pen what eventually would become the New Testament Scriptures. Even in this letter Peter includes the writings of the apostle Paul in the category of the "Scriptures" (2 Pet 3:16). Regardless of whether Peter knew his own letters would one day be included in that same category, he evidently was conscious that God was in the process of expanding his written revelation. Truly the apostolic witness exemplified in verses 16-18 was used for this purpose (cf. John 15:27; Acts 1:21-22). That makes this an important text for contemporary Christians regarding our view of the entirety of Scripture contained in the Bible. So consider in this passage a *reality*, a *reason*, and a *response* for all followers of Christ concerning our approach to Scripture.

First, the reality is that Scripture is superior to our personal experience. In verse 19 Peter says the Scriptures are a more "strongly confirmed" (*bebaioterion*) source of authority than even the personal experience and eyewitness testimony he's just finished recounting. That's an amazing claim! For most people nothing is more authoritative than their personal experience. How often do we hear someone say something like, "I know that's true because I've experienced it"? Peter indicates that such a contention is limited at best. Satan can create experiences and feelings, and he can manipulate circumstances in our lives. So the objective constant of Scripture must be seen to be on a higher plane of authority than personal experience.

Such a contention is consistent with the normal tendency of first-century Jews. They would believe prophecy before they would believe a voice from heaven! So Peter—a Jewish Christian and an apostle with deep regard for Old Testament prophecies—essentially says to his readers, "If you don't believe me, go to the Scriptures." He obviously had complete confidence that Scripture was a reliable source of authority (M. Green, *2 Peter*, 108–9). Furthermore, Peter wasn't comparing the Old Testament Scriptures to the *transfiguration* as a reliable source of authority. He was comparing the Old Testament Scriptures to his eyewitness *experience*. And so should we. Whenever Scripture contradicts our personal experience, we should always put our trust in Scripture. That's part of walking by faith and not by sight!

Second, the reason Scripture is superior is because of its supernatural origin. I'm skipping ahead here and addressing verses 20-21 first simply because they provide the rationale for the counsel found in the second half of verse 19. In these verses Peter is calling attention to the divine source of Scripture. He's continuing his case for the authentication of Christian teaching, namely the return of Christ. He's already provided authentication through his eyewitness of the transfiguration (vv. 16-18). Here he authenticates Scripture by citing its divine origin and authority. Essentially he's saying, "The same God whom the apostles heard speak in the transfiguration spoke also through the prophets" (M. Green, *2 Peter*, 112). In verse 20 he tells us Scripture is authoritative, and in verse 21 he tells us why.

In a backdoor kind of way, Peter tells his readers they shouldn't listen to anyone who tries to make Scripture say whatever they want it to say. Why? Because that not only changes its meaning, but it cancels out its authority. A proper understanding of the prophets' words wasn't derived "from the prophet's own interpretation" (v. 20). This is the only time the word "interpretation" (*epilyseōs*) is used as a noun in the New Testament, but the verb form shows up in Mark 4:34 and Acts 19:39. In both places it means to unravel a problem (Vaughn and Lea, *1, 2 Peter*, 164). This was a clear prohibition against interpreting Scripture on a personal whim, which is exactly what the false teachers were doing by denying Christ's coming. They were negating the authoritative word of the prophets by unraveling the words of Scripture to an end that was convenient for their own agendas. None of us has the right to make Scripture say whatever we want it to say!

Verse 21 spells out for us the gravity of unraveling Scripture to this end. It has everything to do with Scripture's origin. Peter continues by saying, "because no prophecy ever came by the will of man" (v. 21). To say it another way, Scripture didn't originate with humans. Consequently, people have absolutely no right to twist it to say whatever they want. And the stakes keep getting higher in this verse as Peter reveals by whose will prophecy of Scripture actually was produced. It came "from God . . . by the Holy Spirit" (v. 21). Peter clearly identifies God as the origin and source of Scripture, making it a superior source of authority over everything else, including personal experience. Think about what this says about the false teachers' tweaking the Old Testament prophecies about the coming kingdom. God spoke, but they unraveled his words to make them their own. In so doing, they put "new" words—their own words—in the mouth of the God of the universe!

This is exactly what drew such strong rebuke from God against false prophets in the Old Testament (e.g., Jer 23:16; Ezek 13:3). They spoke their own words instead of his. They twisted his words to fit their own agendas and justify their godless living. But before we rush to cast stones at false prophets in the Old Testament and false teachers in the New Testament, let's take a look inward. What's different about the Christian who reads God's Word in her quiet time but then only draws meaning from a topical devotional book that merely addresses one small detail of the passage, and that out of context? What's different about a small group leader who reads a Bible passage and then asks his members to share what it means to them without discriminating between their various interpretations? What's different about a pastor who announces a text for his sermon and then launches off into a tirade on a personal pet peeve that has nothing to do with the passage he read? These are just a few examples of unraveling Scripture incorrectly and thereby undermining its authority and denying its Author. Doing so muffles the voice of God at best and puts words in his mouth at worst. Either way we miss hearing and obeying what God has for us.

How much clearer could Peter have been in authenticating the trustworthiness of Scripture? His readers could have complete confidence that what the Old Testament Scriptures said about the coming kingdom was true. Consequently, they should be compelled to live holy lives as they wait for Christ's return. Subsequently, we can have confidence in what the Bible says about the second coming as well as what it says about every other subject found on its pages. And its truth should compel us to godly living. As the apostle John says, "And everyone who has this hope in him purifies himself just as he is pure" (1 John 3:3).

A final aspect of Peter's authentication was to show that Scripture didn't just fall out of the sky or appear under a rock. It actually was transmitted through human instruments. He said that "men spoke from God as they were carried along by the Holy Spirit" (v. 21). The idea of being "carried along" (*pheromenoi*) was used to describe a ship being moved by the wind (cf. Acts 27:15,17). The language is describing the prophets as raising their sails and the Holy Spirit filling them and blowing their sails in the direction he wanted them to go (M. Green, *2 Peter*, 113).

One of the most important phrases in this passage is "from God" (v. 21). God used human instruments, but the result was a message *from him*. This truth is foundational to what's been called the doctrine of verbal plenary inspiration. It suggests that in the original manuscripts of Scripture—throughout all its pages—the Holy Spirit guided the human authors even in their choice of expressions without ignoring or negating their personalities (Hernando, *Dictionary of Hermeneutics*, 26). The result of this process was that every word of those original manuscripts was perfect and without error, recording the exact message God desired to give to man (Gaebelein, *Meaning*, 9).

God moved some men who uttered truths out of their own background and life situation without ever losing their consciousness or normal mental functions. This was not an act of mechanical dictation but active cooperation of men with God. The result was that these men spoke *from God*, not merely about God (Vaughn and Lea, *1, 2 Peter*, 164–65). Two implications flow from this reality. First, we must approach the Bible as having a specific message from God for us, not as a book of random subjects intended to address every detail of life. Second, when we read the Bible with integrity today, and when we hear it taught and preached rightly, we can be confident that God is speaking.

Third, our response should be submission to Scripture in view of Christ's return. Both the superiority of Scripture as well as its divine origin compel us to pay attention to it and obey what it says. That's why Peter says that "you will do well to pay attention to it" (v. 19). Essentially, this is the main point of the passage. Everything he's written up to this point leads to this command (Schreiner, *1 and 2 Peter*, 321). To "pay attention" (v. 19) means to "pay close attention," and it implies that one will act on the words by embracing and following them. In so doing the respondent will "do well" (v. 19), Peter says. This expression refers to doing what is right and correct. Obeying Scripture isn't simply a good thing to do, but it's the right thing to do (G. L. Green, *Jude*, 227). We don't obey what the Bible says simply because it will benefit us; we obey it because obedience to God is what's right.

But benefit us it does. The exhortation to obey what Scripture says is intensified by the use of a simile: "as to a lamp shining in a dark place" (v. 19). Green likens this to a torch that illuminates a dark room, revealing the dirt inside and making it easier to clean (M. Green, *2 Peter*, 109). Peter may be using the phrase "dark place" to describe either the darkness of the world because of sin or the false teaching that his readers were encountering. The latter seems more likely in context. The heresies that Christ isn't coming back (or has already come back), that there's no impending judgment, and that people consequently have a license for godless living all serve to dim a person's view of the realities of life and the gospel. We can find ourselves groping around in darkness without any spiritual awareness or direction.

The light that only Scripture provides will be necessary "until the day dawns and the morning star rises in your hearts" (v. 19). Both images here naturally refer to Christ's return and the brilliance that will characterize it. In Greek literature the "morning star" was used to refer to royal and divine people. In the Old Testament the Messiah was symbolized by a star (Num 24:17) and the rising sun of righteousness (Mal 4:2). In the New Testament Jesus himself is called the "morning star" (Rev 2:28; 22:16). The phrase "in your hearts" likely refers to our re-creation in Christ Jesus, that inner transformation that's already begun through the work of God's Spirit as we learn and obey Scripture (2 Cor 3:18). When Jesus returns, this process will be completed. As the apostle John says, "When he appears, we will be like him because we will see him as he is" (1 John 3:2). As believers in Christ we look forward to the day our lives will be illuminated by the radiance of his presence in all of his glory. Until he returns, we've been given the divine flashlight of Scripture to transform us into his image and light our path as we walk with him (cf. Pss 19:8; 119:105; Prov 6:23).

Conclusion

I used several different homiletics textbooks in the seminary classroom for about five years before I coauthored the book I currently use. The first semester I required my new book I remember telling my students on the first day of class, "You're liable to hear some of the same things in my lectures that you read in that textbook because everything I know is now in that book!" There was a lot of truth to that. I had incorporated into that book the combination of all the lessons learned in my educational journey, my decade of pastoral preaching experience, and my five years of teaching experience. Why did I feel I needed to give that disclaimer? Because I know some students get frustrated—or even insulted—when a professor says the same things in class that they read in their textbooks. Our tendency is to avoid repetition, or at least push back against it.

However, God knows we need to be reminded of gospel truth. For believers today the same two sources—the apostolic witness and the prophetic word—remain as the solid and enduring sources of what we believe. This dynamic duo has been supernaturally recorded to form the two testaments of our Bible. The dominant component comprising the Old Testament is the written record of the message of the prophets. And the New Testament is largely the witness of the apostles to the life, ministry, and teaching of the Lord Jesus Christ. Together they form the sixty-six books of our Bible and serve as the inspired, inerrant, infallible, sufficient, reliable, and resounding reminder of the glorious gospel of grace!

In these two testaments God has given us a textbook for "life and godliness" (1:3), which contains "very great and precious promises" (v. 4) intended gradually to make us "share in the divine nature" (v. 4) as we wait for "the power and coming of our Lord Jesus Christ" (v. 16). And he makes no apology that the Bible is a book of repetition, whether it be the prophets' reminders about the Mosaic law in the Old Testament, the Gospel writers' reverberation of Jesus's acts and teachings in the New Testament, or the apostolic witness to the same. The Bible says the same thing over and over again from Genesis to Revelation. It gives testimony to the gospel, God's redemption of his creation.

Within that witness is contained the weighty doctrine at hand in 2 Peter. The importance of remembering the certainty of the second coming of Jesus Christ can't be overstated. This doctrine is a key component of the gospel and one of the primary motivations for godly living. Christ's rule and return, including his final judgment of all people, truly is one of those "very great and precious promises" (v. 4) that's foundational to the Christian calling. While we navigate the ups and downs of daily life in our journey through this world, let's set our gaze toward the east and think often of Christ's return. And may the reality that he may appear at any moment compel us to holy living and progressive spiritual maturity.

Reflect and Discuss

1. Why do we constantly need to be reminded of the truth of the gospel?
2. What are practical ways that we, like Peter, can "wake up" one another? How can we "wake up" ourselves?
3. How can we practically avoid "functional amnesia"?
4. What is the significance of Peter's and the other apostles' eyewitness testimony?
5. What part does ancient eyewitness testimony play in modern-day evangelism?
6. How should personal experience be balanced with the Word of God? How does Peter balance it?
7. How does a Christian leader avoid carelessly using Scripture that results in one's "own interpretation" or faulty interpretation? What steps can be made to avoid this at all cost?
8. How does the true teaching that Jesus will return in glory spur us on to godliness?
9. How does verse 21 speak to the doctrine of inspiration? Why is this important?
10. What implications does divine inspiration carry, specifically in how we read and apply the Bible?

Remember Their Motives

2 PETER 2:1-3A

Main Idea: Believers must beware of teachers who discredit the gospel through deception, sexual immorality, and greed.

I. **They Smuggle Destruction (2:1).**
   A. How they work
   B. What they teach
   C. Where they're headed
II. **They Scandalize the Gospel (2:2).**
   A. The temptation to godless conduct
   B. The tarnish to gospel credibility
III. **They Swindle Believers (2:3a).**

Thomas Jefferson first wrote the phrase "All men are created equal" in the U.S. Declaration of Independence in 1776, at the beginning of the American Revolution. It's been said that these simple yet profound words have had the greatest continuing importance of any that came out of the period. But while all men certainly are equal, all prophets are not. And that contention is the common denominator between chapters 1 and 2. Having reminded his readers that the apostolic witness and the prophetic word are the reliable sources for the believer's confidence in Christ's coming (1:16-21), Peter now shifts his focus to remind them about an unreliable source: false teachers. He draws this distinction by using the conjunction "indeed" at the beginning of 2:1. He just told his readers that since the Holy Spirit inspired the prophets, the prophetic Scriptures should be trusted because both their revelation and their interpretation came from God. Now he warns his readers of a sobering reality—not all prophets are from God (Schreiner, *1 and 2 Peter*, 325).

To make his case Peter uses language in 2:1–3:3 that's similar to that used by Jude in his letter. In 2:1 he identifies the culprits as "false prophets" who deny Christ's return as well as other Christian truth. They are to be associated with their counterparts who were "among the people" of Israel in ancient times. Now they've invaded the church and are "among you," Peter says. He sees them as fulfilling the prophecies of the Old Testament, Jesus, and the apostle Paul (see Deut 13:1-5; Jer 23:9-22; Matt 7:15-23; 24:23-26; Acts 20:28-30; 2 Tim 3:1-9; 4:1-4). Their primary target is unsuspecting people who at least profess to be part of the community of faith. So Peter desperately wants his readers to pay attention to the truth spoken by the apostles and prophets over against these heretics who are scavenging their ranks. They are "apostates from the faith, and their aim is to draw disciples after themselves" (G. L. Green, *Jude*, 235).

The stakes of progressive Christian growth discussed in chapter 1 are now raised. If Christ isn't coming back, then the foundation and motivation for godly living disappears. That's the agenda fostered by these false teachers. Although Peter uses the future tense here, the present tense in 2:10b forward indicates he's talking about an impending— and even present—reality both for his readers and for us. "There always have been and there always will be false teachers among the people of God" (M. Green, *2 Peter*, 116). So in 2:1-3 Peter unpacks how these false teachers are motivated by a desire to secretly introduce destructive teaching, smear the gospel, and embezzle money from Christians.

They Smuggle Destruction
2 PETER 2:1

Due to my frequent international travel, not long ago I applied for expedited customs privileges when returning to the United States from other countries. When I went for my interview as part of the application process, the agent asked me if I had ever been guilty of a customs violation. "No," I quickly replied, laughing under my breath at the absurdity of thought. Then he responded, "Well, it says here in our records that in 2002 you tried to bring some switchblades back into the country from the Philippines." As my forehead and palms began to sweat, I suddenly remembered the incident from years before. I had in fact tried to bring some switchblades back into the United States. I had bought them in a market in the Philippines and wanted to bring them home for my sons to add to their knife collections. The problem was I didn't know it was illegal to bring switchblades into our country! I even declared them as being in my luggage when I went through customs. But my ignorance didn't matter to the United States government. Customs agents quickly confiscated my souvenirs, and I now have a record for attempting to bring something illegal into the country!

Needless to say, I was denied expedited customs privileges. But the stakes are much higher for purveyors of false teaching. Their crime is greater, and their fate is worse. So Peter reminds his readers of *how they work*, *what they teach*, and *where they're headed.*

How They Work

My customs record was the result of an innocent mistake. Not so with false teachers. They don't "declare" their false doctrine when passing through customs at the church door. They try to hide it and bring it in by stealth. The verb translated "bring in" is *pareisagō*, which carries the idea of smuggling or introducing something in a deceptive way. While the word doesn't always connote a secretive bringing in, it likely does in this context. These teachers weren't hiding what they were teaching but merely covering up the degree to which their teaching differed from the apostolic teaching (Moo, *2 Peter*, 92). They were sneaking destructive ideas into the community of faith and infiltrating the Christian ranks with unorthodox principles. False teachers never stand up and announce, "I've got some stuff to tell you that's totally false!" No, they introduce their teaching as if it were the real thing, as if it were the guidance that's true and beneficial.

Jesus told us it would be this way. He warned, "Be on your guard against false prophets who come to you in sheep's clothing but inwardly are ravaging wolves" (Matt 7:15). No heretical wolf ever comes displaying his natural appearance, but he disguises himself in the garb of one who will be received by the flock as just another innocent sheep. The apostle Paul was equally burdened with this reality and knew it would be commonplace in the church. He was clear about the true impetus for such deception:

> *For such people are false apostles, deceitful workers, disguising themselves as apostles of Christ. And no wonder! For even Satan disguises himself as an angel of light. So it is no surprise if his servants also disguise themselves as servants of righteousness. Their end will be according to their works.* (2 Cor 11:13-15; cf. Gal 2:4; 2 Tim 3:1-5,13; Jude 4)

The one behind the disguise of any false teacher is Satan himself. He's the one who desires to pull unsuspecting religious adherents into eternal destruction. He is not clothed in a red suit and carrying a fiery pitchfork when he approaches people. He shows up dressed as preachers and small group leaders and student workers. And so our recognition of them can't be based on what they wear or otherwise look like. It has to be based on whether their words square with the Bible.

What They Teach

I assume our government doesn't allow us to bring switchblades into the country because they're considered harmful. That's the way it is with false teaching. What these false teachers were smuggling wasn't to be taken lightly. The words "destructive heresies" indicate fatally ruinous ideas, ones that don't lead to mere temporal destruction but to the second death and eternal exclusion from Christ's kingdom (see 2:3; 3:7,16; cf. Matt 7:13; Rom 9:22; Phil 1:28; 3:19; 1 Tim 6:9; Heb 10:39; Rev 17:8,11). This was and is a matter of eternal life and death! Instruction not rooted in the apostolic witness and the prophetic word—in other words, not rooted in the Bible—is instruction set on turning people away from the true words of life and toward that which will lead to eternal separation from God. Switchblades can only cause temporal death, but instruction contrary to the Bible can lead people to hell.

Ultimately, false teaching that leads people to an eternal hell can only be rooted in one thing: a denial of the person and work of Christ. That's exactly what the heretics in Peter's day were doing. They were "even denying the Master who bought them." The term "Master" (*despotēs*) means "sovereign lord" and is often used in the New Testament to refer to God (e.g., Acts 4:24). But the qualifier here to the one "who bought them" likely makes this a reference to the Lord Jesus Christ (Vaughn and Lea, *1, 2 Peter*, 168; see also Jude 4). The term "bought" (*agorazō*) carries the idea of purchasing from a marketplace" (see Deut 32:5-6; Zeph 1:4-6) as a master of a household might purchase a slave and then assign that slave responsibilities over various tasks. They now owed their complete allegiance to him because they were his personal property.

However, the false teachers refused to submit to Christ's authority yet *claimed* to be part of his household. They claimed Christ as their Redeemer, but they refused his sovereign lordship, thus revealing their true character as unregenerate enemies of biblical truth. Both in conduct and in doctrine, the false teachers were rejecting the life demanded by their Redeemer, thus revealing their true character as unregenerate men (MacArthur, *2 Peter*, 73). A lifestyle of ungodliness always stems from rejecting Christ and his redemptive work, regardless of what one claims.

Ultimately, these false teachers were advocating something that was present in Corinth (1 Cor 6:19-20; 7:23) and is certainly a problem in Christian circles today. I'm talking about the abuse of grace that leads to freedom from holiness. No doubt the liberty afforded by the work of Christ is one of the banners waved by those who embrace such error (see 2:19). But these people refuse to acknowledge and obey the responsibility of holy living that the cross demands. Christianity is most certainly a religion of liberty, but it demands that its adherents willingly and lovingly submit to the one who redeemed them. The designation "servant" was something New Testament leaders gladly imposed on themselves (cf. Rom 1:1; Phil 1:1; Titus 1:1; Jas 1:1; Jude 1). The cross of Christ demands no less from us.

Where They're Headed

I was disappointed when those customs agents confiscated my switchblades that I intended to be gifts for my boys, and I greatly regret that having a customs violation on my record prevents me from obtaining the convenience of expedited customs service; but those consequences for my mistake pale in comparison to the ones awaiting those who intentionally deceive people into denying Christ. Before leaving the false teachers' sinister work of smuggling destruction, Peter tips his hat to a theme on which he will expand later in this chapter—the judgment awaiting false teachers (see 2:4-10). Bauckham identifies three characteristics of false prophets in the Bible, each of which applies to the ones here: (1) they lack divine authority, (2) they promise peace when God threatens judgment, and (3) they will certainly be judged by God (Bauckham, *2 Peter*, 238). The third one is particularly relevant here since these false teachers refused to see the coming of Christ as the climax of human history.

Peter basically says false teachers will reap what they sow, as they "will bring swift destruction on themselves." Because they sow the seeds of destruction within the community of faith, they will reap the very end they wish for their hearers. And the realization of their fate will be "swift," a word that means the approach will come quickly in an unexpected manner. These and all false teachers are headed for a fast-approaching judgment of eternal destruction and separation from God. Michael Green says, "The man who attempts to serve God and self is on the high road to *swift destruction*, for either death or the parousia will cut him off in mid-course" (M. Green, *2 Peter*, 118). Christ is jealous for his bride, the church, and he will defend her by condemning those who seek to mislead his disciples.

Consequently, Christ will not tolerate false teachers among his people, and he expects his disciples to follow suit (cf. Matt 7:15-20; Acts 13:6-12; 1 Tim 1:18-20; 6:3-5; 2 Tim 3:1-9; 1 John 4:1-3; 2 John 7-11; 3 John 9-11; see also Isa 9:15; Jer 28:15-17; 29:21,32; Mic 3:5-7). But Christians and local churches today often do just the opposite. In the name of love, unity, and acceptance, we tolerate any teacher in person, on television, or through podcast who claims to be a believer and has an appealing presentation, regardless of what they are teaching. The result has been the development of a careless indifference to the truth. It's caused many Christians to view biblical absolutes as being archaic and even embarrassing (MacArthur, *2 Peter*, 68). Christ's disciples, and especially those who lead them, must heed Peter's words and take false teaching seriously and deal with it proactively.

Before leaving this verse, an important point of clarification needs to be made. Like other verses in 2 Peter, 2:1 has been the subject of much debate, in this case as to whether these teachers were genuine Christians who lost their salvation. But let's not forget that Peter asserted in his first letter that those who belong to God are being guarded by his power through faith so as to possess their salvation forever (1 Pet 1:5). If we let Scripture interpret Scripture, we're compelled to see Peter's words here as being consistent with the numerous other texts that teach the eternal security of the true believer (e.g., Rom 8:28-39; 1 Cor 1:8-9; Phil 1:6; 1 Thess 5:23-24).

These false teachers—like many church members who follow them—apparently had made a "profession of faith" and for a season had given the impression that they were truly saved. But their ultimate denial of Christ revealed that their profession wasn't genuine. Like so many people today who walk away from the church, it becomes apparent that

> they are wolves in the flock (Acts 20:29-30), that though they called on Jesus as Lord their disobedience shows that he *never* knew them (Matt 7:21-23), that they are like the seed sown on rocky or thorny ground that initially bears fruit but dries up and dies when hard times come (Matt 13:20-22). (Schreiner, *1 and 2 Peter*, 331–32)

The concern of this in 2 Peter 2:1 is twofold. First, it's a warning to unbelievers who are currently interacting with the community of faith that false teaching will lead them to the same eternal destruction that awaits the teachers (see Matt 13:20-22,36-42,47-50). Second, it's a warning to true believers that tolerating false teaching sets them up for shipwrecked faith (see 1 Tim 1:18-20). May these words be a wake-up call for us all.

They Scandalize the Gospel
2 PETER 2:2

I heard an interview one time with a prominent professional athlete who was known for his riotous living, boisterous demeanor, and sexual promiscuity. The reporter asked him about the effect he was having on young people who looked up to him because of his stardom. He responded with the sentiment that he hadn't asked to be anyone's role model and, furthermore, didn't want to be anyone's role model. Not long afterward another athlete responded to the star's flippant dismissal of responsibility. He wisely said, "That's not his call; it comes with the territory." The second athlete was right. Some things in life just can't be separated. Conduct and influence are inseparable. In verse 2 Peter asserts that *godless conduct* among professing Christians will always be followed by damage to *gospel credibility* in the eyes of the world.

The Temptation to Godless Conduct

In every age teachers are role models to their students, not just conveyors of information (Davids, *Letters*, 222). So when it comes to the influence of false teaching, the body count is never minimal. Casualties always abound within the community of faith, and the carnage has a tendency to spread like gangrene (cf. 2 Tim 2:16-18). Peter says that "many" will be deceived by the false teachers and become devoted to their godless conduct. And their influence was all the more tempting because of its erotic nature. The word translated "depraved" (*aselgeiais*) in the New Testament usually refers to sexual sin (Rom 13:13; 2 Cor 12:21; Gal 5:19; Eph 4:19; 1 Pet 4:3). Jude actually uses the idea to compare the sins of false teachers to those of Sodom and Gomorrah:

> *For some people, who were designated for this judgment long ago,*
> *have come in by stealth; they are ungodly, turning the grace of our*
> *God into sensuality and denying Jesus Christ, our only Master and*
> *Lord. . . . Likewise, Sodom and Gomorrah and the surrounding*

> *towns committed sexual immorality and perversions, and serve as an*
> *example by undergoing the punishment of eternal fire.* (Jude 4,7)

Peter will use the word two more times in this chapter to convey the same idea (see vv. 7,18). And in a sex-crazed culture like ours, large numbers of people are ready to jump on the bandwagon when such tantalizing merchandise is being peddled.

This "trendy" nature of following false teaching into godless conduct shouldn't surprise us. Jesus made clear that a whole lot more people will choose the broad road that leads to destruction than the narrow road that leads to true life (Matt 7:13-14; cf. 24:10-12). Much of the fault for this tragic reality can be laid at the feet of false teachers who clothe the broad way in appealing attire and promise that it leads to happiness and fulfillment. MacArthur rightly observes, "Their message of independence, personal freedom, and self-exaltation is inherently appealing to fallen human hearts, who would rather serve themselves than submit to Christ" (*2 Peter*, 76). Jesus was also clear that "not everyone who says to me, 'Lord, Lord,' will enter the kingdom of heaven, but only the one who does the will of my Father in heaven" (Matt 7:21). It doesn't matter what people claim about faith in Christ but what they demonstrate in obedience to him (cf. John 15:14-16; Jas 1:22-25; 1 John 2:3-6; 5:1-5).

The Tarnish to Gospel Credibility

The malignant effect of the temptation to godless living, however, isn't the most devastating result of this strand of false teaching. Its ultimate end is that the gospel "will be maligned" (v. 2) before the world "because of" these apostates who abandon it. The reference to "the way of truth" is clearly a synonym for the gospel. Early disciples of Christ often were referred to as followers of "the Way" (Acts 9:2; 19:9,23; 24:14,22) or the "way of the Lord" (Acts 18:25; cf. v. 26). The designation was a reminder that Christianity isn't so much a set of propositional truths to be believed as it is a way of life to be lived (Davids, *Letters*, 222).

So when a self-identified Christian's way of life is contrary to Jesus's life, it scandalizes the gospel and tarnishes its credibility. Schreiner describes it well:

> The unbelieving world sees the impact on the church and
> responds by maligning and ridiculing "the way of truth." "The
> way of truth" is a reference to the gospel. When unbelievers
> see the moral effect produced by the opponents in the lives of

their followers, they will conclude that the way of truth is a way of error. They will think that any message that leads to dissolute behavior cannot be from God (Schreiner, *1 and 2 Peter*, 332).

The embrace of false teaching always results in the gospel's being maligned. Appealing to Isaiah 52:5, Paul charged the Jews: "For, as it is written: 'The name of God is blasphemed among the Gentiles because of you'" (Rom 2:24). When professing Christians default on their faith, the gospel takes the hit. People will soon forget about the offender, but their distaste for the gospel will hang around for a long time.

The New Testament isn't silent about calling Christians to righteous living for the sake of the gospel's reputation. Christian slaves were to honor their masters so the gospel wouldn't be criticized (1 Tim 6:1). Young believing wives were to live godly lives so people wouldn't revile the gospel (Titus 2:5). Paul said he put no obstacle in anyone's way so no fault would be found with the gospel (2 Cor 6:3). In his first letter Peter told his readers to live honorably and do good so that critics of the gospel would be silenced and put to shame and instead they would glorify God (1 Pet 2:12,15; 3:16). When it comes to the lives we lead, our first concern shouldn't be for our reputation; it should be for the reputation of the gospel. And the only way to make the gospel believable is for Christians to live the kind of righteous lives that make it believable.

So, fellow disciple of Christ, live in such a way "that you may be blameless and pure, children of God who are faultless in a crooked and perverted generation, among whom you shine like stars in the world" (Phil 2:15; cf. Matt 5:16; Eph 2:10; 5:8; 1 Thess 2:12; Titus 2:5,7,14; 1 Pet 2:9-12). If you're a star athlete, you're a role model whether you like it or not. If you're a Christian, you bear the reputation of the gospel, and your godliness—or lack thereof—will always affect it. As you remember the motives of false teachers around you to discredit the gospel, let it compel you to remember the holy life for which that gospel saved you.

They Swindle Believers
2 PETER 2:3A

Bernie Madoff arguably is the most notorious American fraudster in history. In 2009 the former stockbroker, investment advisor, and financier admitted to operating a Ponzi scheme that is considered the largest financial fraud ever. Prosecutors estimated that Madoff swindled about $64.8 billion out of his 4,800 clients. On June 29, 2009, he was sentenced to 150 years in prison. Madoff's arrest and conviction came after his two sons—who were employed by his firm—told authorities their father had confessed to them that the asset management unit of his firm was just a massive Ponzi scheme. They quoted him as saying it was "one big lie."

A discernable link often exists between falsehood and greed. Destroying lives and undermining the gospel weren't the only motives of the false teachers in Peter's day. They were in it for personal gain as well. Peter says "their greed" (v. 3) also drives them to infiltrate the Christian ranks and wreak havoc in people's lives. The verb "exploit" is a commercial term that suggests a monetary motive. The false teachers saw Peter's readers as a source of financial gain. Peter will go on to describe these religious charlatans as having "hearts trained in greed" (2:14). This indictment and characterization of false teachers is common in Scripture (see Jer 6:13; 8:10; 1 Tim 6:3,5,9-11; Titus 1:7,11; 1 Pet 5:1-3; Jude 11,16). They crave wealth and are experts at swindling people in the church out of their money (MacArthur, *2 Peter*, 78).

The approach these tricksters used to cheat people wasn't divorced from their false doctrine. They used "made-up stories" (v. 3)—or cunning precepts they simply fabricated—to swindle the unassuming listeners. They manufactured bogus arguments to sway people over to their side. And these wolves in sheep's clothing were making a good profit off of those who bought in to their teaching and made contributions to them (Bauckham, *2 Peter*, 243). "These teachers were not selling a product to help their hearers. They were hawking defective goods (morally speaking) for their own financial advantage" (Schreiner, *1 and 2 Peter*, 333; cf. 2:14).

This ought to sound all too familiar to believers today. Observe the frequent relationship between false teaching and materialism. Christian television, publishing, conferencing, and numerous other vehicles of mass communication are big business today. When used to disseminate the true gospel with integrity, these avenues are effective means for spreading truth and advancing Christ's kingdom. But when these mediums are infiltrated and hijacked by false teachers, they become ready resources for distributing intoxicating and cancerous information. All the while, the propagation of false teaching yields flowing streams of income that pad perverted pockets.

Obviously the biggest lesson here is the need for us to avoid buying in to false teaching and reaping its devastating spiritual effects. But we also must be discerning when it comes to where we invest our money in "kingdom" work. The satanic agenda to shipwreck faith isn't usually discernable to the naked eye. But the lucrative lifestyles, pretentious presentations, and comic commercialism that characterizes the ministries of some preachers and teachers is often blatant. Their flamboyant auras, atmospheres, and appeals should serve as red flags to the false doctrine lurking in the shadows. I believe this is just one of the reasons that accountable giving through one's local church is the New Testament's primary model. Contributions beyond that practice should always be made only after thorough examination of doctrinal beliefs and careful scrutiny of financial practices.

Conclusion

The first three verses of 2 Peter 2 are incredibly telling and eerily characteristic of our own Christian culture. The tactic of false teachers is to introduce their erroneous doctrine by stealth, not in apparent fashion. They also slander the gospel through sexually licentious lifestyles, and they rip off people's money because of their greed. These verses need to serve as a sobering reminder of Satan's schemes. As Peter previously charged, "Be sober-minded, be alert. Your adversary the devil is prowling around like a roaring lion, looking for anyone he can devour" (1 Pet 5:8). And the believer's primary defense is a working knowledge of and unwavering obedience to the authoritative word of the apostles and prophets recorded in the Bible.

Every generation between Peter's and ours has faced the same challenge. For example, the nineteenth century was at a period when society's views on human freedom were challenging the nature of biblical authority. In October 1855, Vincent van Gogh, the gifted yet conflicted artist, finished an oil painting he titled *Still Life with Bible*. The painting features an open Bible sitting on a table. To the right of the Bible is a burned-out candle in its holder. In the foreground of the painting van Gogh positioned a small yellow book, the binding of which identified it as Emile Zola's *The Joy of Life*. David Helm interprets the scene:

> By placing a burned-out candle beside the Bible and by
> putting both in the background, van Gogh is telling us that
> the time for walking through this world by the illumination
> of the Holy Spirit, who shines down upon God's Word, is past.
> Biblical authority no longer holds sway. People are guided by
> different, if not lesser lights. That is what he is saying. Even

the flaming color of yellow is now reserved for the cover
of another book. Humanity's new pursuit is governed by
whatever brings us *the joy of life*. (Helm, *1 & 2 Peter*, 223)

The apostle's words recorded in 2 Peter 2:1-3 not only described his
own day but predicted the climate of van Gogh's long before it arrived.
In both eras, "people were following another path, carried along by a
candle of a different sort" (Helm, *1 & 2 Peter*, 223). Peter's words, however, merely reflect the reality that every generation will face: the threat
of society to extinguish the light of God's Word and instead chase after
relativism, sexual promiscuity, and monetary wealth. May it never happen on our watch.

Reflect and Discuss

1. Does the hard and sharp language of Peter surprise you? How
   should we respond in order to be in accord with his resolve to
   rebuke and silence false teaching?
2. What are the defining characteristics of a false teacher? Is it easy to
   pinpoint false teaching?
3. What is the difference between a false teacher and a teacher who
   unintentionally teaches something that is biblically inaccurate?
4. With all of the material available through modern-day media, how
   can we practically shepherd our people to discern what is false and
   what is true?
5. Discerning false teaching is a good, godly, and necessary thing.
   However, many times we go overboard, being overly critical of a
   fellow servant of God. How do we navigate the fine line of harshly
   rebuking false teaching without tearing down a true brother?
6. How can we, as teachers of God's Word, avoid careless mistakes that
   may lead to error in interpretation or teaching?
7. What exactly was the message of these ancient false teachers? Is
   this present today? What are examples of prominent false teaching
   today?
8. How can we precisely articulate the gospel of grace without giving
   license to sin?
9. In what way does false teaching rip away credibility from the gospel?
10. What are areas in our own lives that may tarnish gospel credibility?

Remember God's Justice

2 PETER 2:3B-10A

Main Idea: Because God is just, believers are assured of his help for trials and his punishment of the enemies.

I. God Promises His Justice in the Future (2:3b).
II. God Proved His Justice in the Past (2:4-8).
    A. Example 1: Fallen angels (2:4)
    B. Example 2: Noah and the flood (2:5)
    C. Example 3: Sodom and Gomorrah (2:6-8)
III. God Provides His Justice in the Present (2:9-10a).
    A. He rescues the godly from trials (2:9a).
    B. He reserves the godless for torment (2:9b-10a).

The rapid growth in the number of terrorist attacks in our world during the last two decades, as well as the seemingly more frequent occurrence of natural disasters, are just a couple of the things that have caused our culture to question God's integrity, if not his existence. "If God is loving," many ask, "why does he allow innocent people to suffer?" Others pose simpler questions: "Why do bad things happen to good people?" or "Why is there so much suffering in the world?" While these questions aren't new, they do reflect an increasing skepticism in our culture about the justice of God. If God exists, shouldn't he be fair? Abraham himself appealed to this assumed quality when God announced his judgment on Sodom:

> *You could not possibly do such a thing: to kill the righteous with the wicked, treating the righteous and the wicked alike. You could not possibly do that! Won't the Judge of the whole earth do what is just?*
> (Gen 18:25)

It's a good question: If God is good and righteous, shouldn't there be a difference between the way he treats the righteous and the wicked?

Peter's Christian readers were wondering the same thing as their spiritual knees buckled under the weight of false teaching. One argument their opponents were making against final judgment was that it couldn't involve both salvation and condemnation. It had to be either-or. Either the righteous would have to be condemned, or the wicked would have to be saved. And because they deemed neither to be morally acceptable, they concluded that judgment wasn't coming (Davids, *Letters*, 228). So Peter responds by demonstrating that God is fair and just and that he does discriminate in his treatment of the righteous and the wicked. Peter even takes it a step farther to show the immediate, practical implications for the Christian life. The justice of God, he says, assures believers of strong help for their trials while at the same time guarantees that their enemies will be punished.

The structure and flow of 2:3b-10a is important and provides us with a helpful way to develop the text. In the second half of verse 3, Peter suggests that God is just because he promises to condemn the false teachers. Then, beginning with verse 4 and going through the first part of verse 10, he uses a long conditional statement to show that since God has proven his justice in history past (vv. 4-8), he will be faithful to provide it for believers now (vv. 9-10a). In other words, Peter gives us a past-present-future glimpse of God's righteous judgment. He shows us that God will be just in the future because he has been just in the past. Consequently, he can be trusted to be just in the present in dealing with both believers and unbelievers.

God Promises His Justice in the Future
2 PETER 2:3B

Sometimes when I'm joking around with my wife and poking at her about something, she'll retaliate by threatening, "You better sleep with one eye open tonight, buddy!" She recommends that I stay awake and alert. In 2:3, Peter essentially says the same thing about the condemnation that's coming to the false teachers. He personifies God's condemnation and says that it has always had one eye open! He says, "Their condemnation, . . . is not idle, and their destruction does not sleep." The latter phrase suggests drowsiness and—used here with the negative—indicates that God's condemnation isn't nodding off! It's still in effect and has been hanging over their heads for a long time. Far from sleeping, it's imminent (Davids, *Letters*, 224). The picture here is of "eternal damnation as if it were an executioner, who remains fully awake, ready to administer God's just sentence of condemnation on those who falsify His Word" (MacArthur, *2 Peter*, 83–84). God will keep his promise!

Peter no doubt is reiterating here his earlier contention that these false teachers "will bring swift destruction on themselves" (v. 1). But he's also implying an attitude that he'll flesh out more in chapter 3. There he will tell us,

> *Scoffers will come in the last days scoffing and following their own evil desires, saying, "Where is his 'coming' that he promised? Ever since our ancestors fell asleep, all things continue as they have been since the beginning of creation."* (3:3-4)

In other words, they will sarcastically mock the idea that Christ is coming again to execute the judgment of God against the unrighteous. They will say that it's been thousands of years already, and yet there is no sign of his appearing. Consequently, they will continue to justify their ungodly lifestyles and heretical beliefs.

The same is true of the unbelieving world in our day. People deny the return (and even existence!) of Christ. They dismiss the promise of God to bring about his righteous judgment. And they use their denial as a license for selfish and godless living. False teachers—who are to be counted among their ranks—lead the pack of those who operate as if God's condemnation was dozing, if not already fully asleep. Even if they preach the second coming, they don't believe it in their heart of hearts. If they did believe it, they would know that even if God's condemnation appears to be sleeping, then it's sleeping with one eye open. But neither God nor his condemnation sleeps (cf. Ps 121:3-4). He hasn't forgotten his justice, and his righteous judgment is looming. He promises to be just by condemning the unrighteous.

God Proved His Justice in the Past
2 PETER 2:4-8

There's not much I despise more than the barrage of political ads that floods the airways during election season. The character assassination, mudslinging, and name calling that cloud the real issues are a big turn-off for me. But one thing I find of interest in those ads is track records. Periodically, a candidate will rehearse how he or she (or an opponent) has typically voted on particular issues. Track records are important because they assert that how someone has acted in the past is usually a fairly good indicator of how they will act in the future. Peter thought God's track record was important, so he rehearses it here to show that God can be trusted to be fair and just when it comes to his judgment.

Peter already has clearly asserted that the condemnation pronounced against these false teachers "long ago" (v. 3; cf. Jude 4) in the Old Testament is still pending and will eventually consume them. While our English Bibles include his words there as part of verse 3, they fit better as an introduction to what follows in 2:4-8. From the first pronouncement of judgment on the serpent in the garden (Gen 3:13-15), God consistently has condemned all who misrepresent his truth (cf. Isa 8:19-21; 28:15; Jer 9:6-9; 14:14-15; Zeph 3:1-8; Rev 21:8,27). So in 2:4-8 Peter illustrates this reality by offering three Old Testament examples of how God, throughout history, consistently has punished the unrighteous. He speaks of God's condemnation of sinning angels (v. 4), of Noah's generation (v. 5), and of Sodom and Gomorrah (vv. 6-8). In these examples he includes a new twist. Just as God's justice has led him to punish the unrighteous, it has compelled him to preserve the righteous as well. Once again Peter's words in this passage bear a striking resemblance to Jude's letter (cf. Jude 5-7).

Example 1: Fallen Angels (2:4)

The first example Peter provides to verify God's justice in the past is that he "didn't spare the angels who sinned." While he doesn't tell us the specific sin of these fallen angels or a particular incident, it's likely that he's referring to the story in Genesis 6:1-4 where certain angels somehow crossed species lines and had sexual relations with women on earth. Their actions obviously involved both rebellion and sensual lust (cf. Jude 6), which is consistent with both Peter's and Jude's arguments. This sin moved God to "cast them into hell." The phrase is one word in Greek, and it is only used here in the Bible. It means to "consign to Tartarus," which in Greek mythology was the place of punishment of the spirits of the most wicked people (M. Green, *2 Peter*, 122). Peter probably chose a familiar idiom to relate to the large number of converted pagans among his readers as well as to distinguish it from the place of final punishment often referred to with our English word *hell*.

The intended meaning of the word translated "chains" also is uncertain due to textual variations. Some manuscripts use a similar word that is translated "dungeons." But what is clear (and most important!) is that these chains or dungeons provide the context in which these angels are being "kept for judgment." Peter suggests that these unrighteous angels are being held in a place of temporary punishment until the day of final judgment.

No doubt many mysteries exist in Peter's language here. He leaves us with lots of questions. What did these angels do to deserve this punishment? What exactly are the chains that are holding them? Are those chains literal or metaphorical? Where is this place they are being held? Why did Peter use a term from Greek mythology to designate it? In response, let me offer two observations. First, these are not the only unknowns with which the Bible leaves us when it comes to angels and their destiny. After all, Paul rhetorically asked of the Corinthians, "Don't you know that we will judge angels?" (1 Cor 6:3). What in the world is that going to look like? We can't expect to know and comprehend all the details of the angelic economy. Second, the answers to the questions above don't have bearing on the major reason for this part of Peter's example. His point is to argue from the greater to the lesser: If great and powerful angels can't escape God's judgment, how much less will mortal men like false teachers escape (Vaughn and Lea, *1, 2 Peter*, 170)!

The other side of Peter's argument—God's justice for the righteous—can only be inferred here in Peter's first example. He doesn't directly address any *innocent* angels God preserved like he does the righteous individuals in the following two examples, namely Noah (v. 5) and Lot (vv. 7-8). This absence may be due to the author's wanting to make a distinction between corporeal, earthly beings and those that are not. Peter may not have deemed it appropriate to say that angels were either righteous or unrighteous. At any rate, the subsequent examples would suggest that Peter wants us to conclude that other angels didn't sin and, therefore, were preserved by God. Obviously, there are hosts of angels who actually did "keep their own position" and "proper dwelling" (Jude 6), and the context of the current paragraph implies that God was responsible for preserving them in that role (see Schreiner, *1 and 2 Peter*, 335). Conclusion: God has proven his justice from the beginning of time by discriminating in his judgment between angels that sinned and those that didn't.

Example 2: Noah and the Flood (2:5)

Peter's second example of God's justice is drawn from the story of Noah and the flood that obliterated the vast majority of the earth's inhabitants during his day (Gen 6–8). Jesus himself used this event and the subsequent one about Sodom and Gomorrah to warn about God's sudden destruction of sensual people (Luke 17:26-29). Peter's point here is best understood by considering the beginning and end of the verse together: "[God] didn't spare the ancient world . . . when he brought the flood on the world of the ungodly." The words "didn't spare" are repeated from the previous verse and emphasize two realities. First, judgment is indeed a reality. Second, any hope is eliminated that God might show mercy and change his mind about judging the world (Schreiner, *1 and 2 Peter*, 337–38). Peter is making the same point as before. Like the sinning angels, God didn't spare an entire generation that rebelled against him but exercised his righteous judgment on them by flooding the earth.

In this example, however, Peter explicitly identifies the other side of God's righteous judgment, that of protecting the righteous. In the midst of judging the unrighteous with the flood, God "protected Noah." Three specific details are given that provide rich application regarding God's protection of a righteous person. First, he "protected" him. This idea will be further unpacked in reference to Lot in 2:7-8, but here it foreshadows the gospel of grace and hope that only God can provide in Christ Jesus. Second, Noah was "a preacher of righteousness," a designation that isn't so much a reference to Noah's being justified as it is to his service to God. The righteous person's service to God will stand in obvious contrast to the rest of his or her generation. And it will always involve calling others to repentance. Third, God's mercy wasn't just extended to Noah but to Noah "and seven others." The English phrase is a translation of a single word that encompassed Noah's wife, his three sons, and their wives (cf. 1 Pet 3:20). The godly are most often in the minority. False teachers will usually attract a following, and that can become discouraging. But although the godly are often fewer in numbers, God is always faithful to preserve them (Moo, *2 Peter*, 104).

The introduction of this other side to God's justice had to be a comforting thought to Peter's audience, as it should be to us. It is a refreshing drink of cold water in the midst of so much heated talk about judgment. Believers often can grow weary toeing the line of righteousness in a sinful world that stands in the crosshairs of God's condemnation. Sometimes we grow weary of proclaiming the heaviness of judgment that awaits the unrepentant. At other times we grow impatient with Christ's delayed return and find ourselves tempted to dabble in the world. The fact that God has been just in not only punishing the wicked but also in protecting the righteous ought to encourage us to stand by the truth of Scripture and resist the false teaching of the age.

Example 3: Sodom and Gomorrah (2:6-8)

The third and most lengthy example Peter gives of the proof of God's justice involves the destruction of Sodom and Gomorrah and the deliverance of Lot (cf. Gen 18:22–19:29). We're told that when he "reduced the cities . . . to ashes," he "condemned them to extinction" (v. 6). Basically, God torched them and burned them to the ground and sentenced them never to be rebuilt. Of the destruction Philo would later write,

> Even to this day there are seen in Syria monuments of the
> unprecedented destruction that fell upon them, in the ruins,
> and ashes, and sulphur, and smoke, and the dusky flame
> which still is sent up from the ground as of a fire smouldering
> beneath. (*Moses* 2.56)

Peter specifies something in this example that's only implied in the previous two. He highlights the fact that God exercised this condemnation in part as a warning to all who would follow after the way of the ungodly—"making them an example of what is coming to the ungodly" (v. 6). The perfect participle "making" indicates that the destruction of these cities serves as lasting evidence of what will happen to those who live godless lives (Vaughn and Lea, *1, 2 Peter*, 172). And it's clear from the parallel text in Jude 7 that the fiery physical punishment of these people was intended to prefigure eternal punishment in hell's fire. Our present culture needs to heed this example.

> There are curious parallels between our contemporary scene
> and Sodom, for that city was as famed for its affluence and
> softness as for its immorality—and, of course, like any men
> come of age, they thought they had outgrown the idea of God.
> They found out their mistake too late. (M. Green, *2 Peter*, 123)

I pray it's not too late for our generation.

As with the example of Noah, Peter then shows the proof of God's justice to protect the righteous by explaining how God delivered Lot. Again, similar to Noah, Lot likely isn't called "righteous" (v. 7) because he was completely upright but because he was a good man in comparison to the men of Sodom. He also may be categorized as such by virtue of his obedience to God's instructions during the judgment (cf. Gen 19:1-22). Don't forget that Peter's purpose here is not to set these men up as examples of justification before God but to give evidence that God is perfectly able to punish the ungodly while at the same time saving the righteous.

Peter then adds another new component in this third example. He highlights the effect the unrighteous culture was having on Lot. He describes him as "distressed by the depraved behavior of the immoral" (v. 7). The description suggests that his moral compass was "knocked about" by his exposure to his erotic atmosphere, to the point that he became dull to sin and apathetic about God's standards. Lot's waning faith is unpacked for us a bit more in verse 8: "For as that righteous man lived among them day by day, his righteous soul was tormented by the lawless deeds he saw and heard." What Lot saw and heard day in and day out took its toll on him. The exposure to the "lawless deeds" of the unprincipled people of his city literally tortured his spiritual nature. Lot was wearing down when God rescued him.

This commentary in 2:7b-8 about Lot's weakening defense likely is included for a couple of reasons. First, Peter wants to warn his readers about passive exposure to wickedness, especially of the sexual nature (see 1 Thess 4:1-8).

> The portrayal of Lot provides a warning to a generation of people who will view without protest television material that, a generation ago, they would never have considered seeing at a movie. (Vaughn and Lea, *1, 2 Peter*, 173)

We'll never completely be able to avoid hearing and seeing everything that's evil. But the default response to that predicament is not to throw up our hands and welcome the world into our lives and homes. When that happens, we stop crying out to God for his deliverance. Instead, we need to run from godlessness (cf. 1 Cor 6:18; 10:14; 1 Tim 6:11; 2 Tim 2:22), partly because of its devastating effects on our spiritual sensitivity and defenses. We must avoid settling in to our cultural climate. The biggest danger many of us face as believers is not being martyred for our faith but having our faith dulled by exposure to wickedness.

Second, Peter knew his readers could identify with Lot because they were getting frustrated and discouraged by the need to resist the false teachers. Many of them were wearing down, just as we do in our sensual culture. Peter wanted to encourage them and us with a reminder that God has a spotless track record of protecting his people during such trials and temptations. So this description of Lot's injured faith provides a perfect segue to what Peter says next.

God Provides His Justice in the Present
2 PETER 2:9-10A

I did my undergraduate degree in secondary education with a major in English and a minor in math. At the time, I was preparing to teach and coach in a public school. While I enjoy math, I have to be honest and say that the primary reason I went that route for my minor was because I felt it gave me the best chance of getting a job. But I did like grappling with all the axioms, theorems, postulates, corollaries, and hypotheses that guide the field. I especially liked the logic of rules that involved "if-then" statements, or conditional statements. My favorite was "If A=B and B=C, then A=C." The part after the "if" (A=B and B=C) is called a hypothesis, and the part after the "then" (A=C) is called a conclusion. The conclusion ("then") flows directly from the validity of the hypothesis ("if").

In 2:9-10, Peter draws a conclusion to his long "if-then" statement that he began back in verse 4. Beginning there and going through verse 8, he basically says, "If God didn't spare sinning angels, and if he didn't spare the ancient world but preserved Noah, and if he obliterated Sodom and Gomorrah but rescued Lot, THEN . . ." And his conclusion, marked by "then" at the beginning of verse 9, flows directly from the validity of his hypothesis: *Because God—in his justice—has both punished the wicked and preserved the righteous in the past, he can be trusted to do the same in the present.* Peter knew his readers were getting frustrated and discouraged in their ongoing attempts to resist the false teachers, so he encouraged them by reminding them of God's sovereign help for the righteous in times of trial and adversity. Today we have the same confidence. God will provide help to *protect the righteous from trials,* and at the same time he will continue to *preserve the godless for torment.*

He Rescues the Godly from Trials (2:9a)

The first part of Peter's conclusion is that God's track record proves he "knows how to rescue the godly from trials." He picks up the word "rescue" from the discussion of Lot (v. 7), which carries the same idea as "protected" in reference to Noah (v. 5). Two particular explanations about the rest of the statement help us understand what it says. First, the "trials" here are external circumstances, not internal desires. Our internal desires for evil are the result of our sinful hearts (cf. Jas 1:14) and need to be crucified (cf. Col 3:5). But God uses external circumstances to mature our faith and develop our endurance (cf. Jas 1:2-4,12).

Second, the preposition "from" (*ek*) is best understood to mean "out of" instead of "away from." While God will never tempt anyone to sin (cf. Jas 1:13), he never promises to protect us from ever facing trials. In fact, he uses them to accomplish the purposes like the ones mentioned above. And he always protects us in the midst of these trials by providing grace sufficient for each one (cf. Jas 1:5; see also 1 Cor 10:13).

Equally as important as noticing what this statement says is noticing what it does not say. It does not say God always protects his children from harm and even death. Peter's conclusion is that God's track record proves that he "knows how" (v. 9) to rescue his children from trials, not that he always chooses to do so. In the New Testament the term *trials* most often refers to tests a believer experiences as a result of embracing the gospel of Christ and advancing his mission. Jesus actually viewed his entire life as being characterized by such trials (cf. Luke 22:28; cf. Jas 1:2; 1 Pet 1:6). He said his followers would experience the same, sometimes even to death (cf. Matt 10:17-18,21-22; 24:9; Mark 13:9,12-13; Luke 21:12,16,17; John 15:19-20; 16:2; Rev 2:10). While Christians aren't immune to these trials, however, God does promise to give us everything necessary for us to emerge with our faith intact and our salvation untouched. Following Christ sometimes will bring physical harm, emotional stress, economic deprivation, and even physical death; but the sovereign, wise, and good God will always provide us with a "way out" so we can emerge in a better spiritual state (Moo, *2 Peter*, 116).

Putting all this in context, Peter wants to encourage his readers amid the biggest danger in any time of trial, that of apostasy (Luke 8:13; 22:28). Noah and Lot passed this test with flying colors. When the dust settled, they alone stood among the scoffers. Peter wanted us to know that God is faithful and promises to protect his children when they face such temptation (cf. Rev 3:10). He obviously isn't suggesting that God gives us a pass on facing any trials. He's just finished talking about how both Noah and Lot lived among the wicked and were confronted by evil people. Neither is he trying to say that true believers (the "righteous") never sin or that they never get killed along the way of righteous living. He simply wants to comfort us with the truth that God will protect his righteous ones from committing apostasy. When all is said and done, he won't let us forsake him (Schreiner, *1 and 2 Peter*, 343–44).

Before leaving this section, let's take a moment to behold the beautiful picture of the gospel we find in this text. Peter doesn't use examples of self-made, sinless men who earned God's protection. Like

Abraham, these men weren't free from sin (see Gen 9:18-28; 16:1-6; 19:1-38). Peter never says that God rescued Lot *because* he was a righteous man. In fact, Lot comes across as just the opposite—a man of the world who strayed a long way from the God of his fathers (see Gen 13:10-14; 19:16). He probably shouldn't have even been in Sodom in the first place! Although he was hospitable while there, he was weak and morally depraved (Gen 19:6-8). He was so invested in the city that he had to be dragged out when God's judgment fell (Gen 19:16). If that wasn't enough, after he left he proved himself to be a drunk (Gen 19:33,35)! Suffice it to say that this brother isn't a picture of what most of us think of when we think of righteousness!

Neither Noah nor Lot brought anything to the table by which they could rescue themselves or earn God's favor to do it for them. Their rescue operations were entirely due to the unmerited favor of God, which he shows to men because of what he is, not because of what they are or do (M. Green, *2 Peter*, 124; cf. Gen 19:16,19). Both Noah and Lot evidently received by faith God's judgment and instructions (cf. Gen 15:6; Rom 4:3,20-24), and therefore his righteousness was credited to them. God imputed his own righteousness to them because they trusted him.

What a great picture of the gospel! Jesus doesn't save us because we're all cleaned up and deserve his salvation but because we simply act in faith on what he has done for us. So Noah and Lot—like Abraham—are Old Testament illustrations of justification by faith. Like the apostle Paul, they can be said to have been "found in him, not having a righteousness of my own from the law, but one that is through faith in Christ—the righteousness from God based on faith" (Phil 3:9). Peter wanted his readers to know that it would not be by virtue of their inherent goodness that God would deliver them from their present trials or from the condemnation that he will bring on the ungodly. Instead, it will be because of their "knowledge of God and of Jesus our Lord" (2 Pet 1:2).

He Reserves the Godless for Torment (2:9b-10a)

Protecting the righteous in the midst of trials isn't the only thing God's track record proves he can do. Peter concludes he's also capable of keeping the unrighteous on track toward final judgment. God knows how "to keep the unrighteous under punishment for the day of judgment" (v. 9). The verb in this phrase is a present participle and can be interpreted at least two ways. Some believe it suggests that those who die outside of God's protection experience torment while they are waiting for the final judgment. In other words, they're in the process of being punished as they await the "day of judgment," or the final judgment at Christ's coming (Vaughn and Lea, *1, 2 Peter*, 174; cf. Luke 16:19-31). Others note that the present participle in Greek doesn't always indicate current activity. So the statement could simply mean that God holds the unrighteous for the day of judgment, at which time they will be punished (Davids, *Letters*, 232). Theologically, the two interpretations aren't mutually exclusive. Both can be true. God can be keeping the unrighteous for the day he will judge them in the end; in the meantime, he's holding them in some kind of temporary torment.

Actually, a third consideration is possible, which also is compatible with the others. Peter could be referring to God's judgment against sin in this life. Three times in Romans 1, Paul asserts that God "delivered over" sinful people to the consequences of their sin (Rom 1:24,26,28). Having turned from the true God to worship idols, they were handed over to sexual impurity, unnatural passions, and depraved thinking. Because these people chose their own way instead of God's, he allowed them to continue down their own path to its disastrous end. Maybe Peter is thinking about this kind of present judgment. Sin always has terrible consequences for the health of mind and body, and that's a form of punishment (Moo, *2 Peter*, 113–14). Regardless of whether it's one or more of these interpretations, the language here is terrifying. Those who reject God and his ways are doomed for torment.

Under the inspiration of the Spirit, Peter further specifies those who experience this "both now and then" torment. He says they are "those who follow the polluting desires of the flesh and despise authority" (v. 10). To "follow" was to "go after the flesh" and had as its objects two particular sins. To lust after "polluting desires" is synonymous with sexual immorality; and to despise "authority" refers to rebelling against God, whether through rejecting the gospel, church leadership, or just God in general. Possibly the reason Peter includes these qualifications is to set his words in context and ensure his readers know he's speaking of the false teachers in their midst. After all, the contexts of both Peter and Jude indicate that sensuality and rebellion were the dominating characteristics of these peddlers of destruction (see Jude 7-8).

The gospel of Christ shows up not only in God's protection of his children but even here in this terrifying pronouncement of impending judgment. Peter doesn't imply that the false teachers will be punished immediately. After all, the angels, the flood generation, and Sodom and Gomorrah weren't condemned the moment they began to sin. They lived in their rebellion for various periods of time before they were punished. God never wants us to be discouraged or wonder if he is faithful simply because he allows the godless to prosper for a season. What he wants is for us to remember that he graciously gives people plenty of time to repent before their judgment (Schreiner, *1 and 2 Peter*, 344; cf. Gen 15:16; Exod 34:6; Ps 86:15; Rom 9:22; 1 Tim 1:16; 1 Pet 3:20). Peter will say as much later in his letter: "The Lord does not delay his promise, as some understand delay, but is patient with you, not wanting any to perish but all to come to repentance" (3:9). The life, death, and resurrection of Christ are all clear demonstrations of God's patient heartbeat for the lost to repent.

While Peter wanted his readers to know the destiny of the false teachers who were harassing them, the Holy Spirit wants us to remember what awaits all who reject the gospel. If God didn't even spare sinning angels, what makes anyone think he will give a Get Out of Jail Free card to those who follow the company of false teachers today who deny a fixed and final judgment and whose lives and ministries are characterized by sensuality and greed (Helm, *1 & 2 Peter*, 226–27)? The horror of Peter's words compels us not only to stay the course of following the way of the prophets and apostles as recorded in the Bible, but his words also compel us to infiltrate every tribe and nation and tongue to warn them of God's terrifying judgment and offer them his glorious gospel.

Conclusion

For most people in our culture today, the concept of eternal punishment is a tough pill to swallow. The British agnostic Bertrand Russell wrote,

> There is one very serious defect to my mind in Christ's moral character, and that is that he believed in hell. I do not myself feel that any person who is really profoundly humane can believe in everlasting punishment. (*Why I Am Not a Christian*, 17)

Philosopher John Hick said hell attributed to God "an unappeasable vindictiveness and insatiable cruelty" (*Death and Eternal Life*, 200). Even professing Christians aren't immune to the sentiment. Clark Pinnock, a supposed evangelical scholar, asked,

> How can Christians possibly project a deity of such cruelty
> and vindictiveness whose ways include inflicting everlasting
> torture upon his creatures, however sinful they may have
> been? Surely a God who would do such a thing is more nearly
> like Satan than like God. ("The Destruction of the Finally
> Impenitent," 246–47)

Tommy Clayton says these examples are merely representative of the widespread rejection of the doctrine of God's wrath, both inside and outside the church (Tommy Clayton, http://www.gty.org/Blog/B110518).

But like it or not, God's condemnation is real and necessary because it's rooted in his justice. It has rightly been said that the seriousness of a crime is measured not only by its inherent nature but also by the one offended. Our sin has offended the Creator of the universe who is eternal, almighty, glorious, and holy. Consequently, our punishment has to correspond to that offense. And God's justice demands that he not let us off the hook. He "will not leave the guilty unpunished" (Exod 34:7) and ultimately will hold everyone accountable (Gen 18:25; Heb 9:27; 1 Pet 4:5; Rev 20:14). For Christians, Jesus Christ has incurred God's wrath against sin and met his righteous requirement in our stead. When we remember God's justice, we remember his gospel. So now as his redeemed we can find comfort and encouragement in his justice—justice that not only assures us that he's executing a plan for punishing the wicked but that also gives us strong help in our struggle for Christlike living in a secular world.

Reflect and Discuss

1. As believers, what effect does forgetting the return and impending judgment of Christ have on our lives and ministries?
2. Why is it important to know deeply and remember often the righteous judgment of God? How can we consistently remember and apply the truth of God's coming judgment to our ongoing ministries?
3. How do Peter's examples of God's past acts of punishment further his argument? Can we use the same argument today?
4. Is God's "track record" of punishment an important part of the message of the gospel? How so?
5. How does the example of Lot, living in a godless environment, encourage us? How should it concern us?

6. In terms of cultural engagement, what is the balance between being "in the culture" but not "of the culture"?

7. How should we understand God's *ability* to rescue from every trial and God's *choosing* when to rescue from trial? In other words, will God rescue from every trial?

8. If God's promise is not to rescue from every trial, what does he promise?

9. How does the gospel shine through Peter's language of impending judgment? How should God's patience spur us on?

10. While viewing our culture of godlessness, it is easy to become frustrated and discouraged. Why does God not judge immediately? How would it change our mentality if we viewed the lost world in the way that God does?

Remember Their Nature

2 PETER 2:10B-22

Main Idea: Believers must appreciate the seriousness of false teaching by understanding the depravity and doom of its advocates.

I. **Their Depravity Is Extreme (2:10b-16).**
   A. Audacious arrogance (2:10b-13a)
   B. Limitless lust (2:13b-14b)
   C. Greedy gain (2:14c-16)
II. **Their Doctrine Is Empty (2:17-19).**
   A. The presentation of showy speech (2:17-18)
   B. The promise of false freedom (2:19)
III. **Their DNA Is Exposed (2:20-22).**
   A. The presumption (2:20a)
   B. The principle (2:20b-21)
   C. The proverb (2:22)

In the 1970s "Scared Straight" programs began to be used throughout the United States as a means of deterring juvenile crime. They usually involved taking at-risk young people into adult prisons where they would hear about the harsh realities of prison life from inmates. The programs are built on an in-your-face approach, with inmates often screaming and yelling at the youth in hopes of "scaring" them into changing their ways so they don't end up in prison as well. While the effectiveness of these tactics has been debated, it's hard to argue with the premise: awareness inspires reform.

Peter wants to raise awareness in the minds of his readers regarding the deadly influence of the false teachers. So, without using any questionable tactics, he gets up in their faces a little bit in 2:10b-22 and attempts to scare them straight into resisting the heretics. Here he essentially elaborates the first part of 2:10—"those who follow the polluting desires of the flesh and despise authority"—by detailing the sins of the false teachers in order to further justify their condemnation (see 2:4-10). So our author is far more graphic and descriptive here. He doesn't want to leave us with any doubt about the evil of false teachers. He wants believers to appreciate the gravity of their work by fully understanding the extent of their depravity and doom.

We need to acknowledge that 2 Peter 2:10a-22 contains some difficult and challenging issues for both interpretation and theology. Whenever we come to texts like this, it's especially important that we concentrate on the things we know, not the things we don't know. God isn't playing games with his people when it comes to his Word, especially as it relates to false teaching. He wants us to hear his voice, and so we can be confident that everything we need is present and understandable. The stuff we don't know doesn't keep us from discovering the primary issues in the passage. What we can be sure of is that the depravity of these false teachers is off the charts, their teaching is hollow, and their true nature will be revealed.

Their Depravity Is Extreme
2 PETER 2:10B-16

We live in a culture where the status quo is refusing to settle for the status quo. I'm not talking about a redemptive quality that drives us to new heights of advancing good but something that simply makes us not OK with being "average." So we buy wide-screen TVs because regular screens aren't big enough. We go to restaurants that have megabars because the food selection on a single serving isn't sufficient. We participate in extreme sports because the exhilaration and risk involved in traditional sporting activities are too low. High-definition is no longer good enough; now we have ultra HD. We gravitate toward prefixes like *hyper* and entertainment that's "epic." Bigger is better, and reaching beyond the accepted norm is more enviable.

While this fascination with the extreme may be innocent (and even productive) in some areas, worldliness isn't one of them. Some professing Christians seem to be driven by unhealthy aspirations to live on the edge of places they should never go. The Reformers used the term *total depravity* to describe their conviction that sin corrupts the entire human nature. All of us have it, and even the smallest dose would keep us out of heaven if it were not for the redeeming work of Christ. But some so-called disciples of Jesus live to take their depravity beyond the norm. Presuming on grace and revolting against legalism, they're on a mission to live "off the charts" when it comes to sin. Like the original *Star Trek* crew, they want to "boldly go where no man has gone before."

The false teachers of Peter's day were like this. They had taken depravity to a new level and were doing everything they could to influence others to join them. So Peter elaborates on 2:10a by showing that the degree of these false teachers' depravity extends beyond even what was normal for their pagan culture. The rhetorical skill the apostle uses in 2:10b-16—word nuances, word plays, puns, and even alliteration—is virtually undiscernible in our English translations. But using these literary devices, Peter circles back to 2:1-3 to show the intemperance of the false teachers regarding the three sinful qualities that most succinctly characterize their lives and ministries: arrogance, sensuality, and greed.

Audacious Arrogance (2:10b-13a)

The first example of their extreme evil is that these false teachers exercise an unrestrained license in how they interact with authority. They "are not afraid" before "the glorious ones," but instead they "slander" them (v. 10). Bible scholars are uncertain about the precise identity of these "glorious ones" (*doxai*), debating whether this is a reference to angelic beings (good or bad) or church leaders. While a good biblical case can be made for either, it seems more likely that Peter is referring to evil, or fallen, angels. He appears to be contrasting these glorious ones reviled by the false teachers with the apparent good angels that he commends in 2:11. Jude's example of Michael (a good angel) not rebuking Satan (an evil angel) also supports this understanding (see Jude 9). Evidently, it's wrong for the false teachers to malign evil angels because they—even in their fallen state—still bear the image of the glory of their Creator (Moo, *2 Peter*, 121).

But to spend too much time on the unknown risks missing Peter's point, which is the extreme arrogance of these false teachers in verbally usurping the authority of those who at present hold a higher rank. While the Bible is clear that in the future believers will hold a higher position than the angels, that order apparently is reversed until the final judgment. The speech of these false teachers regarding the angelic beings is "bold" and "arrogant" (v. 10), two words that overlap in meaning and are probably best understood dynamically as "boldly arrogant." These heretics demonstrate audacious arrogance in their blatant disregard for and defamation of those in authority over them.

Peter strengthens his argument in the next verse by comparing this haughtiness with the humility exemplified by "angels" (v. 11). Although they are "greater in might and power," they exercise holy restraint in passing judgment on the false teachers and, instead, yield that judgment to God. The phrase "before the Lord" is probably best understood this way as supported by Jude's example. He says that even "when Michael the archangel was disputing with the devil in an argument about Moses's body, he did not dare utter a slanderous condemnation against him but said, 'The Lord rebuke you!'" (Jude 9). False teachers have an amazing confidence in deriding authority figures, but their confidence unfortunately isn't tempered with any wisdom or humility (Schreiner, *1 and 2 Peter*, 347).

If "the glorious ones" (v. 10) are, in fact, celestial beings, there's an important lesson here for Christians who like to dabble in the paranormal and take demonic activity too lightly. Because Jesus and the apostles cast out demons and because these adventurous Christians are now in Christ, they feel like they have the same right and authority to talk to demons and put them in their place. So pronouncements like "I rebuke you, Satan!" or "I rebuke that spirit of jealousy!" are commonplace in their vocabulary. This text should serve as a warning to us about flippantly throwing our spiritual weight around. If Michael was careful not to overstep his authoritative bounds, good angels—who are "greater in might and power"—control themselves from passing sentence, and Peter condemned false teachers for rushing in where angels fear to tread, then surely it behooves us to exercise some righteous restraint when it comes to how we talk to demonic forces. Paul seemed to describe our position here as one more of defense than offense (cf. Eph 6:10-20). Let's not go looking for trouble.

At the same time, the opposite is true as well. The rational, scientific, material world in which we live naturally and subtly suggests the supernatural world is a myth. Demons are something we only read about in the Gospels and view as entertainment in a Hollywood movie. But we don't really take them seriously as if they had any real bearing on our daily lives. Christians today need to consider seriously the possibility of real demonic influence in things like horoscopes, occult-themed video games, secretive clubs and organizations, and even movies and TV shows that feature the paranormal. The apostle Paul warned the Corinthians—who prided themselves on their "knowledge"—that their participation in idol feasts actually exposed them to demonic influence (see 1 Cor 10:14-22). Why should we think our exposure will do any less? We can't afford to ignore the real spiritual power that may be at work in some of the things we pass off as trivial entertainment. This issue is tough because so many of us have friends and loved ones who are involved in them. But the stakes are high here!

> Reference to the spirit world in such societies and
> activities may appear to be purely superficial or of simple
> entertainment value. But we must always reckon with the
> possibility that below the surface may lurk genuine demonic
> influence. (Moo, *2 Peter*, 134–35)

If "the glorious ones" just happen to be church leaders, as some suggest, the New Testament still isn't silent in helping us make application. The false teachers certainly were countering the teaching of the prophets and apostles. While they were rejecting the equivalent of biblical authority in our day, they were undermining God's ordained church leaders in their own day. Such rebellion is clearly contrary to New Testament instruction. The early church "devoted themselves to the apostles' teaching" (Acts 2:42). Paul exhorted the Thessalonians,

> *Now we ask you, brothers and sisters, to give recognition to those who*
> *labor among you and lead you in the Lord and admonish you, and to*
> *regard them very highly in love because of their work.* (1 Thess 5:12-13)

He charged young Timothy,

> *The elders who are good leaders are to be considered worthy of double*
> *honor, especially those who work hard at preaching and teaching.*
> (1 Tim 5:17)

The author of Hebrews wrote:

> *Remember your leaders who have spoken God's word to you. As you*
> *carefully observe the outcome of their lives, imitate their faith. . . .*
> *Obey your leaders and submit to them, since they keep watch over*
> *your souls as those who will give an account, so that they can do this*
> *with joy and not with grief, for that would be unprofitable for you.*
> (Heb 13:7,17)

It is to the advantage of all believers in Christ to align themselves under the loving leadership and faithful biblical instruction of their local church's God-ordained leaders.

As we return to the somewhat difficult language in 2 Peter 2, it's comforting to know that we're not the only ones in the dark about some of the issues at hand. Apparently, this is "what [false teachers] do not understand" (v. 12) as well. And yet they go on opening their big mouths "like irrational animals—creatures of instinct born to be caught and destroyed." Like animals, the false teachers operate on the basis of desires and feelings instead of reason. They follow their flesh, not their minds. Peter's point is that the false teachers don't know when to shut up about things they know nothing about. Claiming to be wise, they're really showing themselves to be fools.

The inability to button their lips ultimately will make these false teachers victims of their own fleshly drives, just like irrational animals. Just as wild animals die by the bow or rifle of a hunter, these guys will fall prey to their own unrestrained passions: "In [the animals'] destruction, they too will be destroyed" (v. 12). This tragedy is intensified with a string of participles at the beginning of the next verse. The clause "paid back with harm for the harm they have done" is merely a colorful way of saying these teachers will reap what they sow (Bauckham, *2 Peter*, 265). This is a graphic and accurate picture of a man who chooses to live like a beast! First, he gets captured. Then he's actually destroyed by his passions. Although he started out in pursuit of pleasure, in the end he even loses that! What he enjoys for a short time ultimately "ruins his health, wrecks his constitution, destroys his mind and character and begins his experience of hell while he is still on earth" (M. Green, *2 Peter*, 130). The off-the-charts arrogance of those who peddle heresy will come back to bite them.

Limitless Lust (2:13b-14b)

Peter's second example of the extreme evil of the false teachers is that their lust has no limits. Four statements flesh out this unbridled sensuality. First, "they consider it a pleasure to carouse in broad daylight." These guys don't get enough riotous and lascivious partying at night; they have to keep going in the daytime! Or they can't wait until the sun goes down, so they crank the party up during the day! Either way, when most people are at work, these guys are rabble-rousing (cf. Eccl 10:16; Isa 5:11; Rom 13:12-13; 1 Thess 5:17). Much like the Corinthians, who were tolerating sin "that is not even tolerated among the Gentiles" (1 Cor 5:1), these false teachers partook of a kind of daylight debauchery that wasn't even condoned by the degenerate Romans of the day (M. Green, *2 Peter*, 132; see also Acts 2:15). Their sensuality has no limits and is simply unquenchable.

Second, the false teachers likely were perverting the communion memorial in the church. The word "deceptions" (v. 13) is actually replaced in some manuscripts with "love feasts." This term is an obvious reference to the meal that traditionally accompanied the Lord's Supper and one that appears to have been a favorite target for abusers (see Jude 12; cf. 1 Cor 11:17-22). Even if the preferred word is "deceptions," it still likely refers to licentious conduct taking place "while they feast with you." As if it were not enough for these teachers to be partying both day and night, their self-indulgence was being practiced at the common meal of the community that was part of the Lord's Supper celebration (Davids, *Letters*, 239)! That's why Peter refers to the false teachers as "spots and blemishes." Because they are associated with the community of faith, they stain and defile the body of Christ. Peter will finish his letter by exhorting his readers to be just the opposite—"without spot or blemish" (2 Pet 3:14; cf. Eph 5:27)—as they remember the Lord Jesus. But there's no sacred ground for these false teachers. They even tarnish the feast that's intended as a memorial to him!

Peter's third reference to the limitless lust of these false teachers is the carousel of adultery that constantly plays in their minds. They have "eyes full of adultery" (v. 14), which either refers to their obsession with adulterous women or to their inability to look at any woman without seeing her as a candidate for infidelity. These guys are always sizing up women for their potential sexual performance. Peter is making an insightful observation about the human mind. If lust is dwelt upon and acted upon, eventually it will dominate one's thinking (M. Green, *2 Peter*, 133). It becomes a stronghold, leaving captives who "never stop looking for sin." They're in bondage to it! Boundless lust will always leave a man restless and longing for more, always pushing him beyond his own borders to explore new territory of sexual immorality, only to find himself entrapped there. While the word translated "never stop looking" is rare, it's related to the verb Peter uses in his first letter when he says that whoever has died to sin "is finished with sin" (1 Pet 4:1). He's talking there about the victorious living of the believer in Christ. The only way out for a person who denies Christ and becomes a prisoner to sin is to repent and be identified with him in his death and resurrection.

Fourth and finally, the severe lust of the false teachers is manifested in their refusal to travel their journey alone. Peter says, "They seduce unstable people" (v. 14). While some interpreters see this as a reference to the object of their lust, it seems more likely that it speaks of their influence. These guys want others to join them on their perverted path, and they know how to get them to do it. Likely they are enticing people to adopt their insatiable sexual appetite by promising them that they could live for sexual pleasure without any worry of punishment. The term "seduce" is a fishing metaphor that means "to catch with bait." Like skilled fishermen, they lure unsuspecting people who've not been firmly established in their faith to take their bait and get hooked on their evil practices. Sin loves company, and these false teachers will do whatever it takes to coax people into their net and join them in their sin.

Our hedonistic culture compels us to worship the God of pleasure, even in Christian homes and churches. And it's easy for us to become enslaved to limitless lust. But pleasure in this life is a goal that we'll never attain. It's bound by the law of diminishing returns. Douglas Moo observes:

> The food that used to satisfy no longer does, so we search
> for ever more exotic and more expensive dishes. What once
> entertained us now seems blasé; so we demand new media,
> bigger TVs, more stations. The spousal sex that used to satisfy
> our natural urges is no longer enough; as a result, we try sex
> with others and explore various deviant practices to bring
> the excitement back. Pleasure, in other words, is a goal never
> reached; it is always somewhere in the distance, urging one on
> to new and usually more sinful practices, never quite satisfying.
> (Moo, *2 Peter*, 135)

While God created us to find pleasure in things like sex and food and entertainment within his prescribed parameters, he never intended for our pursuit of that pleasure to dominate us. That's a line that's easy to blur—and to cross—if we're not spiritually perceptive.

Greedy Gain (2:14c-16)

The third example Peter gives of the extreme evil of the false teach-ers is their instinctive greed. He says they "have hearts trained in greed" (v. 14). In other words, they're experts in it! The word "trained" (*gegumnasmenēn*) is the word from which we get our word "gymnasium" (cf. 1 Tim 4:7; Heb 5:12; 12:11). These men worked out for this, devot-ing time and energy to developing muscles of greed. They "had trained themselves in the unbridled desire for more and more of the forbid-den" (Vaughn and Lea, *1, 2 Peter*, 179). While the word "greed" can be used in reference to both money and sex, Peter's earlier reference in 2:3 as well as his example of Balaam that follows seem to point toward the former. These false teachers have practiced exploitation and swindling to the point that it's second nature to them. It's now a habit; it's the way they think . . . and act.

This impulsive greed—like the other sins of the false teachers—doesn't fly under the radar of the divine Judge. Peter pronounces them "children under a curse!" (v. 14), an expressive Hebrew idiom that basically means "God's curse is on them." Their extreme evil has led them down a path to a place of being under God's curse. Don't overlook the fact that the theme of impending judgment just keeps on surfacing in Peter's letter. This reality was the primary truth these false teachers were denying. Peter wants to wake his readers up so they (and we!) will take it seriously and resist these men (Schreiner, *1 and 2 Peter*, 353).

Peter now sets out to illustrate the immoral greed of the false teachers by comparing them with the hireling prophet Balaam in the Old Testament. While some commentators separate 2:15-16 out as a distinct aspect of the heretics' extreme, it seems more natural that Peter is using it to support his point about greed. The fact that Balaam was greedy is evident from Numbers 22–24, and Peter acknowledges as much by saying that they "have followed the path of Balaam, the son of Bosor, who loved the wages of wickedness" (v. 15). Additionally, Jude associates Balaam with greed in his denunciation of false teachers, saying they "have plunged into Balaam's error for profit" (Jude 11). So Balaam essentially "becomes the prototype of an unprincipled false teacher seeking gain" (Vaughn and Lea, *1, 2 Peter*, 179).

Specifically, Peter associates the false teachers with Balaam because he agreed to prophesy at the bidding of Balak, king of Moab, in return for personal gain (cf. Num 22:15-20). So Peter says of the false teachers, "They have gone astray by abandoning the straight path" (v. 15) in the same way as Balaam. To identify the specific nature of their sin, Peter then summarizes the infamous story of Balaam being rebuked by his donkey (cf. Num 22:21-35). On the way to his spiritual treason, the angel of the Lord blocked his donkey's path, causing the animal to turn aside and mash Balaam's foot against a wall. Unable to see the angel, Balaam struck the donkey to get him back on track. Eventually the donkey actually spoke up in protest. Then Balaam's eyes were opened to see the angel, who rebuked him for "his lawlessness" (v. 16; see Num 22:32).

Here Peter makes the connection and drives his point home: "A speechless donkey spoke with a human voice and restrained the prophet's madness" (v. 16). There's a play on words here with "lawlessness" (*paranomias*) and "madness" (*paraphronian*). Balaam wasn't literally insane. But the suggestion is that all who pursue lawlessness are really out of their minds because unrighteousness always leads to punishment (Schreiner, *1 and 2 Peter*, 355). And Peter doesn't want his readers to be deceived by the pretentious arguments being posed by the false teachers. So he points out that God gave a donkey a "human voice" and used it as his mouthpiece. Why? To show the superiority of his voice over "the prophet's madness." Imagine that: a donkey—which is most often thought of as being a brute beast—has more prophetic vision than a prophet of God whose moral compass had been disturbed by his greed for personal gain! Bottom line: God's words must always be heeded over the absurd, deceitful claims of those who speak only for personal gain (M. Green, *2 Peter*, 136).

Like the demonic and the sensual, Peter's rebuke of the false teachers regarding greed also comes with a warning to Christians. How easy it is for us to come to the place where we begin to make family and career decisions based solely on their financial benefit to us. So the decision to take a job in another city is driven by the lure of a bigger paycheck instead of what's best for our family or even more what's best for the mission of Christ. And the purchase of a bigger home or nicer car is determined simply on the fact that we can afford it instead of on the potential opportunity to leverage our livelihood for global disciple making. And saving for retirement is based more on providing us with the luxury we think we deserve instead of positioning us for greater ministry involvement and gospel advancement. Beloved, we've been left on this planet not to build a nest egg or advance a career but to fulfill the Great Commission. Nothing stands in the way of that for many Christians more than the greedy pursuit of more stuff and more comfort.

Their Doctrine Is Empty
2 PETER 2:17-19

Marriage proposals are much more complex than they used to be. Some young men today hire photographers to hide in the bushes and take pictures of them as they pop the question amid a Hollywood production of events. Others pay big bucks to get down on one knee while a mass of spectators watch on the jumbotron at an athletic event. We weren't that smart—or resourceful—in my day. I asked my wife to marry me sitting in a '67 Camaro in the parking lot of the Atlanta airport. She came into town to visit me at one point during our long-distance relationship, and

I couldn't wait any longer. So just to have a little fun, I placed the empty ring box on the console of my sports car. When she got in, she picked it up and excitedly asked, "Is this for me?" I affirmed that it was and told her to open it. Her excitement immediately tanked when she opened the box and discovered it to be empty. As she looked up at me in utter disappointment, I held out the ring and asked her to be my wife. I loved watching her momentary distress be instantaneously transformed into great joy!

A ring box isn't supposed to be empty, especially at the moment of proposal. Its size, décor, and company logo all indicate there's something of great value inside. In the hands of an eager young man down on one knee, that box promises great thrill for the girl who's about to receive what's in it. What a letdown to find it empty! But an empty ring box (even one used as a lighthearted, harmless trick) is a far cry from hollow religious teaching that can damn people to an eternal hell. That's what false teachers do. Their speech, presentation, and promises all give the impression that something desirable is inside. But the Word of God says their doctrine is empty. In 2:17-19, Peter identifies two manifestations of the hollow claims of heretical teachers: showy speech and false freedom.

The Presentation of Showy Speech (2:17-18)

The first manifestation of the vain teaching of these heretics has to do with ostentatious orality they employ, showy speech that has no substance. These men are described as "springs without water, mists driven by a storm" (v. 17). The first expression refers to a well, and the second to a cloud. The common denominator, of course, is that both items promise something they actually don't deliver. The well is dry, and the cloud is driven away by the wind before it has a chance to produce any rain. Both a well and a cloud, by their nature, hold the promise of providing water for weary travelers or dry crops. But neither lives up to its billing. Jude combines the two expressions in referring to the false teachers as "waterless clouds" (Jude 12). Both writers are describing the promise of the heretics to provide new sources of life for people. But there's no substance to their promises. All they do is leave naïve people thirsting for satisfaction.

Standing in stark contrast to the dearth of satisfaction in false teaching is the eternal refreshment of the water of life, Jesus Christ. He told the Samaritan woman,

Everyone who drinks from this water will get thirsty again. But whoever drinks from the water that I will give him will never get thirsty again. In fact, the water I will give him will become a well of water springing up in him for eternal life. (John 4:13-14)

Only in him can anyone find lasting satisfaction. "The one who believes in me," Jesus said, "as the Scripture has said, will have streams of living water flow from deep within him" (John 7:38). Through his death and resurrection, he bought the right to put the life of God back inside those he saves. And that life is a never-ending source of gratification for the otherwise thirsty soul, both now and forever!

Deceivers, on the other hand, have a reservation with "the gloom of darkness" (v. 17; cf. Jude 13). Just as their depravity is extreme, so will be their punishment. They won't just experience "darkness" in the final judgment but "gloom." It will be thick, eternal darkness. Peter pulls no punches in announcing the terrifying nature of the punishment of false teachers. He's obviously talking here about the darkness of hell, the eternal destination of the wicked that's characterized by both fire (see Matt 13:42; 25:41) and darkness (see Matt 8:12; 22:13).

But how exactly do these false teachers get away with such fraud? Peter says they speak with "boastful, empty words" (v. 18). In other words, they employ showy, arrogant speech that actually is hollow. It's a shell without anything inside other than foolishness. They try to make their words sound weighty and important, but those words are really nothing more than mere stupidity. Yet their stupidity isn't without effect. There are always some whom "they seduce, with fleshly desires and debauchery" (v. 18). Their shameless immoral appeals play tricks on some ignorant and immature souls the same way a fish is tricked into biting the fake, plastic plug cast by a skilled fisherman.

These duped individuals likely are new or at least immature believers. Peter describes them as "people who have barely escaped from those who live in error." The word "barely" is a rare word used only here in the New Testament. It communicates the idea that it hadn't been long since these people had escaped the clutches of their pagan counterparts, "those who live in error" as citizens of the wicked Roman culture. So the false teachers were luring some relatively new Christians into their immorality. These new believers were jumping out of the frying pan of paganism and into the fire of heretical religion!

The Promise of False Freedom (2:19)

A second expression of their empty doctrine was giving people a false sense of freedom. On one occasion Jesus told his disciples to let the Pharisees alone because they were blind guides who led people to share in their fate. He said, "And if the blind guide the blind, both will fall into a pit" (Matt 15:14). On this point the Pharisees were precursors to the false teachers of Peter's day. These heretics are slaves leading people into the very pit of slavery. "They promise them freedom," Peter writes, "but they themselves are slaves of corruption." They have been overcome by their own evil conduct and, consequently, have become slaves to it. Now they're compelling others into that same bondage but passing it off as freedom. They "were prisoners talking to others of a freedom that they didn't have" (Vaughn and Lea, *1, 2 Peter*, 182).

A proverbial statement serves to conclude Peter's argument and solidify his point: "People are enslaved to whatever defeats them." These false teachers are

> so thoroughly dominated and controlled by their sinful
> nature (John 8:34; Rom 6:16) that their teaching is void of any
> divine power. Although they offer freedom, they are slaves to
> sin, utterly unable to bestow true spiritual freedom because
> they reject Jesus Christ—the only one who can truly liberate
> the soul (John 8:31-32,36; Rom 8:2; Gal 5:1; Heb 2:14-15; cf.
> Jas 1:25). (MacArthur, *2 Peter*, 105–6)

Not much has changed. Today Christianity often is viewed as a restricted life confined to following a bunch of rules. Believers are seen as being enslaved to someone else's bidding. The banner cry of modern individualists is, "Live your life the way you want to live it!" But all the time these false freedom fighters are luring people into a life of slavery to sin and bondage to corruption. As people gradually succumb to spiritual and moral decay by their own immoral choices, they ultimately lose even the illusion of freedom and fall into unqualified bondage to their sin. That's why we need a Savior. Against the tide of false teaching that leads to damnation, we need to hear Jesus pronounce over us, "You will know the truth, and the truth will set you free. . . . So if the Son sets you free, you really will be free" (John 8:32,36). And he has set us free indeed through his life, death, and resurrection. He's broken the chains of sin and corruption, and he's put his life back inside of us! If you're in Christ, beloved, "the law of the Spirit of life in Christ Jesus has set you free from the law of sin and death" (Rom 8:2; cf. Rom 6:18; 2 Cor 3:17; Gal 5:1).

Every Christian, as well as every Christian church, needs to do some honest self-evaluation at this point as well. We need to ask, What powers have mastered us? We can't afford to allow our banner cry of "Freedom in Christ!" to actually keep us from experiencing it. Jesus himself suggested it was possible to try to remove a splinter from someone else's eye, all the while having a plank in your own (cf. Matt 7:1-5). It's not uncommon for believers to become so busy pointing fingers at the evils of a corrupted culture that they fail to see slavery to sin in our own lives and churches (Davids, *Letters*, 247–48). It's easy, for example, to rebuke the world for things like gay marriage and transgender accommodation and yet avoid calling into account Christians who are guilty of things like gluttony and materialism.

Their DNA is Exposed
2 PETER 2:20-22

While I don't watch a lot of TV, I do enjoy a couple of the crime shows like *Criminal Minds* and *Law & Order: Criminal Intent.* I like to watch how smart people figure out things by unraveling a web of complex details. But sometimes it's easy for the cops to match people with their crimes because of things like DNA. DNA is the abbreviation of deoxyribonucleic acid, which is the hereditary material in humans and almost all other organisms. Nearly every cell in a person's body has the same DNA. Yet the DNA of every person who's ever lived is different because everybody gets a random mix of the genes from their parents, and that mix is never the same.

However, spiritual DNA is different. Since the fall of mankind, all of us have inherited the same sin-infected genes. Because we all have this sin nature, we all sin, and we all die as a result of our sin (cf. Rom 3:11-12,23; 5:14). For those in Christ, however, our tainted spiritual DNA has been replaced with the righteous DNA of Christ (cf. 1 Cor 15:22,45). Those outside of Christ remain enslaved to their unregenerate DNA. Peter just finished saying as much about the false teachers and their converts: "They themselves are slaves of corruption" (v. 19). Now he proceeds to show how the corrupted spiritual DNA of these people continues to show its ugly head.

Bible scholars have debated whether 2:20-22 is referring specifically to the false teachers or to the converts they were enticing (see vv. 18-19). The fact that the whole chapter is aimed at the false teachers, and that some form of the word translated "defeats" is repeated in verses 19 and 20, implies the false teachers are in view. At the same time, the word "For" at the beginning of verse 20, as well as the repetition of the same word translated "escaped" (vv. 18,20), suggests that Peter may have the converts in mind. But this is likely another one of those places where trying to be too definitive misses the point. Whether it's the false teachers or those seduced by them,

> The fate of those who had apostatized stands as a warning
> to those wavering under the influence of the teachers. Peter
> wanted his readers to see that those who commit apostasy
> are very unlikely to return to the truth. The decision is of
> great consequence, and those who are wavering must see that
> heaven and hell are at stake. (Schreiner, *1 and 2 Peter*, 360–61)

What the false teachers had done, their converts were in danger of copying! Peter's warning can be organized around three categories: the presumption, the principle, and the parable.

The Presumption (2:20a)

Peter first talks about a gross presumption these apostates had made at some point in the past. Because they had "escaped the world's impurity," or the world's contaminating moral influence, they had assumed they were truly saved when they really weren't. How did they make such a damning mistake? The heretics' escape had come about "through the knowledge of the Lord and Savior Jesus Christ," but it resulted in that "they are again entangled in these things and defeated." That's not much of an escape; in fact, it's no escape at all! The word "knowledge" is *epignōsis*, that full and complete knowledge of God in Christ. These people had come to the place where they understood the gospel. They actually got it. But the word "entangled"—another fishing metaphor—indicates they once again had been duped by their flesh and by the world.

So whatever "knowledge" of Jesus these folks had, it never took root. It only affected them short term, maybe with some intellectual grasp of Christian truth followed by a superficial change of behavior. But it evidently wasn't the real deal. If it had been a true knowledge of Christ

Jesus, it would have had lasting effect on their intellects and wills. Their imperfect knowledge only caused a brief change. They proved by their defection that they weren't true Christ followers. Their profession was false. They made a tragic mistake about the genuineness of their spiritual condition.

This text is important for our understanding about the doctrine of the security of the believer. Some have suggested that this passage teaches that Christians can lose their salvation. But Peter isn't in any way, form, or fashion unclear regarding his convictions about this subject. He opens his first letter by contending that believers "are being guarded by God's power through faith for a salvation that is ready to be revealed in the last time" (1 Pet 1:5). And he begins this second letter by claiming that God's "divine power has given us everything required for life and godliness through the knowledge of him who called us by his own glory and goodness" (2 Pet 1:3). Peter unapologetically declares that God calls believers and, therefore, will guard them so they will definitely reach their final salvation and participate in his divine nature. So why would he contradict himself at this point, teaching in one place that believers are secure and in another that they aren't?

At the same time, Peter is equally firm on his conviction regarding the absolute necessity of the perseverance, endurance, or continuation of the saints. At the heart of the doctrine of eternal security is the relationship between endurance and authenticity. In the parable of the sower, two of the four kinds of soil on which the seed of the gospel fell represent people who initially give visible evidence of truly receiving it. However, that visible manifestation of life fails to endure and, consequently, proves their life to be inauthentic (see Mark 4:5-7). Later in his ministry, Jesus said that "the one who endures to the end will be saved" (Matt 10:22). Of those who abandoned the community of faith, John says,

> They went out from us, but they did not belong to us; for if they had belonged to us, they would have remained with us. However, they went out so that it might be made clear that none of them belongs to us.
> (1 John 2:19)

Other New Testament writers concur that endurance is the clear determinant of the authenticity of one's salvation (see Rom 2:7; Heb 3:14; Jude 20-21; Rev 2:7,10,17,26; 3:21).

Peter's words in 2:20 are a needed reminder that things like walking an aisle, making a "profession" of faith, praying a prayer inviting

Jesus into your heart, joining a church, or even being baptized don't guarantee entrance into heaven. Peter has taught throughout the letter that only those who continue to live a life of godliness will get eternal life (see 1:5-11). Perseverance is the mark of whether a person has the real deal (Schreiner, *1 and 2 Peter*, 363). If you are truly saved, you will endure. If you endure, you are truly saved. But if—like these apostates—you have "escaped the world's impurity through the knowledge of the Lord and Savior Jesus Christ," and yet "are again entangled in these things and defeated," then something is amiss with the genuineness of your professed faith.

The Principle (2:20b-21)

The false presumption made by those who had walked away from the church leads Peter to articulate a simple principle: it's better never to have known the gospel than to have known it and rejected it. For people who have known about Jesus and rejected him, "the last state is worse for them than the first" (v. 20). Why? Because the human heart is adversely affected by rejecting truth that is fully known and understood. "Cynicism and bitterness multiply in the soul of individuals who turn from God's grace back to sin. Re-entanglement with evil produces scoffers and skeptics" (Vaughn and Lea, *1, 2 Peter*, 183). In short, it's far more difficult than ever before for such a person's heart to be softened to the gospel. With knowledge comes responsibility, so that an individual is now more responsible for having known and rejected the truth.

Peter uses a number of proverbial statements in this passage, some of which he seems to draw from Jesus. Our Lord told a parable about an evil spirit that had been cast out of a man and then wanders around looking for a new place to inhabit. Finding no new home, it goes back to its previous dwelling, but this time seven other spirits join it in inhabiting the man (cf. Matt 12:43-45). Jesus concludes, "That person's last condition is worse than the first" (Matt 12:45). Similarly, in his parable of the faithful and wise manager, Jesus indicates that to know truth and reject it deserves a harsher punishment:

> *And that servant who knew his master's will and didn't prepare himself or do it will be severely beaten. But the one who did not know and did what deserved punishment will receive a light beating. From everyone who has been given much, much will be required; and from the one who has been entrusted with much, even more will be expected.* (Luke 12:47-48)

Our Lord's brother communicates a similar principle when he says, "So it is sin to know the good and yet not do it" (Jas 4:17). The bottom line: with greater knowledge comes greater accountability!

Peter feels the gravity of this principle merits restatement, so he says, "For it would have been better for them not to have known the way of righteousness than, after knowing it, to turn back from the holy command delivered to them" (v. 21). The "way of righteousness" simply refers to the pathway of salvation through faith in Christ. And because the verb translated "to have known" is a perfect infinitive, these false teachers evidently had known about this way and had been fully aware of and yet ultimately snubbed it. Peter likely uses "the holy command" as a synonym for the gospel. It's an allusion to the laws of God delivered to people for their good (cf. Deut 10:13). These apostates had received the gospel and understood it to be for their good, but then they took what was good and rendered it bad. It would have been better for them to still be in the position of never having known the gospel with the prospect of still rendering a right verdict when the opportunity came.

To render as bad what God has rendered good is at the heart of the unpardonable sin (cf. Mark 3:21-30; cf. Heb 6:4-6; 10:26-31; 1 John 5:16). To blaspheme against the Holy Spirit is to decree all of God's goodness to actually be bad. It's to declare darkness to be light and bondage to be freedom. Such revolt is unforgivable because there's no longer any basis to acknowledge one's sinfulness before God. The sacrificial death of Jesus Christ, the gracious gift of repentance, the loving conviction of the Holy Spirit, and the merciful patience of God have all been spurned. Consequently, nothing remains to serve as the backdrop of righteousness by which an individual's sinfulness can be discerned. The situation is hopeless because the sin is unforgivable—"unforgivable not because God is unwilling to forgive, but because the man who persists in such self-delusion refuses to accept the forgiveness which God patiently proffers to rebels" (M. Green, *2 Peter*, 142).

The Proverb (2:22)

Peter finishes his weighty condemnation by illustrating this principle with a twofold proverb, one that parallels the lives of those who turn away: "'A dog returns to its own vomit,' and, 'A washed sow returns to wallowing in the mud'" (v. 22). The first part of the proverb is similar to Proverbs 26:11, but the second part doesn't appear to have a biblical parallel. The Jews considered both dogs and sows—or pigs—to be unclean, so Peter's use of them here was intended to stir up disgust in his Hebrew readers. Dogs and pigs will always revert to the bent of their natures. The nature of a dog will compel him to eat his own vomit, and the nature of a pig will compel her to return to her mud hole. It doesn't matter if the dog throws up something that's made him sick, and it doesn't matter if you give the pig a bath. Those activities have no lasting effect. These animals will naturally go back to what they were temporarily rid of. Their natures remain unchanged. Their innate DNA is exposed.

Jesus used both dogs and pigs to describe people who are completely out of touch with God (cf. Matt 7:6). Peter's purpose here isn't much different. Even though some people temporarily demonstrated some embrace of the gospel, they ultimately renounced Christ and went back to their old way of life. They simply demonstrated their true nature as loving the sickness and filthiness of their sin. This two-faceted proverb clearly exhibits the foolishness, disgrace, and desecration that characterizes a person who willingly goes back to the moral filth of worldliness after having learned about forgiveness and deliverance through the gospel of Christ.

It's easy to see how the use of phenomenological language in 2:20-22 has caused some to interpret these verses as teaching that true believers can lose their salvation. Peter uses "Christian lingo" to describe those who fall away because they appeared at one time to be genuine Christ followers. Schreiner likens it to them confessing Christ as Lord and Savior, being baptized, and joining the church. So Peter describes the false teachers—and some of their converts—in Christian terms simply because they were still participating in the community of faith after demonstrating some evidence of genuine faith. But now they've revealed that they weren't ever part of the people of God because they haven't remained true to the faith. Peter's proverbial illustration of the dog and pig clearly indicates that those who fall away never really change their nature (Schreiner, *1 and 2 Peter*, 364–65). Their true spiritual DNA is ultimately exposed.

Conclusion

I remember walking into the auditorium one Sunday to preach in one of the churches I used to pastor. A dear senior adult lady met me at the door and paid me what she thought was a compliment: "I listened to my two favorite preachers on television this morning." And then she told me who they were—me and one of the most popular prosperity gospel preachers of our day! Because our broadcast was on a one-week delay, she could watch both of us before coming to our Sunday gathering. I was tempted to just smile, thank her, and move toward my seat in preparation for the beginning of the service. But it struck me that the stakes were too high. So I gently said to her, "Do you really think that he and I are saying the same thing?" The shocked and bewildered look on her face confirmed my suspicion. She hadn't been assessing the content of either preacher's sermons according to God's Word. She was choosing favorites based on other criteria.

Peter unleashes some heavy artillery here on the false teachers. Why? Because he's a shepherd—a pastor—who's tired of his sheep being ravaged by men full of arrogance, lust, and greed who are masquerading in religious clothing. While his words at times seem harsh, they must be judged against the dire consequences of speaking softly or saying nothing at all. Michael Green's warning is on target:

> It does our generation little credit that such passion for truth and holiness strikes an alien note in our minds. Peter's plain speaking in this chapter has a very practical purpose, just as Jesus' warnings had: "What I say to you I say to everyone: 'watch!'" We would be mistaken to assume, "It could never happen to us." Both Scripture and experience assure us that it could. "So, if you think you are standing firm, be careful that you don't fall" (1 Cor 10:12). Covetousness, sophistical arguments, pride in knowledge, gluttony, drunkenness, lust, arrogance against authority of all kinds, and, most of all, the danger of denying the lordship of the Redeemer—are these not all the paramount temptations of money-mad, sex-mad, materialistic, anti-authoritarian, twentieth-century man?
> (M. Green, *2 Peter*, 144)

The contemporary church needs to be scared straight. We need to stop playing "Mr. Nice Guy" when it comes to false teaching. Pastors need to call some names and warn their people to shun the men who bear them. Believers need to take more seriously the detrimental influence false teachers have on ungrounded Christians and the damning effect they have on unsuspecting non-Christians.

Reflect and Discuss

1. In what ways do false teachers actually embody the opposite of a life that's being sanctified?

2. In a culture that generally despises authority, do Christians sometimes find themselves influenced by this attitude? What is the Christian's proper understanding of God-ordained authority?

3. If it is possible that Peter's "glorious ones" may be referencing Christian leaders, how then should we treat our pastors? What is the nature of the pastor's biblical authority, and how should we respond to it?

4. To what degree should believers in Jesus Christ delve into the demonic spiritual world?

5. What is the proper way to address a friend, family member, or a member of your congregation who consistently listens to false teaching? How much of a person's teaching should you listen to before drawing a verdict? Where is the line?

6. How does Peter demonstrate the difference between genuine faith versus phony faith? How do we deal with others when it's unclear? What is our biblical responsibility to others here?

7. Peter says that false teachers' hearts are "trained in greed." How can we, as true believers and even teachers of the Word, protect our hearts from greed? Further, how can we detect when we are making decisions based on our own greed, even when we may not realize it?

8. Peter submits that the false teachers "promise them freedom, but they themselves are slaves of corruption." In other words, these false teachers were making empty promises, which then led to sinful bondage. Who are the specific false teachers that are popular today, and how should we warn our people about them?

9. What is the danger of knowing the gospel yet still walking away from it?

10. Will our culture be held more accountable for rejecting the gospel? How should this motivate us?

Remember That He'll Be Back

2 PETER 3:1-10

Main Idea: Believers must hold fast to the promises of Christ's return in the face of the world's mocking.

I. **God's Word Says It (3:1-2).**
   A. Why we need to be reminded (3:1)
   B. What we need to remember (3:2)
II. **God's Enemies Scoff at It (3:3-4).**
   A. Their agenda (3:3)
   B. Their argument (3:4)
III. **God's Nature Supports It (3:5-10).**
   A. God is sovereign (3:5-7).
   B. God is timeless (3:8).
   C. God is merciful (3:9).
   D. God is just (3:10).

The declaration "I'll be back" is a catchphrase associated with Arnold Schwarzenegger. The Austrian-American actor used some variation of it in a number of his movies. He first used it in his role as the title character from the 1984 science fiction film *The Terminator*. In the scene Schwarzenegger's character, the Terminator—an android assassin—was refused entry to the police station where his target was being held. He surveys the counter, then promises the police sergeant, "I'll be back." A short time later the Terminator drives a car into the station, obliterates the counter, and massacres the staff.

Jesus made the same promise to his followers. He said, "I'll be back," and he said it in no uncertain terms (see John 14:3; cf. Acts 1:11). But people need to understand that when Jesus makes good on his promise, it won't be Hollywood science fiction, and he won't be acting. It will be a real, physical, catastrophic event. And when it happens, he will destroy the world as we know it and bring judgment against those who've opposed him.

God knew that the longer Jesus tarries the greater chance his followers will have of becoming discouraged, and the more discouraged they become, the greater chance they have of falling prey to false teachers who scoff at his return. So he gives us 2 Peter 3 to help us navigate that temptation. And he does it with great tenderness. Peter says, "Dear friends, this is now the second letter I have written to you" (3:1). He calls his readers "dear friends" (*agapētoi*) as he summons them to remember Christ's coming, an intimate address he'll use throughout the chapter with other exhortations (see 3:14,17; cf. Jude 17). The term expresses heartfelt affection. Parents use it to refer to their children. Mourners use it for loved ones who've passed away. Couples use it to signify their undivided loyalty to one another. Even Solomon used it to convey the intimate relationship he had with his lover in the Song of Songs (Helm, *1 & 2 Peter*, 243). Peter's heart is for his readers. Michael Green says,

> In this chapter Peter returns from harrying the heretics to encourage the faithful. . . . The vehemence of his attack in the last chapter, and the repetition of his reminders here, alike spring from a pastoral heart of love towards his flock. (*2 Peter*, 145)

Our Father is deeply and affectionately desirous that we never lose our conviction that Jesus will come back. So he inspires Peter to write with the purpose "to stir up your sincere understanding by way of reminder" (v. 1). He wants to disturb any complacency and make clear the spiritual urgency of holding fast to the blessed hope being undermined by false teaching. This theme is clear in the chapter. In the second half of the chapter, Peter will address "what sort of people you should be" (v. 11) while waiting for Jesus to come back. But first he tackles the scoffer's accusatory question, "Where is his 'coming' that he promised?" (v. 4). Here he continues his purpose of reminding his readers about this cataclysmic event by drawing a contrast between how God speaks of Christ's return and how the world scoffs at it.

God's Word Says It
2 PETER 3:1-2

I don't know a lot about rodeos, but I've watched enough of them to know that bull riders are my heroes. These guys are real men. They get on a crazy mad bull and attempt to stay on him while the huge critter attempts to buck them off. The rider has to stay on top of the bucking bull by holding onto the bull rope with one hand, without touching the bull or himself with his free hand. Oh, and did I mention that the rope is wrapped around the chest of the bull directly behind the bull's front legs? No wonder he's so mad! If the cowboy can do all that for eight seconds, then it's a qualified ride. If he gets bucked off before eight seconds, it's a no score. So it doesn't take a rocket scientist to figure out that one of the keys for these tough guys is to hold on to that rope really tightly and not let go!

Peter's immediate concern is the devastating effect that loosening one's grip on what God says about Christ's second coming can have on our lives. So he calls his readers to hang on tightly to what they've been taught. Verses 1-2 are saturated with one thing—the importance of remembering. Peter calls attention to the fact that this is "the second letter" he's written and that he's doing it "by way of reminder" to the people he's shepherding. And that's all driven by his conviction that his readers should "recall" the promise of Christ's return. It's like he's asking us, "What part of 'remember' don't you get?" Nobody can read these verses and have to ask, "What's your point, Peter?" While believers should always be learning new things about their faith and discovering new ways to serve the Lord, we also need to be reminded of basic spiritual truths. And we never outgrow that need. While the gospel is still embedded in the database of our minds, it can cease to have an active influence over us (Moo, *2 Peter*, 162).

Remembering the gospel in an effectual way isn't automatic. We have to be stimulated, and that's what we must do for one another on a regular basis. Remembering the gospel is weighty business! Our losing sight of the hope we have in Christ's return is something the enemy wants. It threatens the stability of our faith like few other things can. Peter knew that the prophets of denial would appear along the way and that we would have to fight hard not to be unsettled by their vigor in attacking the Christian belief in Christ's return. So he answers two questions: Why do we need to be reminded about it? and What specifically do we need to remember?

Why We Need to Be Reminded (3:1)

The first issue Peter addresses is why we need to be reminded at all. Most of us could easily say, "What's the big deal?" Every self-respecting follower of Christ knows he's coming back. So, why does Peter write— not one but two—letters and include in both of them reminders about

Christ's return? First of all, this chapter as a whole is clear in suggesting that it's entirely possible for believers to stumble at the world's scoffing when it comes to the second coming. Take a quick look ahead and notice the development of Peter's thought. He says in verse 5, "They deliberately overlook," speaking of the scoffing unbelievers. But then in verse 8 he says, "Don't overlook," speaking to believers. Then in verse 17 he says, "Be on your guard, so that you are not led away by the error of lawless people and fall from your own stable position." Peter knows that the longer our Lord tarries, and the more the unbelieving world scoffs at his delay (and even the idea that he's coming at all!), the easier it will be for us to get discouraged, lose hope, and become unstable in our faith.

This issue has extraordinary gravity when it comes to the believer's walk with Christ. So Peter says here that in both of his letters he wants "to stir up your sincere understanding." The adjective "sincere" signifies that which is pure, right, and good. Qualifying the noun "understanding," the idea suggests a healthy way of thinking. But it's speaking of more than a purely mental process; it involves the ability to discern spiritual truth and apply it (Moo, *2 Peter*, 162). "To stir up your sincere understanding by way of reminder," then, involves more than the mental act of "recalling" what had once been learned about the second coming. It's the dynamic process of applying the truths to the new situations and problems that the believer confronts. Peter—returning to the theme of 1:12-15 in his first epistle—is stimulating us to wholesome thinking by reminding us about the promises of Christ's return. "In biblical thinking reminders grip the whole person, so that we are possessed again by the gospel and its truth, so that we are energized to live for the glory of God" (Schreiner, *1 and 2 Peter*, 370).

What We Need to Remember (3:2)

The second issue Peter tackles is what, specifically, believers need to remember. He says we need to "recall the words previously spoken by the holy prophets and the command of our Lord and Savior given through your apostles" (cf. Jude 17). Peter is reaching back here to where he appealed to apostolic (1:16-18) and prophetic (1:19-21) testimony to verify the future coming of the Lord. Peter is emphasizing that the teaching of the apostles actually represented the words of Jesus Christ as Lord and Savior. The words of Jesus Christ have been transmitted accurately by the apostles (Schreiner, *1 and 2 Peter*, 370-71).

The exhortation here is a reminder that we can be confident that Scripture declares Christ's return repeatedly. The Old Testament prophets spoke about the end of history, the day of judgment, and God's great salvation. And the apostles reiterated those themes. In Acts 3:17-21 Peter references Jesus's return and says the prophets talked about the same thing "from the beginning." He's likely referring there specifically to Old Testament passages that predicted Messiah's coming and his subsequent judgment (e.g., Isa 13:10-13; 24:19-23; 34:1-4; 51:6; 66:15-16; Ezek 30:3; Dan 7:9-14; Joel 2:31; Mic 1:3-5; Zeph 1:14-18; 3:8; Zech 14:3-5; Mal 4:1-5).

The New Testament continues the emphasis on Messiah's coming. Jesus himself addressed it numerous times (e.g., Matt 16:27; 24:29-30; 25:31; 26:64; Mark 13:3-27; Luke 12:40). The apostle Paul repeatedly confirmed his belief in Christ's glorious return (1 Cor 4:5; 15:23-28; 1 Thess 1:9-10; 3:13; 4:14-16; 2 Thess 1:7-8,10; 2 Tim 4:1,8; Titus 2:13), and the apostle John followed suit (Rev 1:7; 16:15; 19:11-16). Actually, twenty-three of the twenty-seven books in the New Testament explicitly reference Jesus's return, and two others allude to it. Only Philemon and 3 John don't mention it. In the 260 chapters of the New Testament, Jesus's apostles make reference to his second coming about 300 times. So the Bible declares Christ's return over and over again. We believe Jesus is coming again because the Bible features it so much!

The Bible not only convinces us that Jesus is coming back; it compels us to live holy lives while we wait. The word "command" in this verse likely doesn't refer to the promise of Christ's return but to the moral norms expected of believers. It's used approximately sixty times in the New Testament and always refers to some kind of demand or requirement (see 2:21). Peter isn't referring to a series of dos and don'ts but to the basic command for believers to conform to the image of Christ, becoming holy even as the God who called them is holy (Moo, *2 Peter*, 164; cf. Matt 5:48; 1 Pet 1:15-16). This is exactly what the false teachers were ignoring—the need for believers to obey God's call to holiness as taught by Christ and handed down by the apostles.

Peter is again returning here to his previous declaration (1:12-21), namely the connection between progressive godly living and the second coming of Christ. He asserts that the moral standard for believers is summed up in the teaching of Jesus Christ, while the false teachers were known for their self-indulgent lifestyles. In chapter 2 he described their perverted doctrine and subsequent immoral lifestyle. Now he appeals to his readers to return to the teaching of the prophets and the apostles who often spoke of the day of the Lord and, in view of that day, urged God's people to practice godliness. The repeated emphasis in the Bible on the coming of our Lord constrains us to holy living!

God's Enemies Scoff at It
2 PETER 3:3-4

"Haters gonna hate" is a popular catchphrase used to express consolation, voice encouragement, or dismiss criticism. The term started showing up in hip-hop lyrics in the early 1990s. *The Right Rhymes*, a hip-hop dictionary, traces the term back to the 1991 song "Psycobetabuckdown" by Cypress Hill. Throughout the early '90s it appeared in a number of other songs by various artists including Too $hort, 2Pac, and Sir Mix-A-Lot. In more recent years it was featured in the 2014 hit by Taylor Swift, "Shake It Off." The phrase implies that criticism says more about the critic—or "hater"—than the person being criticized. The same is true for those who scoff at the idea that Jesus will one day come again. Their scoffing tells a lot about them.

While God repeatedly testifies to the veracity of Christ's return in his Word, he also wants his people to know that critics and skeptics will always be ready to dismiss it. The phrase "Above all" (v. 3) isn't talking about chronological sequence but rather about first importance. Above all else Peter doesn't want us to be surprised by the presence and prevalence of false teachers because Jesus and the apostles expected resistance. They clearly prophesied that in the "last days"—the days between the resurrection and ascension of Christ and his second coming—mockers and deceivers would be the order of the day (e.g., Matt 24:3-5,11,23-26; Acts 20:29-31; 1 Tim 4:1ff.; 2 Tim 3:1ff.; Jas 5:3; Jude 18). In fact, their presence is a sign that Christ's coming is near, and their skepticism ironically serves as a sign of its imminence (M. Green, *2 Peter*, 149)! So to help us recognize and resist them, Peter shows us their agenda and summarizes their argument.

Their Agenda (3:3)

Before identifying the scoffers' arguments and developing his own counterarguments, Peter warns us about the false teachers' agenda. The bottom line is that they deny the return of Christ in order to indulge their own sinful desires without having to face any consequences. Notice that the real reason they scoff at the return of Christ is not because they're really smart. Regardless of their intelligence, what's really going on here is spiritual warfare. Peter says they actually are "following their own evil desires." He'll later say that they "deliberately overlook" (v. 5) indicators that Christ will return, and he will call them "ungodly" (v. 7), "untaught and unstable" (v. 16), and "lawless" (v. 17). He's not describing people here who are smarter and more rational than Christians. He's describing people who are deceived by the enemy and following the passions of sinful flesh. They are cynics who practice self-indulgence, ultimately opposing God's judgment against their hedonistic lifestyles.

Here Peter directly connects two of his most important themes: the false teachers' skepticism about the return of Christ in glory (see 1:16-21) and their contempt of holiness (2:1-22). And it shouldn't surprise us that these two qualities frequently go together. Michael Green says:

> Anthropocentric hedonism always mocks at the idea of ultimate standards and a final division between saved and lost. For men who live in the world of the relative, the claim that the relative will be ended by the absolute is nothing short of ludicrous. For men who nourish a belief in human self-determination and perfectibility, the very idea that we are accountable and dependent is a bitter pill to swallow. No wonder they mocked! (M. Green, 2 Peter, 150)

False teaching isn't guarded by any moral standards but is championed by grace abusers who live to satisfy their own selfish desires. This should be enough to negate whatever argument they make. "Before we hear the content of their teaching in v. 4, we are prepared to dismiss their perspective, since the false teachers were mockers and licentious" (Schreiner, 1 and 2 Peter, 372).

Their Argument (3:4)

The scoffers of Peter's day thought they had a rational argument against the return of Christ. Their question, "Where is his 'coming' that he promised?" is not an innocent request for information about the time or the nature of Christ's return. The form of the question often is found in the Old Testament to express unbelief and mockery (e.g., Pss 79:10; 115:2; Jer 17:15; Ezek 12:22; Joel 2:17; Mic 7:10; Mal 2:17). In asking the question, the false teachers were implying that it was past due and insinuating that it wasn't going to happen at all (Moo, 2 Peter, 166).

The rhetorical question of the false teachers is followed by the unfounded assertion that "all things continue as they have been since the beginning of creation." They simply say we've always lived in a closed system, an orderly world that's bound by certain laws of nature. They claim our routine and regularity really are not subject to any major outside interruptions. It seems rational to them that all of that will continue, and they think it irrational that anything catastrophic like Christ's coming and a chaotic end of the world will disturb it. It just makes sense to God's enemies that things will keep hopping along as they have for centuries, and it makes no sense that anybody's god suddenly will appear in the sky and turn everything upside down.

This mockery is still around today. Sceptics often talk about the chain of cause and effect in a closed universe governed by natural laws, where miracles, almost by definition, cannot happen. The laws of nature, we're told, disprove any doctrine of divine intervention that supposedly will wind up the course of history (M. Green, *2 Peter*, 151). Adherents of uniformitarianism—the belief that what's governed natural processes in the past will continue to govern them in the present—deny divine intervention throughout world history, including what the Bible says about a six-day creation and a global flood. It's true that in recent years there's been a renewed interest in the possibility that vast geological changes in the earth's history have been caused by catastrophes rather than gradual evolutionary processes (catastrophism). But these new catastrophists aren't at all ready to throw in their hats to embrace the biblical account of a catastrophic six-day creation or Noah's flood (MacArthur, *2 Peter*, 114).

Few believers would argue that there's a general uniformity in the world that results from God's care for his creation (Gen 8:22). If that weren't the case, chaos would result. And if the current escalation in the frequency of natural disasters is any indicator, it may be that God is slowly and sovereignly removing his providential grip on the universe. But a biblical view of creation sees it as an open system in which God has put in place orderly processes of natural causes but reserves the right to interrupt those processes to accomplish his sovereign purposes. Many false teachers of our day go beyond this, embracing a belief in natural order that precludes God's catastrophic intervention in history. In doing so, they deceive themselves and deny the teaching of Scripture, including the promise of Christ's return (MacArthur, *2 Peter*, 114–15).

God's Nature Supports It
2 PETER 3:5-10

If "haters gonna hate" and "scoffers gonna scoff" because their actions reveal their character, then it makes sense that God's actions tell us a lot about him as well. So Peter proceeds to remind Christ followers of some truths about God's nature that counter his scoffers. He addresses some things about who God is as well as things he has done, is doing, and will do in the future. In other words, these attributes reflect who God is and how he acts according to who he is. All of these attributes are things that scoffers "deliberately overlook" (v. 5) and about which Peter exhorts his readers, "Don't overlook" (v. 8). So take a look at four reminders, each of which appeals to the character and nature of God and forms an argument for the plausibility of Christ's return.

God Is Sovereign (3:5-7)

Peter first asserts that God has sovereignly manipulated his creation in the past to accomplish his purposes. He starts with this subject and spends the most time on it for two reasons: it's foundational for the other reminders, and it's the aspect of God's nature that the scoffers most obviously overlooked. There was a fundamental flaw in the scoffers' worldview, and it came about by their own willful decision to ignore the teachings of the prophets and apostles (see v. 2). The phrase "they deliberately overlook" (v. 5) syntactically makes more sense if the word "this" is the object of the clause. And since the word "overlook" is best translated "maintain," the idea is "When maintaining this, they overlook the fact . . ." (Bauckham, *2 Peter*, 297). The word "this" refers back to verse 4—the scoffers forgot something crucial when they maintained that God doesn't intervene in the natural order of his creation. Peter has charged believers to remember what was said by the prophets and apostles when formulating our position on the second coming. The scoffers obviously forgot some important facts when formulating theirs (Schreiner, *1 and 2 Peter*, 375).

But what exactly did they forget? Peter points out that the scoffers overlook that the sovereign hand of God actually has interrupted chaos with order and interrupted order with chaos several times before in history. And that track record suggests he'll do it again in the future. The bottom line is that it's foolish to suggest that things have stayed the same throughout history and that they will stay the same in the future. The scoffers "mistake was to forget the laws of nature are God's laws; their predictability springs from his faithfulness" (M. Green, *2 Peter*, 151). So Peter proposes that because God intervened cosmologically at creation (v. 5) and at the flood (v. 6), he surely can be expected to do it again when Christ returns (v. 7).

God first brought the order of creation out of the chaos of a water-covered cosmos (cf. Gen 1:1-2). Peter says, "The heavens came into being long ago and the earth was brought about from water and through water" (v. 5). When he says the earth was formed "through water," he's obviously drawing from the Genesis 1 account where watery chaos covered the earth. God brought order to this chaos by making the sky to separate the waters above and the waters below (Gen 1:6-8). And the waters on earth were allocated in such a way that dry ground came into existence (Gen 1:9-10). The scoffers apparently ignored this early creation account of God's interrupting what had been the natural, albeit chaotic, order.

They also had a memory lapse about when God later messed up the orderliness of his creation by flooding the earth during Noah's day (cf. Gen 7). Peter says, "The world of that time perished when it was flooded" (v. 6). God even used the same substance that brought order to the world—water—to destroy it! The wording of this verse implies that the flood wasn't merely a natural disaster, but it was God's judgment on the world. It was a foretaste of what God will do when Christ comes in final judgment. Nonetheless, it was another example of how God has interrupted the creative order for his sovereign purposes. This fact conveniently had slipped the scoffers' minds. While certainly much has been the same since creation, there hasn't been full continuity. We're actually in the second age of the world, an age that began after the flood when God restrained chaos and reset the world to its original order (Davids, *Letters*, 271).

After demonstrating that God's sovereign hand has interrupted the routine of history several times, Peter then declares that he will do it again at Christ's return (v. 7). God's judgment through the flood set the precedent for another age to begin when he judges the earth with fire. Like the original creation, this demarcation between ages will involve "the present heavens and earth," which "are stored up for fire, being kept for the day of judgment and destruction of the ungodly." Instead of using water, this time God will use fire because he promised after the flood not to destroy the world with water again (cf. Gen 9:11-17).

This is the only place in the Bible we're told the world will be destroyed by fire. However, the Old Testament often associates fire with enforcing judgment and even makes some references to that happening at the end of the world (e.g., Deut 32:22; Ps 97:3; Isa 30:30; 66:15-16; Ezek 38:22; Amos 7:4; Zeph 1:18; Mal 4:1). While the fiery destructions in the Old Testament refer to the destiny of people as opposed to the cosmos, Peter doesn't seem to separate the two. The "day of the Lord," as it was often called in the Old Testament, will be the day of judgment and the day of destruction for the ungodly. When it comes, it will be too late for the false teachers to realize and correct their oversight that God does in fact sovereignly interrupt the general order in creation (Schreiner, *1 and 2 Peter*, 377–78).

One more important note should be made about God's sovereign activity in these verses. His "holy interruption" comes about by the power of his word. This truth shows up in all three of these verses. Peter points out that "by the word of God the heavens came into being long ago and the earth was brought about" (v. 5), and "through these" same divine words he brought about the flood that destroyed the earth (v. 6). Furthermore, "by the same word, the present heavens and earth are stored up for fire" (v. 7). The truth of the matter is that any order that's ever been in this world has been due to the word of God (cf. Ps 75:3; Col 1:17; Heb 1:3). Truly, God's sovereign activity throughout history at the very least should have made the catastrophic events surrounding Christ's return a strong possibility for the gospel detractors.

God Is Timeless (3:8)

Peter's treatment of the remainder of God's attributes that counter the scoffers is marked by two qualities. First is his appeal for Christians to not "overlook" these attributes of God like the scoffers were doing (see v. 5). He knew we would be susceptible to brain lapses because of false teachers who will constantly bombard us with the argument that Christ's lengthy delay undermines the assertion that he will ever return. The second quality is another expression of Peter's pastoral heart for his readers. Again he calls us "dear friends" (*agapētoi*; cf. 3:1,14,17) because he wants us to remember that he's speaking from a sincerely burdened heart for our well-being.

In 3:8 Peter specifically puts on the table God's boundless nature regarding time in order to dispute the scoffers' argument. He draws on Psalm 90:4 to remind his readers that—because God is omniscient and omnipresent—he views all time as equally near. He urges us not to overlook the fact that "with the Lord one day is like a thousand years, and a thousand years like one day." Peter likely had been accused of appealing to the relativity of time to justify the delay in Christ's coming. But Michael Green points out that he actually was just leaning on Jewish exegesis of the psalm passage—"with thee the hours are as the ages, and the days are as the generations" (M. Green, *2 Peter*, 157; see 2 Baruch 48.12–13). God's eternal nature is being contrasted in the verse with the temporal nature of human beings. Marking time is irrelevant to him because he transcends it. So, if the passing of time doesn't diminish God in any way, and if he transcends time so that its passing doesn't affect who he is, then we shouldn't be concerned about any perceived delay of Christ's return (Schreiner, *1 and 2 Peter*, 379–80).

Like all New Testament writers, Peter believed Christ was coming soon. But he wisely refused to put a date on it. He was willing to live in the tension between the nearness of our Lord's coming and the uncertainty about when it would happen. He was OK knowing that God isn't bound by time like we are and, therefore, relates to it differently than we do. Consequently, even now the seeming delay in Christ's return isn't proof that it won't actually occur. After all, if to God a day is like a thousand years and a thousand years is like a day, then it's only been a couple of days since he was here the first time!

God Is Merciful (3:9)

Some of the scoffers apparently were saying the delay in Christ's return was evidence that God made a promise he can't keep. Peter rebuts by suggesting that instead of the delay being evidence of God's unfaithfulness, it's actually evidence of his mercy. He says, "The Lord does not delay his promise, as some understand delay, but is patient with you." Here Peter reaches back specifically to the promise of Christ's coming mentioned in verse 4 but also to the general assurance of his "very great and precious promises" in 1:4. Against that backdrop he draws an implication from 3:8 that if God doesn't mark time like we do, then it's obvious that he's not slow about keeping his promise (cf. Hab 2:3). The phrase "as some understand delay" is best understood as a reference to the false teachers (Moo, *2 Peter*, 187). Peter appeals to believers not to misunderstand the seeming "delay" of Christ's return like those guys are doing.

In contrast to God's being slow to keep his promise, Peter asserts that he's actually "patient with you." God's patient and long-suffering nature is a common theme in the Bible. It was part of his self-revelation to Israel: "The LORD—the LORD is a compassionate and gracious God, slow to anger and abounding in faithful love and truth" (Exod 34:6). Moses appealed to this quality when he prayed for God to forgive Israel: "The LORD is slow to anger and abounding in faithful love, forgiving iniquity and rebellion" (Num 14:18). This aspect of God's nature was so prevalent that Jonah even complained about it to justify his desertion: "I knew that you are a gracious and compassionate God, slow to anger, abounding in faithful love, and one who relents from sending disaster" (Jonah 4:2). Similar to his patience, the Bible contains numerous references to God's being "slow to anger," represented in the Septuagint by the same Greek root as the word used here in 2 Peter 3:9 (e.g., Exod 34:6; Neh 9:17; Pss 86:15; 103:8; 145:8; Joel 2:13; 4:2; Nah 1:3). Furthermore, God considers his long-suffering nature so crucial that he requires it of his children, who are to be like their Father (cf. 2 Cor 6:6; Gal 5:22; Eph 4:2; Col 1:11; 3:12; 1 Tim 3:10; 4:2; Heb 6:12). "One cannot properly claim to follow a Father who is patient and slow to anger if one is herself impatient and quick to anger" (Davids, *Letters*, 279).

However, God's patience isn't without redemptive motive. He's patient, Peter says, because he's "not wanting any to perish but all to come to repentance." God's patience as a means of provoking repentance also is a familiar biblical concept (cf. Joel 2:12-13; Rom 2:4). Instead of casting doubt on his promise, God's seeming delay actually highlights his heart! His waiting isn't due to his impotence but to his mercy. Ironically, what the false teachers were using as an argument against God's promise was the very thing that should have led them to repentance!

Don't miss the fact that God desires people to repent because the stakes are so high. Peter says that he's "not wanting any to perish." The word "perish" (*apolesthai*) typically refers to eternal punishment, and here it contrasts with the word "repentance" (*metanoia*), which is necessary for eternal life. Peter wants believers to remember that what's at stake here is God's desire for people to be saved from his wrath that results in hell! He says God is not wanting any to experience that end. The word "wanting" isn't a word indicating mere preference, like I might *want* a certain gift at Christmas. Instead, it expresses a conscious choice in which God desires that not one person would perish under his judgment but that all would come to repentance (cf. 1 Tim 2:4). That includes the scoffers! Mistaking God's patience for incapacity or impotence is a grave error with eternal consequences.

Before leaving this attribute of God's mercy, we must acknowledge here another mysterious tension in which believers are called to live. Does God's desire that not "any" should perish but that "all" should repent mean that his will is for everyone *without any exception* to repent? Or does it reflect his displeasure in the perishing of some even though he decrees it as such (see Ezek 18:32)? We find a similar debate over the reference to "everyone" in 1 Timothy 2:4, where Paul says God "wants everyone to be saved and to come to the knowledge of the truth." As we're all aware, many people push back on the idea that God ordains that only some will be saved, citing both Peter and Paul. Others, however, wholeheartedly embrace the idea based on other biblical texts (e.g., John 6:37,44-45,65; 10:16,26; Acts 13:48; Rom 8:29-30; 9:1-23; Eph 1:4-5,11).[1] But to debate that here is to miss the point of God's mercy. It is

> better to live with the tension and mystery of the text than
> to swallow it up in a philosophical system that pretends to
> understand all of God's ways. God's patience and his love
> are not illusions, but neither do they remove his sovereignty.
> (Schreiner, *1 and 2 Peter*, 382–83)

This verse contains wonderful—yet urgent—news for those who are without Christ. God as merciful is manifested in his patience with people to repent of sin, trust Jesus to save them, and thereby avoid the eternal condemnation of God. The absence of his appearing is not the result of unfaithfulness on his part. It's not due to some inability or inadequacy that he has. And it's certainly not an indication that he's not coming at all. It's because he's waiting . . . and he's waiting for those who have yet to believe. The apostle Paul asked, "Or do you despise the riches of his kindness, restraint, and patience, not recognizing that God's kindness is intended to lead you to repentance?" (Rom 2:4). We must plead with unbelievers not to presume on his kindness but to know that he's being patient because he loves them and desires them to repent and trust Jesus today!

---

[1] See also John Piper, "Are There Two Wills in God?" in *Still Sovereign*, ed. T. R. Schreiner and B. A. Ware (Grand Rapids, MI: Baker, 1995, 2000), 107–31.

God Is Just (3:10)

Peter completes his response to the scoffers by reminding us that God is a righteous judge and he will bring about what is just and fair. The announcement that "the day of the Lord" is coming closes the loop Peter formed in 2:3-10, specifically when he said of the false teachers, "Their condemnation, pronounced long ago, is not idle, and their destruction does not sleep" (2:3), and God knows how "to keep the unrighteous under punishment for the day of judgment" (2:9). In the Bible the day of the Lord culminates "the last days," or the time between Jesus's first and second comings. It's marked by the catastrophic and extraordinary intervention of God in history for the purposes of decisive judgment against his enemies and gracious salvation of his people.

A quick glance at the whole of 3:10, however, indicates that Peter primarily has condemnation in mind (Moo, *2 Peter*, 189). MacArthur observes that the testimony of Scripture is that the day of the Lord will culminate in God's "final judgment of the wicked on earth and the destruction of the present universe . . . a day of unparalleled judgment, darkness, and damnation, a day in which the Lord would completely destroy His enemies, vindicate His name, reveal His glory, and establish His kingdom" (MacArthur, *2 Peter*, 123-24; see Isa 2:10-21; 13:6-22; Joel 1–2; Amos 5; Obad 15; Zeph 1:7-18; Zech 14; Mal 4; 2 Thess 2:2; Matt 24:29-31).

The warning that this day of God's justice "will come like a thief" reflects the unexpected nature of the timing of Christ's coming and the unpreparedness of people to face God's judgment (cf. Matt 24:43; Luke 12:39). The arrival of this terrible day won't be accompanied by any more warning than that of a midnight burglar who comes by stealth to rifle through your belongings while you sleep. Using the same image, Jesus warned his hearers to prepare for this sudden arrival:

> *Therefore, stay awake, for you do not know on what day your Lord is coming. But know this, that if the master of the house had known in what part of the night the thief was coming, he would have stayed awake and would not have let his house be broken into. Therefore you also must be ready, for the Son of Man is coming at an hour you do not expect.* (Matt 24:42-44 ESV; cf. Rev 3:3; 16:15)

Paul picked up the same simile, saying the day of the Lord will happen when people least expect it and are least prepared for it:

> *For you yourselves know very well that the day of the Lord will come just like a thief in the night. When they say, "Peace and security," then sudden destruction will come upon them, like labor pains on a pregnant woman, and they will not escape.* (1 Thess 5:2-3)

Circumstances will say otherwise, supposed "signs of the times" won't be sufficient, and false teachers will be proclaiming that all is well. But the day of the Lord will come, and it will come without warning. And because people won't see it coming, they won't prepare for it.

Peter then reminds his readers of what they knew from the Old Testament as well as from their Lord: the day of Lord will come with dramatic and catastrophic effect! Isaiah prophesied that it will be a day when "all the stars in the sky will dissolve. The sky will roll up like a scroll, and its stars will all wither as leaves wither on the vine, and foliage on the fig tree" (Isa 34:4; cf. Isa 13:10-13; 24:19; 64:1-4; 66:16; Mic 1:4). Jesus described it as a time when "the sun will be darkened, and the moon will not shed its light; the stars will fall from the sky, and the powers of the heavens will be shaken" (Matt 24:29), and he declared that "heaven and earth will pass away" (Matt 24:35). He also said, "Then there will be signs in the sun, moon, and stars; and there will be anguish on the earth among nations bewildered by the roaring of the sea and the waves" (Luke 21:25). Scripture describes that day as not just a time of disrupting the universe's order but of utterly destroying it.

This horrific time is described in the present passage as having three particular effects. First, we learn that "the heavens will pass away with a loud noise." The word translated "loud noise" is a colorful, onomatopoeic term that can refer to the swish of an arrow through the air, the rumbling of thunder, the crackle of flames in a fire, the scream of a whip as it descends, the rushing of mighty waters, or the hissing of a serpent (M. Green, *2 Peter*, 161–62). It's as if Peter attempts to unite many horrifying properties into one in order to describe the extreme nature of the sky's demise. And if that weren't enough, we're told next that "the elements will burn and be dissolved" as well. Fire as a picture of enforcing judgment is found throughout the Old Testament (e.g., Deut 4:24; Mal 4:1), and it's frequently used to describe Christ's return in the New Testament, including here in 3:7,10,12. The "elements" could either mean the physical elements of earth (i.e., air, earth, water) or the heavenly bodies (i.e., sun, moon, stars, etc.). Regardless, these first two descriptions together unfold the utter destruction of the heavens and the elements of the world.

The third and final description reveals that not only will the physical elements of the universe be wrecked, but its wicked inhabitants will be destroyed as well. The phrase "the works on it will be disclosed" suggests that God's judgment will end with a definitive pronouncement of a just and fair penalty on mankind's sin. The exact meaning of "disclosed" is uncertain, but it seems to allude to the revealing of the deeds of men and women. The word suggests that both the inhabitants of the earth and their deeds will be "laid bare" (NIV) in God's court. The whole world will pass away, and only man will be left to give an account of himself to his Creator (see Bauckham's discussion, *2 Peter*, 319–20). When Christ comes, it will be clear that God is acting with righteous judgment against sin as he said he would.

People have debated whether what's being described in 3:10 is literal or figurative. Admittedly, Peter's language isn't entirely clear regarding all the detail we'd like to have. After all, he is attempting to describe the indescribable! Personally, I lean toward his description here being literal for numerous reasons, the most significant of which may be the immediate context. Peter obviously uses "water" in 3:5-6 in reference to a literal event. So it would seem odd for him to switch to figurative language in verse 7, where he introduces the element ("fire") that obviously causes the effect here in verse 10 ("burn"). But whether the description is literal or figurative, what's certain is that the judgment of God against sin will come; and when it does, it will be purifying, awful, and devastating. Peter's "main purpose is to lift up the eyes of his readers to the climax of history" (M. Green, *2 Peter*, 161). And he wants us to know that when we see it, it will be completely fair in light of God's holy justice (see 2 Thess 1:5-12).

Conclusion

I've found myself longing for Jesus's return more in recent years than I remember doing in a long time. I longed for Jesus to come back when I saw the news recently about a young man driving his vehicle into a crowd of people who were protesting a white supremacist rally in Virginia, killing one person and injuring nineteen others. When I heard recently that North Korea has now developed a hydrogen bomb more powerful than the ones we dropped on Japan during World War II, I longed for Jesus to come back. When I heard about a Christian brother getting gunned down in cold blood in Benghazi, leaving behind a young wife and son, I longed for Jesus to come back. When I heard about an ISIS sympathizer killing forty-nine people in an Orlando nightclub and wounding fifty-eight others, I found myself longing for Jesus to come back. And these are just a few of the more recent occasions that have caused me to look toward the eastern sky and say, "Come quickly, Lord Jesus."

But I must admit that every time I hear about how messed up our world is, and every time I look toward the east and Jesus isn't there, I stare in the face of discouragement and doubt. I face the temptation to buy into the same thing so many people in our day believe: he's not coming. And as more time passes, more and more Christians run the risk of wandering. And the closer we get to his coming, the more people will ridicule and attack this truth that we believe and value.

However, while the world trashes what we treasure, the Word of God and the nature of God both assure us of Christ's return. So in 2 Peter 3:1-10 Peter makes another installment in his theme of promise. In 1:4 he submitted that God "has given us very great and precious promises." Those promises no doubt include the promise of Christ's return and the inauguration of his eternal reign. The verbal form of the word *promise* then shows up in 2:19 in reference to the empty promises of freedom made by the false teachers, who ironically are slaves themselves. In this current passage Peter picks up the theme by using the same word (3:4) specifically to reference Christ's second coming (Davids, *Letters*, 263–64). Although false teaching tries to undermine our belief in God's promises, he will be faithful to fulfill all that he's committed to his children. Jesus will make good on his promise, "I'll be back!"

Reflect and Discuss

1. Peter is adamant about reminding his readers about the gospel. Why is constant reminding of gospel life important?
2. What are daily strategies for remembering the gospel? How can we help others do this?
3. Which are the only two books of the New Testament that do not mention the return of Christ? What should this stark proportion (25 out of 27 books) tell us about the importance of this cosmic and cataclysmic event?
4. Are there those today who scoff at the return of Christ? What should our response to them be?
5. We worship a God who is patient and slow to anger. As a worshiper of this God, would you consider yourself to be patient and slow to

anger? In light of 2 Peter 1:4, how do we become more like God in these ways?

6. Peter says that God "wants all to come to repentance." What, then, should our desire be? How does this motivate us to share the gospel?

7. We often rightly exclaim, "Come, Lord Jesus!" With that ultimate desire tugging at us, what should our response be to his delaying? How should it change us knowing that his delay in returning is due—at least in part—to his patience?

8. Why did God include in his Word graphic and grave pictures of his judgment? What are his purposes in describing his judgment in such terms?

9. Peter says that the works of the false teachers will "be disclosed" under God's judgment. Will believers' works also be disclosed? What other Scriptures come to mind? Compare and contrast the judgment of believers and unbelievers at the return of Christ.

10. Regardless of whether the description of the destruction of physical creation is literal or figurative, what message does God want us to know about his power as it will be demonstrated through the final judgment?

Remember How You're to Wait

2 PETER 3:11-18

Main Idea: A right understanding of the second coming enables believers to stand firm as they await Christ's return.

I. **Be Godly (3:11-14).**
   A. Our response is practical righteousness.
   B. Our reason is perfect righteousness.
II. **Seize the Day (3:15-16).**
   A. The exhortation to believers (3:15a)
   B. The corroboration of the apostle Paul (3:15b-16a)
   C. The distortion of false teachers (3:16b)
III. **Don't Cave In (3:17-18).**
   A. Be on guard (3:17).
   B. Grow in Christ (3:18).

Like most young pastors, I didn't have a lot of experience when I served my first church. No place was that more evident than in wedding rehearsals. I didn't have any idea what I was doing. I would tell the wedding party to go to the back of the church and then proceed to march in when the music cranked up. Seemed like a logical plan. But I quickly discovered that everything went downhill when the bridesmaids and groomsmen began to ascend up to the stage. Chaos ensued. They always looked confused and disoriented. Why? Because they didn't know where on the stage they were supposed to end up. Then a seasoned pastor gave me some advice. He encouraged me to begin on the stage, showing everybody where they're supposed to stand when they get there. Then they know where they're going when they march in. Made complete sense. And it worked! What you believe about where you're going to end up has bearing on how you march in!

The same is true for our eschatology. What we believe about the end of the world will determine how we march toward it. Beginning with 3:11, Peter transitions to the last section of his letter. He starts moving from argumentation to application, and his application reflects his heart for us to live in view of our firm conviction that Jesus is coming back. So he offers us three applications regarding how we're to wait for Jesus in view of what we believe about his return.

Be Godly
2 PETER 3:11-14

We've all heard the logical argument, "If it looks like a duck, walks like a duck, and quacks like a duck, then it's probably a duck." What a person says or does is a fairly good indicator of who that person is. The reverse is true as well: "If it doesn't look like a duck, walk like a duck, or quack like a duck, then it's probably not a duck." That's what Peter is saying about false teachers and their disciples. If a person doesn't walk like a Christian and talk like a Christian, then he or she probably isn't a Christian. These heretics reject the idea of a second coming, a day of judgment, and a future new world. And their libertine lifestyle and ethic give clear evidence of their belief about the end times. Because they dismiss the future coming of Christ, they live however they want to live. What we believe about where life is headed has a direct influence on our morality—or lack thereof.

So Peter's first application to believers about how we should live while we wait for Jesus is to be godly. He says that if you walk like a Christian and talk like a Christian, then it's a pretty good indication that you're a Christian. Peter's words remind us of Christ's coming so we will live in a way that pleases God and avoid his condemnation. And a future judgment wasn't an idea he had to dream up to foster godly living. The condemnation and salvation that is coming with Christ's return was his conviction (Schreiner, *1 and 2 Peter*, 393). And it was one he shared not only with his fellow apostles but with the Old Testament prophets as well. Based on that conviction, he tells us to exercise practical righteousness now in preparation for perfect righteousness in the future.

Our Response Is Practical Righteousness

The basic idea of 3:11-14 is that a right view of Christ's second coming should lead to ethical living in the present. Although it's not in the same grammatical form, his exhortation in 3:11-14 could be likened to an "if-then" statement similar to his argument about God's track record of justice in 2:4-10a. In these verses he's basically saying, "IF Jesus is coming back to judge the wicked and deliver the righteous, THEN you should live righteously while you're waiting." For Peter it's a no-brainer: if the end of the world is imminent, and the present heavens and earth as we know them are going to be abolished, and Jesus is coming back to judge the living and the dead, then it just makes sense that his readers should respond by living godly lives. Consider how his argument is developed.

First of all, notice how Peter's "IF" statement—or condition—is reflected in each of the four verses:

> *Since all these things are to be dissolved in this way . . .* (v. 11)

> *. . . as you wait for the day of God and hasten its coming. Because of that day, the heavens will be dissolved with fire and the elements will melt with heat.* (v. 12)

> *But based on his promise, we wait for new heavens and a new earth, where righteousness dwells.* (v. 13)

> *while you wait for these things . . .* (v. 14)

All four of these references reach back to verses 7 and 10 and reiterate the prediction that on the day of the Lord a fire will consume the existing world. The phrase in 3:11 noted above is a present participle and designates a future destruction that is total and complete, involving a burning of the present elements of the world (Bauckham, *2 Peter*, 323; cf. 3:12).

But then look at how these conditional references are framed up by Peter's "THEN"—or conclusion—statement found at the beginning and end of the section:

> *It is clear what sort of people you should be in holy conduct and godliness.* (v. 11)

> *Therefore, dear friends, . . . make every effort to be found without spot or blemish in his sight, at peace.* (v. 14)

Since this earth isn't our final home, Peter urges us to strive to be found godly, diligent, spotless, blameless, and at peace with God when Jesus comes back in judgment. He describes people whose contemporary lives represent God's worship and character with phrases like "holy conduct and godliness" (v. 11) as well as "without spot or blemish" (v. 14). That's practical righteousness right now in the day in which we live. It's behavior: the way we act, the things we do and don't do. If we live this way, then we will "be found . . . in his sight, at peace" (v. 14). "Peace" (*eirēnē*) describes the state of being right with God and entering into his presence with joy as opposed to experiencing his wrath like the false teachers (Bauckham, *2 Peter*, 327; see also Moo, *2 Peter*, 208). Evidently, while we're made righteous because of Christ's righteousness, our practical righteousness will have at least some bearing on our eternal reward.

The call to practical righteousness in these verses is grounded on the eschatological future noted in the "THEN" statements highlighted previously (Schreiner, *1 and 2 Peter*, 388). And this call to practice holy "conduct" (v. 11; cf. 1 Pet 1:15) to some degree frames up Peter's entire letter (cf. 1:3,6-7). From the beginning he asserted that God has given us everything we need for life and godliness, making it a Christian virtue of first importance that all believers should zealously pursue. What we believe about what's going to happen in the future should dictate how we live in the present. Our belief about eternity demands the response of practical righteous living.

Our Reason Is Perfect Righteousness

While practical righteousness certainly is the logical response to the imminent return of Christ, Peter doesn't call us to such a lifestyle primarily because of impending punishment. A second coming that only brings destruction would leave believers miserable, and it wouldn't reflect the whole gospel or be a noble motive for living in grace. The term translated "wait for" (*prosdokaō*) shows up three times in three verses (vv. 12,13,14) and provides a different slant on the believer's reason for responding with righteous living. It indicates the eager anticipation we ought to have for Jesus to come back and make good on all of God's promises. This is a term of expectation and longing! But expectation and longing for *what*? Is it merely the punishment of the wicked and the destruction of the world we're waiting for? No, it's something more.

The believer's real motivation for righteous living is the promise of "new heavens and a new earth, where righteousness dwells" (v. 13). What we're anticipating is not primarily the punishment of the wicked but a new world for us, one that's transformed into a place where righteousness is the order of the day! While it's difficult for us to know whether Peter was saying that God will completely wipe out the old heavens and earth and make brand-new ones or that he'll purify the old ones and create new ones out of the same elements, we can be confident that a new physical universe will be born (Schreiner, *1 and 2 Peter*, 392).

When that happens, God's intention for creation will finally be realized, and the loop of the Bible will be closed (cf. Gen 1:1; Isa 65:17; 66:22; Rev 21:1–22:5).

The practical righteousness we practice now is primarily done in anticipation of the perfect righteousness we'll experience when Christ returns. Preparing for perfect righteousness in the future results in practicing personal righteousness in daily life right now! The fact that we're headed for life with Christ in eternity demands daily conduct that is conducive for such. Without the hope that life is going somewhere, there's nothing left to live for; but if we have that hope, there's everything to live for! Look at everything you're doing and not doing in your life today, and then ask, "Does this reflect the life that I'll have in eternity?" If not, pause from reading this book right now, repent, and correct your course!

Not only is righteous living spurred on by an anticipation of perfect righteousness, but perfect righteousness evidently is spurred on by righteous living! Sounds crazy, huh? The most natural sense of the verb translated "hasten" (v. 12; cf. Luke 2:16; 19:5-6; Acts 20:16; 22:18) suggests that Peter seems to think that we can speed up Christ's coming by living godly lives (Moo, *2 Peter*, 198; cf. Matt 6:10; 24:14; Acts 3:19-21). Some would say such an idea undermines God's sovereignty. But God himself knows in advance what his people will do (see Bauckham, *2 Peter*, 313, 325); furthermore, the Bible is clear that he even foreordains it (e.g., Prov 16:33; Isa 46:9-11; Lam 3:37-38; Amos 4:13; Eph 1:11). These mysterious truths, however, don't negate Peter's assertion that such practical godliness in some way hastens Christ's coming. Once again he summons us to live in the tension between divine sovereignty and human responsibility. Here he calls us to the latter—living righteously in view of prompting Christ's return!

Seize the Day
2 PETER 3:15-16

I love the movie *Dead Poets Society*. The 1989 film, set in 1959, tells the story of English professor John Keating, who inspires his students at a boys' school to love poetry and to overcome their reluctance to make changes in their lives. At one point in the movie, Keating—played by Robin Williams—is showing his students some pictures on display in a school trophy case. The pictures are of deceased alumni from years gone by. Hoping to impress on the boys the brevity of life and the need to make the most of their lives, he whispers in their ears as they stare at the old pictures, "If you listen real close, you can hear them whisper their legacy to you. Go on, lean in. Listen, you hear it?—*Carpe*—hear it?—*Carpe, carpe diem*, seize the day, boys, make your lives extraordinary." Keating didn't want his students to miss the opportunity to take advantage of the short time they had.

Peter didn't want his hearers to miss their opportunity. So his second application is for believers to seize the day in order to maximize our gospel influence and make the most of the time before Jesus comes back. So, under the inspiration of the Spirit, he exhorts us to pursue salvation for ourselves and others, supports his exhortation with the truth found in the writings of the apostle Paul, and then warns us about those who seek to distort that truth.

The Exhortation to Believers (3:15a)

As we wait for Jesus to return, Peter not only wants believers to live righteously but also to "regard the patience of our Lord as salvation." As he's already asserted, Christ's delay in returning to judge the earth is the result of God's patience (v. 9). But false teachers consider it an indication that he isn't coming at all and, therefore, justify their immoral conduct. Peter exhorts believers to have a different attitude—one that sees God's "patience" as an opportunity to pursue "salvation" as opposed to godless living.

The idea of counting God's patience as salvation could mean a couple of things. First, it could be a call for believers to engage in aggressive evangelism so as to reach as many people for Christ as possible before it's too late. Without a doubt, pursuing the salvation of others is one of the most important things we should be doing while we're waiting for Christ to come back. Such aggressive witness is not only crucial for the souls of men and women, but Jesus declared that it actually must happen before he returns: "This good news of the kingdom will be proclaimed in all the world as a testimony to all nations, and then the end will come" (Matt 24:14). So it shouldn't be a surprise that Peter might possibly be encouraging believers to pursue the salvation of everybody on the planet while they have the chance.

A second possible meaning of the exhortation to "regard the patience of our Lord as salvation" is for professing Christians to be sure of their own salvation. This understanding is consistent with what Peter has already said. Early in his letter, he encourages his readers to

> make every effort to confirm your calling and election, because if you do these things you will never stumble. For in this way, entry into the eternal kingdom of our Lord and Savior Jesus Christ will be richly provided for you. (1:10-11)

Peter uses the word *salvation* four other times in his two letters, and all of them refer to ultimate deliverance from sin and death at the end of life (1 Pet 1:5,9,10; 2:2). This understanding is consistent with the general idea of salvation in the New Testament. We've already seen in this book that Peter evidently thought that at least some of his readers were in danger of buying into the deceptive words of the false teachers and thereby showing themselves to be truly unregenerate (see 1:3-11). Consequently, he wants each of us to take the opportunity we have, while waiting for Christ's return, to confirm our relationship with Jesus (Moo, *2 Peter*, 208–9).

The Corroboration of the Apostle Paul (3:15b-16a)

Regardless of whether Peter's talking about bold evangelism or assurance of salvation (or both!), he reinforces his exhortation by saying the apostle Paul warned his readers about the same things: "Just as our dear brother Paul has written to you according to the wisdom given to him" (v. 15). His reference to Paul as "our dear brother" underscores the affection and graciousness he felt toward him as a colaborer in the gospel. These two apostles were the primary leaders in the early church. Both had been present at the Jerusalem Council (Acts 15:6-21), and both had ministered with Silas (cf. Acts 15:40; 1 Pet 5:12). Over two decades earlier, Paul had even confronted Peter for refusing to eat with Gentile believers (Gal 2:8-9,11-21; cf. 1 Cor 1:12; 3:22). These two men had been through some stuff together, so Peter appeals to Paul's writings to corroborate his plea.

If—as some have argued—Peter wrote his second letter to the same people in Asia Minor as his first letter (cf. 1 Pet 1:1; 2 Pet 3:1), his readers likely would have been familiar with a number of Paul's letters since he had written many of his letters to people in the same area (e.g., Galatians, Ephesians, Colossians). Regardless, Peter's reference to "these things in all his letters" (v. 16) suggests his readers are somehow familiar with a lot of what Paul had written. While we can't be entirely sure about which letters Peter is referring to, we can conclude that the themes of the necessity of godly living and the certainty of God's patience are found in a number of Paul's letters.

Before going any further in verse 16, I think it's best to reach down to the end of the verse and note that Peter considers Paul's writings to be of the same nature as "the rest of the Scriptures." In the language of the New Testament, the word translated "rest" or "other" refers to other of the same kind, evidenced by instances in the New Testament where it's used as an adjective (e.g., Matt 25:11; Acts 2:37; 2 Cor 12:13; Gal 2:13; cf. Rom 1:13; 1 Cor 9:5; Phil 4:3). Additionally, the word translated "Scriptures" (*graphē*) is found fifty times in the New Testament and references the Old Testament Scriptures. It comes from the verb meaning "to write" (*graphō*) that occurs about 180 times in the New Testament, half of which refer to the written Word of God. Consequently, we're on solid ground in believing that Peter considered what Paul wrote to be Scripture that carried the same authority as the Old Testament (Moo, *2 Peter*, 212). Having this understanding helps us feel the weight of what Peter is saying in the rest of this verse.

The Distortion of False Teachers (3:16b)

Knowing that Peter's talking here about inspired Scripture, his next words are a great encouragement to me. He acknowledges that "there are some matters [in Paul's letters] that are hard to understand." The term "hard to understand" is used of things that are difficult to interpret (Bauckham, *2 Peter*, 331). Let me be really transparent for a moment and say that I'm super glad Peter makes this observation. I'm encouraged that I'm not the only one who doesn't understand everything he reads in the Bible! Even at several places in this epistle we've run across words or phrases or verses where we don't have all the information we'd like to have, or where we've just had to admit that we simply don't know the exact meaning that's intended. We have to be OK with those times, being confident that none of the "unknowns" rob us of anything that's essential for "life and godliness" (1:3). But we can be encouraged that Peter—under the inspiration of the Holy Spirit—concedes that at times some of the stuff Paul wrote is difficult to interpret.

Although some things in the Bible are difficult to interpret, misinterpretation of Scripture is never excusable (Schreiner, *1 and 2 Peter*, 396). It's better for us to admit that we don't know what a text means than to distort the meaning of a text and make it say what we want it to say. That's what the false teachers and their converts were doing. Peter says these "untaught and unstable will twist" both Paul's writings and the rest of Scripture to justify their immoral behavior. And in so doing they were undermining both the commission to bold evangelism and the assurance of salvation. The word "untaught" denotes a lack of information, and "unstable" indicates a vacillating spiritual character. The verb "twist" speaks of wrenching someone's body on a torture rack, painting a vivid picture of how the false teachers manipulated certain issues in order to confuse and deceive the undiscerning (MacArthur, *2 Peter*, 135).

Beloved, don't miss the haunting negative influence of false teaching that's being revealed here at the end of Peter's letter! The ignorance and instability of the people being described here wasn't merely due to the lack of instruction. Peter began his letter by referring to believers as firmly "established" (*estērigmenous*, 1:12) in the truth. But then he said the false teachers enticed "unstable" (*astēriktous*, 2:14) souls. Now we are being told here that the "unstable" (*astēriktoi*) distorted Paul's writings (Schreiner, *1 and 2 Peter*, 397). There will always be those within the community of faith who aren't established in the gospel. They become the targets of false teachers. And when the unstable fall prey to heresy, they themselves begin to do the same thing with the Bible that their teachers do—they twist it to justify their immoral lifestyles. May God give us grace to zealously establish every man, woman, boy, and girl in the glorious gospel!

This errant use of Paul's writings—or any part of the Bible for that matter—is no innocent offense. Both the false teachers and their disciples twist the Scriptures "to their own destruction." The word "destruction" is used in some form frequently in 2 Peter to refer to God's judgment against the wicked (2:1,3; 3:6-7,9). These hermeneutical gymnastics landed these heretics in hell! They twisted Paul's words to justify their licentious lifestyles. They were dulling the sharp edge of gospel mission as well as the confidence of its adherents. Luther reasonably suggests they were abusing Paul's teaching on justification by faith and freedom from the law to enjoy a life of moral laxity (Luther, *Commentary*, 286). This wasn't a question of minor doctrinal errors but of using misinterpretations to justify immorality. And Peter is consistent in identifying eschatological condemnation as the destiny of those who choose such ungodliness (Bauckham, *2 Peter*, 334).

When all is said and done, it's clear that we don't need to spend a lot of time trying to determine whether Peter wants us to turn up the heat on our bold evangelistic efforts or to give concentrated time to solidifying the assurance of our salvation. Why? First of all, both exhortations are common to the New Testament, including Peter's writings (e.g., 1 Pet 2:9-12; 2 Pet 1:8-11) and Paul's writings (e.g., Rom 2:4; cf. Rom 3:25-26; 9:22). Second, if we think about it closely, the same issue is at the heart of both exhortations: true salvation! Peter wants all people to hear the gospel and be saved and to be sure they're saved. And that includes those of us inside the church who already believe we're saved but are being bombarded with false teaching, tempted by a sexually licentious and materialistic culture, and living day after day wondering when Jesus is coming back. So let's hear Peter as saying both: use this time to leverage our lives to get the gospel to every person who hasn't heard it and intentionally lean in to growing in Christlikeness in order to confirm our calling and election. "Regard the patience of our Lord as salvation." *Carpe diem*! Seize the day, Peter says!

Don't Cave In
2 PETER 3:17-18

I think human pyramids are fascinating to watch (and I underscore the word *watch*!). I must admit that the sinister side of me likes to watch them because of the possibility that they may fall down in a mound of mangled bodies! If you've seen one of these acrobatic formations, you know they're made up of three or more people in which two or more people support a tier of people on top of them, who in turn may support rows of people on top of them. The brave souls up top usually kneel or stand on the shoulders, backs, or thighs of the people below them. Crazy, huh? For obvious reasons, they usually put the people who don't weigh very much higher in the formation, and they put the bigger and stronger people closer to the base. That way the chances of falling are reduced!

Peter was concerned about the weight of false teaching on the Christ followers he was shepherding. He didn't want them to fall. So his third application—which actually doubles as the conclusion of his letter—calls on believers not to cave in under the weight of the scoffing of the wolves who wore sheep's clothing. The apostle's closing thoughts are marked first in verse 17 by the emphatic "You" at the beginning of the verse in the original language (see NASB, ESV), a construction that underscores the urgency and necessity of the reader's response. That's followed by the transitional "therefore," which identifies everything that's been said up to this point as the reason for what he's about to say. And what he's about to say is couched in two imperatives that provide a simple yet pointed summary of the entire letter. First, the readers must be on guard so that they don't fall prey to the false teachers and prove themselves to be imposters when Jesus comes (v. 17). Second, they must grow in Christ Jesus in order to remain on that crucial watch (v. 18).

Be on Guard (3:17)

Peter's first appeal is for his readers to be on guard. He wants his readers to take care "so that you are not led away by the error of lawless people and fall from your own stable position." The word translated "fall" is a reference to apostasy (cf. Rom 11:11,22; 14:4; 1 Cor 10:12; Heb 4:11; Rev 2:5), and the participle translated "led away" serves to indicate how that can actually happen to people. Apostasy happens when someone lets their guard down, so they end up being swept away by the "error" taught by rebellious false teachers and, thereby, fall away (Schreiner, *1 and 2 Peter*, 400; cf. 2:18). These teachers are called "lawless" people, which literally means "without law or custom" and came to mean "morally corrupt" (MacArthur, *2 Peter*, 136). Apostasy happens when these peddlers of perversion are successful in luring someone to adopt their same perverted moral character.

This deadly proselytizing is the reason Peter is so zealous for us never to let our guards down. He suggests that believers have a biblical responsibility to watch themselves so they don't depart from the Christian faith. And his entire letter is clear that those who depart—like the false teachers—are destined for eternal damnation. Again, as we've previously noted, any person who ultimately does fall away reveals that they weren't truly saved in the first place (see the discussion on 2:5-13; cf. 1 Cor 11:19; 1 John 2:19). His plea here is similar to the one he made earlier in his letter:

> *Therefore, brothers and sisters, make every effort to confirm your*
> *calling and election, because if you do these things you will never*
> *stumble. For in this way, entry into the eternal kingdom of our*
> *Lord and Savior Jesus Christ will be richly provided for you.*
> (2 Pet 1:10-11)

He wants all his readers to make it to the finish line in full stride, proving the authenticity of their faith.

So how do professing believers avoid falling away? The opposite of falling away is to maintain our "own stable position"—or secure situation. And we do that by paying attention to instructions and heeding warnings. Doing so doesn't stifle confidence but actually is the means to it. Peter wasn't trying to throw cold water on our assurance but to strengthen it by calling us to heed what we've been taught. The phrase "you know this in advance" refers to the advance warning his readers had been given through the Old Testament prophets and the teaching of the apostles (1:16-21; 3:2), as well as what Peter had previously written in this letter (Moo, *2 Peter*, 213). Today we have all this in our Bibles. If we fall away, Peter reminds us, it won't be because we haven't been warned. We will be without excuse. So it's important for us to keep this on our radar because, if we're not careful, it's possible for us to stumble at false teaching. And the longer Christ delays, the easier it will be for us to trip up and cast our lot in with the scoffers and doubters.

Grow in Christ (3:18)

Endurance doesn't exist in a vacuum. You can only keep your guard up so long if that's all you've got. The negative of saying no to false teaching has to be partnered with a positive. So Peter makes a second appeal to us: grow in Christ. The idea of growing in Christ is broken down into two facets. The noun "grace" and the phrase "knowledge of our Lord and Savior Jesus Christ" are best understood as separate but related ideas (Moo, *2 Peter*, 214). In other words, the first part of Peter's admonition is simply to "grow in grace." The second part is to *grow in the knowledge of Christ.*

Peter begins his ending by telling us to "grow in . . . grace." Like many believers, I grew up thinking grace was something that was limited to my conversion. We sang, "Amazing grace, how sweet the sound that saved a wretch like me!" I learned the little acronym G-R-A-C-E, which represented **G**od's **R**edemption **A**t **C**hrist's **E**xpense. And all of that is good and right, but it's not enough. From the outset of his letter, Peter presents grace not as a static reality limited to the time we first confessed Christ and were forgiven of our sins but as a dynamic infusion of God's help for living the gospel life from beginning to end. He rightly began his letter by highlighting grace as the saving righteousness that gives faith to believers (1:1). But he didn't stop there. He immediately prayed that the grace of Christ would be multiplied in our lives (1:2). Then he declared that the grace of the Lord Jesus has given us everything we need for godly living (1:3-4) so we will experience God's saving promises to the max.

Grace is the amazing gift of God's resources given to believers in order that they might live out the gospel. It's the foundation of the Christian life, and Scripture constantly and consistently calls us to grow in it, to be nurtured in it, and to be strengthened by it (e.g., 2 Cor 6:1; 9:8; 12:9; 2 Tim 2:1; 1 Pet 4:10). Maybe we need an additional acronym for G-R-A-C-E—God's Resources Applied to the Christian Experience! God has given us all the resources of heaven to grow in the image of Christ and remain steadfast in him. If we don't grow and progress in grace our entire lives, we run the risk of being carried away by the lawlessness of false teachers (Schreiner, *1 and 2 Peter*, 401).

Not only do we need to grow in grace, but we need to grow in the "knowledge of our Lord and Savior Jesus Christ" as well. The language of the New Testament indicates that Jesus is the object of the phrase—he is the one we are to know. As we've seen, the knowledge of God in Christ is a major theme in 2 Peter. We've learned that grace and peace will be magnified in knowing Jesus Christ as God and Savior (1:2). Everything we need for life and godliness is available through knowing him (1:3). Growing in the knowledge of Christ is essential for living out the gospel life (1:5-6). Growing in godliness is the only way to demonstrate that the knowledge of Christ is fruitful (1:8). We've seen that the opposite is true as well. People who walk away from Christ after coming to a knowledge of him find themselves worse off than people who never confessed him (2:20-21).

Peter is intentional about closing his letter with this theme of growing in the knowledge of Christ. He understands that knowing Christ is one of our primary goals for Christian development as we move toward a full knowledge of him—"For now we see only a reflection as in a mirror, but then face to face. Now I know in part, but then I will know fully, as I am fully known" (1 Cor 13:12). But he also knows that as believers we need to be able to distinguish between true knowledge of Christ and "irreverent and empty speech and contradictions from what is falsely called knowledge" (1 Tim 6:20), which was championed by the false teachers. Both knowing Christ and knowing about Christ not only help us grow in grace, but they help us keep our guard up against heresy and apostasy. Michael Green says, "The more we know Christ, the more we will invoke his grace. And the more we know about Christ, the more varied will be the grace we invoke" (*2 Peter*, 176). Growing in the knowledge of Jesus Christ is absolutely essential for maturing in Christ and warding off false teaching.

Peter concludes his letter—and his exhortation to grow in Christ—with a doxology. He says, "To him be the glory both now and to the day of eternity." A doxology is an ascription of glory, offering renown to one to whom it is due. Although Peter uses some familiar terms here, his ending is somewhat unusual for a number of reasons, not the least of which is that he ends with a doxology. Most New Testament letters end with greetings, references to fellow workers, requests for prayer, or blessings for grace (for other exceptions, see Rom 16:25-27; Phil 4:20; Jude 24-25). But neither the uniqueness of Peter's ending nor the familiar terms he uses should deflect our attention from the weight of his words. Consider some other distinctive qualities of the way Peter brings his letter to a close, as well as the reasons he likely did so.

Notice that Peter's doxology is to Christ (see also 2 Tim 4:18; Rev 1:5-6), while most doxologies in Scripture normally ascribe glory to God. This shouldn't surprise us, however, because he presents a high view of Jesus, starting with the beginning of his letter (Moo, *2 Peter*, 215; cf. 1:1). Peter held a conviction that all glory goes to Christ because both our salvation and our ability to hold on to that salvation are his doing. He didn't call on us to exercise self-effort in order to save ourselves. He told us that God grants grace so we can grow in our knowledge of him. Peter simply believes that the one who does the work deserves the glory (Schreiner, *1 and 2 Peter*, 402).

Another uncommon characteristic of Peter's ending is that he ascribes glory "to the day of eternity." Most New Testament authors usually ascribe glory to God with something like "forever" (e.g., Jude 25). But the context of Peter's letter—and especially of this last chapter—helps us understand this different slant. His reference to the "day" likely has an eschatological meaning, namely "the day of the Lord" or "the day of God." He's been telling us that when Christ comes back he will inaugurate a new age, an age (or "day") that will last forever. The false teachers denied that this day would ever come, but Peter has reminded us that it will in fact come. And, when it does, it will usher in the eternal glory of our Lord and Savior, Jesus Christ. So the glory belongs to Jesus Christ both now and forever. We glorify him as we long for that day, and as we wait for it with anticipation and holiness (Moo, *2 Peter*, 215; Schreiner, *1 and 2 Peter*, 402).

So we say with Peter, Amen: So let it be!

Conclusion

That seasoned pastor taught me to begin a wedding rehearsal with the end in mind. Start where you're going to end up, he told me. It seems that Peter did the same thing in this letter—he ends up where he started. He started by praying, "May grace and peace be multiplied to you through the knowledge of God and of Jesus our Lord" (1:2). He ends by exhorting us to "grow in the grace and knowledge of our Lord and Savior Jesus Christ" (3:18). He began by acknowledging the God who "called us by his own glory and goodness" (1:3). He ends by blessing that same God and saying, "To him be the glory both now and to the day of eternity" (3:18). He started by calling believers to mature in Christ so they will never fall under the weight of false teaching (1:5-11). He ends by appealing to us to do the same thing (3:17-18).

In some respects that's the way it is with the gospel—it starts and finishes at the same place. It was inaugurated at the first coming of Christ; it will culminate with the second coming of Christ. These two advents certainly have some things in common, not the least of which is the fulfillment of Old Testament prophecies about the coming King. But the two comings also are different. The first time Jesus came, he came as a suffering and humiliated servant to die for the sins of the world. But when he comes again, he will come as the reigning Lord in all of his glory and honor, and he will punish the wicked and gather his followers to himself. Jesus is the coming King of kings and Lord of lords! And until he comes, he expects his followers to live worthy of his arrival and subsequent reign. Since we are assured of the certainty of Christ's return, we must live this life in light of it. As the apostle Paul said,

> *If then you have been raised with Christ, seek the things that are above, where Christ is, seated at the right hand of God. Set your minds on things that are above, not on things that are on earth. For you have died, and your life is hidden with Christ in God. When Christ who is your life appears, then you also will appear with him in glory.* (Col 3:1-4 ESV)

This is the gospel, beloved. Remember it . . . and live it.

Reflect and Discuss

1. Is there any persistent sin in your life that does not represent your eternity with Christ? If you've identified something, what should you do?

2. Peter says that our godly living hastens the return of Christ. In other words, the godlier we live, the faster Jesus comes back. In what ways does this motivate you to live a godly life?

3. How should God's patience in enacting his judgment push us into passionate evangelism? How should God's patience in enacting his judgment remind us to constantly "confirm [our] calling and election" (1:10)?

4. What is significant about Peter's reference to the apostle Paul? What is significant about Peter's reference to "the rest of the Scriptures" (3:16)? What is the relationship between the two?

5. How should Peter's admission that some of Paul's writings are hard to understand encourage us?

6. As Bible teachers, how do we balance the things that are hard to understand with an effort to give God's people proper interpretation? In other words, how do we focus on what we can understand and apply without glossing over what we are unsure about?

7. Peter submits that unstable people in the community of faith are targets of false teaching. How do we cultivate believers who are "established" and "stable" in the gospel?

8. It is possible that the false teachers were taking Paul's teaching on justification and twisting it to give license to immoral living. How do we guard our own hearts from loose interpretation that allows sin to creep in?

9. Peter submits that grace is much more than just something needed for salvation. In what ways does God's grace strengthen us in living the Christian life? Why is the Christian life impossible without God's sustaining and continual grace?

10. Considering the entirety of 2 Peter as your backdrop, how does the glorious return of Christ affect your life today?

Jude

Happy to Be a Slave of a Great Master

JUDE 1-2

Main Idea: Because of the mercy, peace, and love of God shown through Jesus Christ, Christians can rejoice in their status as the Lord's servants.

I. **Know Who You Are in Christ (1).**
   A. You are purchased.
   B. You are called.
   C. You are loved.
   D. You are protected.
II. **Know What You Have from Christ (2).**
   A. Enjoy abundant mercy.
   B. Enjoy abundant peace.
   C. Enjoy abundant love.

I have, since I was a little boy, been a fan of Tarzan, especially the old black-and-white movies that starred the Olympic-gold-medal swimmer Johnny Weissmuller. Altogether he appeared in twelve movies between 1932 and 1948. Throughout those movies fans experienced many occasions of anxiety and excitement as Tarzan faced and escaped danger. Nothing, however, stressed me out as much as when he, his wife Jane, and their son named "Boy" would take a swim. Why? Because there, lurking in the bushes along the shore, were deadly crocodiles that would slip into the water with the clear intent of doing serious bodily harm with extreme prejudice to Tarzan and those he loved. Fortunately, Tarzan was always smart enough and strong enough to save the day. Not once did he lose.

Tragically, the same cannot be said for the church of the Lord Jesus Christ. Far too often false teachers have slipped into the waters or, as Jude 4 says, "come in by stealth," damaging and devastating and deceiving the body of Christ. To this danger Jude, the half brother of Jesus, gives his attention in this short, twenty-five-verse letter. Hoping to write a word of encouragement about "the salvation we share," Jude is redirected by the Holy Spirit to bring a word of warning, calling all believers "to contend for the faith" (v. 3).

Jude's strategy is well thought out and planned. Throughout the body of the letter, he will expose the false teachers for who they are, and he will prescribe a plan of attack that allows us to take the fight to these spiritual terrorists. However, he lays the foundation for the battle both at the beginning and at the end of the letter with a word about our security: we are safe in Christ (vv. 1,24). Such safety is possible for those who are happy to be a slave—a slave to a great Master, a slave to the King. And such safety is an ever-present reality for those who know *who they are* in Christ (v. 1) and know *what they have* in Christ (v. 2). Jude is Christ focused and gospel centered every step of the way as he makes his argument.

Know Who You Are in Christ
JUDE 1

Jude (lit. *Judas* or *Judah*) is immediately identified as the author of this short book. Five men bear this name in the New Testament, but this Jude makes clear his identity: he is a servant of Jesus Christ (a strong statement but not much help when it comes to identification!) and a brother of James. So Jude is the half brother of Jesus and the full brother of James. Four brothers of Jesus are noted in Matthew 13:55 (James, Joseph, Simon, and Judas). He may have been the youngest of the brothers; and like the rest of our Lord's family, Jude did not believe in him during his earthly ministry (John 7:5). In fact, Mark 3:21 says they believed he was out of his mind, mentally unstable! However, the resurrection changed everything, and now Jude is glad to claim his brother as his Lord and Messiah. Indeed, his first affirmation of his new identity (and ours!) in Christ is striking.

You Are Purchased

Jude presents himself as "a servant of Jesus Christ" (lit. "of Jesus Christ a slave" [*doulos*, not *diakonos*]). "Of Jesus Christ" is brought to the front of the sentence for emphasis. His relationship is not one of a brother to a brother but of a slave to a master.

What it must have been like for him to grow up with Jesus (a perfect brother!) and now to follow and worship him! What humility Jude displays! But what an honor it was for him and is for us to be slaves to the King! First Corinthians 6:20 tells us we belong to him because we were "bought with a price." First Peter 1:19 informs us "the precious blood of Christ" was used to purchase us. Therefore we are not our own; we belong to him, and Jude was happy to embrace his brother as his King.

You Are Called

Curtis Vaughan, the wonderful Greek scholar for many years at Southwestern Baptist Theological Seminary, noted that "called," which is actually the last word in verse 1 in the Greek text, is a substantive or verbal adjective and the participles "loved" and "kept" modify or refer to those who have been called (Vaughn and Lea, *1, 2 Peter*, 209). So our calling is central to our identity in Christ.

Jude does not use the word "called" to mean "invited" (Schreiner, *1, 2 Peter*, 429). Here the word means the effectual calling of God that opens the heart to freely respond to the gospel. In Scripture there are two types of calling. There is a *general call* (see Matt 11:28-30), and there is an *effectual call* (see Rom 8:30). There is a mysterious wonder in this truth that the sovereign God effectually brings persons to salvation in perfect harmony with their freewill response to the gospel. There is a marvelous complementarity and mind-bending mystery.

Timothy George has well said,

God created human beings with free moral agency, and
He does not violate this even in the supernatural work of
regeneration. Christ does not rudely bludgeon His way
into the human heart. He does not abrogate our creaturely
freedom. No, He beckons and woos, He pleads and pursues,
He waits and wins. (*Amazing Grace*, 86–87)

Those who have been called are on the receiving end of this wonderful wooing and precious pursuing.

You Are Loved

"Loved" is the preferred reading over "sanctified" (KJV, NKJV). Both "loved" and "kept" are in the perfect tense, affirming that both are settled realities for the Christian. The emphasis here is that we are loved—abidingly so—by the Father.

This is the only place in the Bible where this phrase "loved by God the Father" appears. There is a sense in which God loves all persons indiscriminately as his creatures (John 3:16), but there is also a sense in which God especially loves his children.[2] It is comparable to the difference between the love I have for my friends and that which I have for my wife and sons. For those who are in Christ, he is now our Father, and he loves us with a perfect and permanent Fatherly affection. This love is not whimsical, fleeting, or conditional. You can do nothing to make him love you *more*, and you can do nothing to make him love you *less*. No, as 1 John 4:10 beautifully puts it, "Love consists in this: not that we loved God, but that he loved us and sent his Son to be the atoning sacrifice for our sins."

You Are Protected

Again, the word translated "kept" is in the perfect tense, and it is one of Jude's favorite words. It appears in verse 1, twice in verse 6, and again in verses 13 and 21 (five times total). The word means "to protect, keep from harm, or preserve." Here the emphasis is that we are kept safe in our salvation by Jesus Christ. Hebrews 7:25 links our eternal security to the intercessory prayer ministry of Jesus. Jude 24 says he will keep us from stumbling and will present us to the Father "without blemish and with great joy."

Scripture's witness on this crucial doctrine of God's preserving work is clear: By his work on earth, Jesus obtained my salvation. By his work in heaven, Jesus maintains my salvation. God is preserving fallen angels and apostates for judgment (vv. 6,13). God is preserving you and me for glory!

Know What You Have from Christ
JUDE 2

Jude has a love for triads, or groupings of three. In verse 1 he told us we are called, loved, and preserved. Now in verse 2 he selects three of the abundant blessings that flow into the life of every single person who has trusted Jesus Christ for salvation. He wants mercy, peace, and love to be "multiplied," or increased. Moo says he desires that we are "filled with" these Christian graces (*2 Peter, Jude*, 224).

---

[2] Two excellent works on the doctrine of God's love are D. A. Carson's *The Difficult Doctrine of the Love of God* and *Love in Hard Places*. See Works Cited.

Enjoy Abundant Mercy

Jude's greeting is unique, with "mercy" leading the way. The word translated "mercy" (*eleos*) is found about six hundred times in the LXX and seventy-eight in the New Testament. It is a characteristic of God that moves him to seek a relationship with persons who have no right to be in relationship with him. The word speaks of compassion, lovingkindness (Hb *chesed*). It is gracious, undeserved, and unmerited; yet it is not blind, dumb, or ignorant. It is something in God that moves him to do for us what we cannot do for ourselves and we do not deserve.

In Romans 9:23 those who trust Christ are called objects of mercy. In Matthew 5:7 the merciful are told they will receive mercy. In Jude 21 we are told to look for the mercy of our Lord Jesus Christ. In verse 22 we are admonished to extend that same mercy to those who are doubting and in verse 23 to those who have been defiled and devastated by sin. We receive mercy, and we give mercy. We gladly give to others what we have received from Christ.

We enjoy from God what that certain man going down to Jericho received from the good Samaritan, who when he saw him beaten and left for dead had compassion and went into action (Luke 10:30-37). God saw us beaten by Satan and left for dead by sin; and he went into action and sent his Son, binding our wounds, healing our souls, and making us his own!

Enjoy Abundant Peace

The word for "peace" in Greek, *eirēnē* (occurring ninety-one times in the New Testament), cannot be separated from the Hebrew word *shalom*. Wholeness, completeness, prosperity, and success are just a few of the concepts that emanate from this word. In Judges 6:24 God is called "Yahweh-shalom," informing us that God alone is the source of peace. In Isaiah 9:6-7 God's coming Messiah is designated as the "Prince of Peace."

Hartmut Beck and Colin Brown note that "*shalom* includes everything given by God in all areas of life. . . . *Eirene*, therefore, coming as it does from God, approximates closely to the idea of salvation" ("Peace," 777). No wonder Paul can say in Romans 5:1, "Therefore, since we have been declared righteous by faith, we have peace with God through our Lord Jesus Christ." Here is our *external* peace.

Again in Philippians 4:6-7 Paul, while in prison, can write, "Don't worry about anything, but in everything, through prayer and petition with thanksgiving, present your requests to God. And the peace of God, which surpasses all understanding, will guard your hearts and minds in Christ Jesus." Here is our *internal* peace.

And to all of this Moses can add in Numbers 6:24-26, "May the LORD bless you and protect you; may the LORD make his face shine on you and be gracious to you; may the LORD look with favor on you and give you peace." Here is our *eternal* peace.

God is the Lord of peace. Jesus is the Mediator of peace. We are the heirs of peace. Thus Jesus can say in Matthew 5:9, "Blessed are the peacemakers, for they will be called sons of God."

Enjoy Abundant Love

Throughout this letter Jude reminds his readers that they are loved by God (vv. 1,2,3,17,20). God is ascribed many attributes in the Scriptures. He is directly said to be

- holy (Lev 11:44-45; 19:2; 1 Pet 1:16),
- spirit (John 4:24),
- light (1 John 1:5), and
- a consuming fire (Deut 4:24; Heb 12:29).

But the apostle John sums God's character up as *love* when he says "God is love" (1 John 4:8,16), and Jude prays that his readers would see this love from God as ever real and ever increasing toward them. To say that God is love is to affirm that he always desires and seeks our highest good, even at great sacrifice to himself. C. H. Dodd says, "But to say, 'God is love' implies that *all* His activity is loving activity. If He creates, He creates in love; if He rules, He rules in love; if He judges, He judges in love" (*Johannine Epistles*, 110; emphasis original).

In John 17:23 we are told, amazingly, that as the Father has loved the Son so he has also loved us. In Romans 8:31-39 we are informed that nothing can separate us from the love of God that is ours in Christ Jesus. And in 1 Corinthians 13:8 Paul reminds us that because love is at the center of who our God is, it will never fail, never end! Jude knows the power of this love, and he wants his readers to know it as well.

Conclusion

What a joy to be a slave—a slave of a great Master, a King whose name is Jesus! He has purchased and called. He loves and protects. He showers his children with mercy and blesses them with peace. Because we are his, we have *internal* security in our hearts, *external* security in the world, and *eternal* security in heaven. Could anything be more wonderful than being a slave of such a great King?

Reflect and Discuss

1. What are some ways false teachers may "come in by stealth" and harm the church?
2. Why is it necessary to have assurance of our security in Christ before we attack spiritual threats to the church? What are the dangers of not having this security?
3. Why is it significant that Jude identifies himself specifically as a slave and not simply a servant?
4. How is it that believers are preserved in the Christian life? Can a Christian do anything to keep himself in the family of God?
5. What specific ways have you received mercy from the Lord? From other people?
6. What specific ways is the Lord leading you to show mercy to others?
7. How does *shalom* in the Old Testament relate to our salvation in Christ?
8. When have you experienced the peace that comes from knowing Christ as Lord and Savior?
9. Why can John say that God is love? How is it that all of God's acts are loving?
10. Read all of Jude. How does the greeting relate to the rest of the book?

Contending for the Faith of Jesus

JUDE 3-4

Main Idea: Because of the constant threat of false teachers and enemies of the gospel, Christians must continually defend and obey the Christ-centered, Christ-exalting faith that has been passed on through the true Church.

I. **Know What You Believe (3).**
    A. The faith must be defended.
    B. The faith has been delivered.
II. **Know How to Live (4).**
    A. Beware of those who deceive the church.
    B. Beware of those who distort God's grace.
    C. Beware of those who deny our Lord.

All of the Akins are big fans of the smash-hit television show *24* that ran on FOX from 2001 to 2010, returning for a shortened season in 2014. If you had called our house on Monday nights from 9:00 to 10:00 in those years, all you would have heard is the voice-mail greeting! In the show Kiefer Sutherland starred as Jack Bauer, a counterterrorist agent who defends the USA against those who would harm her. Commentator Hugh Hewitt correctly observed that the work of Jack Bauer is messy and intense. He also notes it is judgmental and almost entirely without moral ambiguity.

> One fan, Melinda Penner, blogged this on the program's appeal: "I love the show because it's morally smart. Jack [Bauer] almost unfailingly makes the correct and necessary decision given the moral dilemmas he's faced with. But it also shows the cost of having engaged evil and the horrible choices it presents. ("Reality TV")

Such is the world of international terrorism. Such, in many ways, is the world of spiritual terrorism as well. Jude writes his epistle to warn the church about spiritual terrorists, spiritual subversives who stealthily crept inside the church with WSDs (Weapons of Spiritual Destruction).

These are Satan's missionaries whose motto is, "If I can't get them from without, I will get them from within."

Theologically, we refer to such persons as "apostates," a word that means "those who have fallen away." Though they try to stay with us personally and corporately, theologically and spiritually they have left and followed after false and destructive teaching. Adrian Rogers pointed out these are persons who *received* the truth, *rejected* the truth, *ridicule* the truth, and eventually will attempt to *replace* the truth ("Snakes in the Garden").

We see the effects of this tragic progression in schools like Harvard, Yale, Princeton, Dartmouth, Columbia, Brown, and the University of Chicago, all of which were founded to train ministers to propagate the gospel. Today, none of them stands for historic Christian orthodoxy.

We also see the demise and death of once great denominations that no longer send gospel missionaries, who deny the inerrancy of Scripture, reject the exclusive claims of Christ, ordain practicing homosexuals to the ministry, advocate same-sex marriage (and perform same-sex weddings), and turn a deaf ear to the holocaust of abortion. Consider the following statistics about the last part of the twentieth century:

Between 1965 and 2003 membership in the following denominations declined as follows:

- Christian Church (Disciples of Christ)—57.2 percent, to 770,793;
- Presbyterian Church (U.S.A.)—43.5 percent, to 2.4 million;
- United Church of Christ—37.4 percent, to 1.3 million;
- Episcopal Church—35.8 percent, to 2.3 million;
- United Methodist Church—25.4 percent, to 8.25 million;
- Evangelical Lutheran Church in America—12.3 percent, to 4.98 million;
- American Baptist Churches—6.9 percent, to 1.43 million.

On the plus side, the Assemblies of God registered a spectacular 377 percent increase, to 2.72 million; the Southern Baptist Convention, a 52.6 percent increase, to 16.43 million; and the U.S. Catholic Church, buoyed by Hispanics, 45.4 percent, to 67.25 million. (Plowman, "Beginnings and Ends")

Sadly, this strategy of infiltration by the devil's deceivers is even in full swing within the camp of evangelicalism. A major emerging church leader called for a five-year moratorium on the issue of homosexuality as sin because he said there is no clarity on the issue. Today 25 percent of "self-described born again adults rely on means other than grace to get to heaven" (Barna, "One-Quarter"). And recently the most popular television preacher (I use the word loosely) in America said in a large rally where I live in Raleigh, North Carolina, "You are the apple of God's eye. The Scripture says God has already approved you and accepted you." He used Mark 1:11 for support, a text where God says to Jesus, "You are my beloved Son; with you I am well pleased." He then said, "God is saying to you, you are my Son, whom I love; with you I am well pleased. If God approves of you, why don't you approve of yourself?" No wonder one attendee said he came because "I leave feeling better than when I came" (Shimron, "Evangelist Stirs Hope"). People come in to many such rallies feeling bad and lost, and they leave *feeling* much better, but they are still lost! This brand of Christianity presents no gospel, no substitutionary atonement, no heaven, no hell, no sin, and no Savior!

There is today a great need for evangelicals to heed the words of Jude and "to contend for the faith that was delivered to the saints once for all" (v. 3). There is a fight for the faith, a struggle to preserve and pass on what has been delivered to us, and it is time to step up.

Know What You Believe
JUDE 3

In his short epistle, Jude gives seven charges to believers:

1. *Earnestly contend* for the faith (v. 3).
2. *Remember* the teaching and warning of the apostles (v. 17).
3. *Build yourselves up* in the most holy faith (v. 20).
4. *Pray* in the Holy Spirit (v. 20).
5. *Keep yourselves* in the love of God (v. 21).
6. *Look* for the mercy of the Lord to bring you to eternal life (v. 21).
7. *Show mercy* to Christians who are doubting, snatch unbelievers from the fire, and cautiously show mercy to the corrupt (vv. 22-23).

Jude's first challenge comes early in this twenty-five-verse letter and begins the body of his message.

The Faith Must Be Defended

"Dear friends" appears three times in Jude (vv. 3,17,20). Some translations render the phrase simply "beloved." Already we have been told we are loved by the Father (v. 1), and Jude has prayed for love's multiplication in verse 2. It is a term of tenderness as well as transition.

Jude tells us he was eager to write about the salvation we hold in common (Gk *koines*). He actually desired to write a different kind of letter, one that expounded on our redemption in Christ. However, necessity was laid on him by the Holy Spirit, so instead he wrote an apologetic, a defense of the faith, exhorting, encouraging, and urging his readers "to contend for the once-delivered-to-the-saints faith" (literal translation).

The word "contend" is a translation of the Greek word *epagonizesthai*, from which we get our word *agonize*. The word appears in both military and athletic contexts. It means "to fight or struggle with intense effort." Jude calls on us to strive after and fight for the faith, and his words suggest that he knows it will not be an easy battle; it will be agonizing at times.

No doubt the "faith" Jude had in mind is the gospel of Jesus Christ and all that derives from his person and work. A brief survey of this letter informs us what Jude was concerned about: the security of the believer (vv. 1,24), the grace of God (v. 3), the lordship of Christ and all its implications (v. 3), immoral living (vv. 4,7,8,10,13,16,18,19,23), unbelief (v. 5), a rebellious spirit (vv. 6,8,11), materialism (v. 11), deception (vv. 12,16), divisiveness (v. 19), and ungodliness (vv. 4,15,18).

Jude understood the faith to be both theological and moral. He understood clearly the rebellious nature of the human heart and the moral havoc that reigns from a rejection of Christ's lordship. Because of the tendency of the human heart to wander, Jude knew that the faith would need to be explained and defended continually. This is not a time for cowards or the weak hearted. This is not a time for the timid or thin-skinned. This is not a time for retreat, compromise, or surrender. The faith must be earnestly defended.

The Faith Has Been Delivered

The faith has come, and it has come once and for all. It is not up for debate or discussion. Paul affirms in Ephesians 4:5 there is "one faith." It is a signed, sealed, and settled reality. Adrian Rogers said of this faith, "It is divine in its conception. It is complete in its content. . . . It is absolutely unique in its character" ("Battle for the Bible").

It has been "delivered" (NIV, "entrusted") once for all to the saints. In saying "once for all," Jude suggests that it is complete. It needs no corrections and no additions. Christians need not seek any fuller revelation. It has come to us decisively in Jesus Christ. God has, as a sacred trust, passed on the precious, soul-saving faith to us. How dare we neglect it? How dare we change it? How dare we deny it?

What is the faith that has been delivered? I believe there are twelve nonnegotiables to which Scripture and the history of the church give eloquent witness.

1. The inerrancy and infallibility of Holy Scripture
2. The full and eternal deity of Christ
3. The miraculous virgin birth and sinless life of Jesus the Messiah
4. The historical creation of man and woman made in God's image
5. The sanctity of all life from conception to natural death
6. The sacredness of marriage between a man and a woman
7. The sinfulness of all human persons
8. The substitutionary death of Christ for sinners
9. The bodily resurrection of Christ from the grave
10. Salvation by grace alone through faith alone in Christ alone
11. The exclusivity of the gospel of Jesus Christ for sinners
12. The return of Christ and the assignment of all people either to eternal blessedness in heaven or eternal condemnation in hell

There is a faith that has been delivered.

Know How to Live
JUDE 4

Belief and behavior go hand in hand. Theology matters, for what you believe will determine how you live. We live in a time when far too many preachers and theologians are not content to be delivery boys of the good news. No, they want to be editors of the good news. Unfortunately, they do not always display their true colors. Like the wolves in sheep's clothing that Jesus warned us about in Matthew 7:15-20, they slip into our churches and distort the truth and destroy the unsuspecting and ill prepared.

In light of such dangers, Jude trumpets a threefold warning we dare not neglect.

Beware of Those Who Deceive the Church

Jude warns that some have "come in by stealth," sliding in through a side door, sneaking in over the fence, worming their way in through the crowd. These spiritual deceivers find their way into our Christian communities at all levels. They never walk proudly and honestly through the front door, declaring themselves to be a threat. Rather, they covertly slip in the back door because there is too often no rear guard.

They look like—and for a while *act* like—friends, but all the while they are enemies dedicated to our destruction. Much like the false prophet of Revelation 13:11, who looks like a lamb but speaks like a dragon, these foes mean to deceive and destroy, though they present themselves as tender and harmless.

Beware of Those Who Distort God's Grace

These false teachers are destined for condemnation, "for the judgment on the great day" (v. 6). God was not surprised by their arrival, and neither should we be. Their end was determined long ago, and it is sure. They will suffer the vengeance of eternal fire (v. 7) as ordained by God and predicted in verses 5-16.

God's condemnation of them is just and fair for two reasons: their character and their conduct. Their character is described as "ungodly," a description that appears six times in Jude. The word means "without worship or reverence." So these men failed to appropriately revere and worship the one true God.

Their conduct deserves condemnation because they turn "the grace of our God into sensuality" (NIV, "into a license for immorality"). They take the grace and goodness of God in the free gift of salvation and use it as an occasion for sin. Douglas Moo says the word "connotes especially sins of the flesh: sexual misconduct, drunkenness, gluttony"(*2 Peter, Jude*, 230). These are antinomians who want no rules, no restraint, and no one telling them what they should or should not do.

Sadly we are seeing a revival of such thinking in our own day even among professing evangelicals. Claiming to revel in grace, they sneer at calls to holiness, purity, and forsaking the ways of the world. "What's the big deal about alcohol and tobacco abuse, pornography, and a little profanity? Am I supposed to believe that God cares about these things?" YES! And to think he does not is to distort his grace that saves and to transform it into a license for sin. May it never be among us (Rom 6:1-2)!

However, we must be careful. We should flee such behavior not because we have to in order to earn God's acceptance but because we want to as those who have already been accepted! The grace of God in Christ frees us from the power of sin over us. Freedom in Jesus is not the liberty to do what I *want* but the power to do what I *should*. Pure, undiluted grace will make me fanatical not about rules but about Christ and his moral perfection and beauty!

Beware of Those Who Deny Our Lord

Jude takes us straight to the question of who Jesus is and what he has done. It is and will always be the great dividing line. These dangerous men and women will not worship Jesus as Lord. "Deny" is the last word of verse 4 in the Greek text, placed there for emphasis. The one they deny is "our only [*monon*] Sovereign [*despotēn*] and Lord [*kurion*]" (NIV).

In the context, what they deny is not his deity, his person, or his work. What they deny is his lordship. They separate his being Savior from his being Lord. By their sinful life and exploitation of grace, they deny his lordship *in* and *over* their lives. They are a law unto themselves, accountable to no one, including the Sovereign Lord Jesus Christ.

Jude justly condemns them. Deny Jesus as Lord, and you forfeit him as Savior. One goes with the other. They are a package deal, not to be separated.

Conclusion

My good friend and pastor James Merritt has well said, "It is right to fight when you fight for what's right" (unpublished sermon notes). We must fight for the faith, and we must contend for the truth; but we must contend for the faith without being *contentious* about the faith. We fight because we must, not because we want to and enjoy it. How do we do this? Hear the wisdom of the apostle Paul in the last letter he ever wrote:

> *But reject foolish and ignorant disputes, because you know that they breed quarrels. The Lord's servant must not quarrel, but must be gentle to everyone, able to teach, and patient, instructing his opponents with gentleness. Perhaps God will grant them repentance leading them to the knowledge of the truth. Then they may come to their senses and escape the trap of the devil, who has taken them captive to do his will.* (2 Tim 2:23-26)

Reflect and Discuss

1. Why do many institutions that began as training grounds for ministers end up denying the faith?
2. What popular expressions of cultural Christianity have you seen that actually contradict the orthodox teachings of the Bible?
3. What's wrong with preaching and teaching that tells people that there's nothing wrong with them?
4. Why does the faith need to be defended? Is it at risk of being defeated?
5. Why does Jude suggest this defense must be earnest (KJV)? How can this earnest defense also be loving?
6. Think about how the faith was delivered to the apostles. How was it delivered to you? How can you be a part of delivering it to others?
7. Write your own list of nonnegotiable elements of the true faith delivered to the saints. What Scriptures would you use to defend your answers?
8. What are some ways enemies of the faith can slip in by stealth? How can the church try to prevent that from happening?
9. Why is it an affront to God's grace to use the gospel as a license to sin? How would you explain the Christian's obligations to live a holy life?
10. Why is it impossible to claim Christ as Savior and not also as Lord?

Three Truths Never to Forget

JUDE 5-7

Main Idea: Learning from those who have rejected the Lord, Christians must continually run to and cling to the mercy of God available in Christ Jesus.

I. **Remember the Danger of Unbelief (5).**
   A. Do not trust in the security of a past experience.
   B. Do not doubt the power of God today.
II. **Remember the Dishonor of Rebellion (6).**
   A. Accept God's plan for your life.
   B. Respect God's power over your life.
III. **Remember the Destiny of the Immoral (7).**
   A. Sexual perversion can consume you.
   B. Eternal punishment can claim you.

With each passing day, it seems, our culture moves further and further away from the God revealed in the Bible. Unbelief, rebellion, and immorality (the three sins Jude highlights in vv. 5-7) characterize with greater intensity and influence our way of life. The evidence is so prevalent one hardly knows where to begin. Of course, as you would expect, the world of sex tops the charts.

Hollywood elites were giddy with praise several years ago over *Brokeback Mountain,* a gay-cowboy love story that shocked the sensibilities of many cultural conservatives. About the same time, Willie Nelson brought out a gay-cowboy love song he had written over twenty years ago entitled "Cowboys Are Secretly, Frequently Fond of Each Other." More recently, pop culture is giving us more and more songs like Katy Perry's "I Kissed a Girl [and I Liked It]" and books like E. L. James's *Fifty Shades of Grey.* Same-sex marriage is now the law of the land; and to speak against it is to quickly be marked as bigoted, narrow, and intolerant. All of these developments work to subvert God's good design for sexuality within the context of a one-man, one-woman lifelong marriage relationship.

But Hollywood isn't the only perpetrator. The *Los Angeles Times* reported several years ago about "condom parties" or "glove affairs" that are being hosted by some middle schools (Hoder, "Sex Education"). At these parties students as young as twelve and thirteen years old receive gift bags with condoms, pamphlets on various sexual acts, and toy syphilis lesions.

We could look elsewhere for more examples, and our search would be unending. But the point has been made, and the evidence is clear: our culture has turned its back on God and his Word, shunned his standards, and mocked his character. And the culture is where it is today, in part, because the church is where it is. Unbelief, rebellion, and immorality run to and fro across the land and within the congregation of God's people. So we must ask, What does God think about our current situation, and what will God do? Jude 5-7 provides the answer to these questions with three truths we ought never forget.

Remember the Danger of Unbelief
JUDE 5

Verses 5-7 flow directly from Jude's warning in verse 4 about false teachers. Indeed, judgment opens and closes the literary unit of verses 5-16. The false teachers were marked out, designated for condemnation long ago because their sin resembles the sin of three well-known events in Old Testament history: God's condemnation of Israel for unbelief, God's condemnation of fallen angels for rebellion, and God's condemnation of Sodom and Gomorrah for immorality.

Jude begins with Israel because they were God's chosen people and because unbelief is at the heart of all sin. Jude says, "Now I want to remind you, although you came to know all these things once and for all." This reading connects his reminder to the "faith that was delivered . . . once for all" of verse 3. These historical events are not "new news" to them anymore than the gospel was now "new news" to them. Still, in our human sinfulness we are prone to forget, to neglect lessons and truths from the past. This can be fatal, as Jude makes clear, so he sounds the call: "Remember!" Jude begins with his first of seven Old Testament references in this epistle.

Do Not Trust in the Security of a Past Experience

God saw the plight of his chosen people, and he "saved," delivered, or rescued them out of Egypt. He sent plagues on Egypt, parted the Red Sea, destroyed Pharaoh's army, and provided manna, quail, and water. He was their glory cloud by day and pillar of fire by night. So Israel had an amazing past, a marvelous legacy. The book of Exodus is a witness to God's grace and salvation.

However, the issue for them and the issue for us is this: Are you trusting God *today*? Are you trusting God *now*? Not once does the Word of God tell us to look back to a past experience for our security. Paul says in 2 Corinthians 13:5, "Test yourselves to see if you are in the faith. Examine yourselves."

Walking an aisle, praying a prayer, signing a card, going into water— these are not the avenues of assurance. Today, right now, are you looking to the cross? Are you trusting Christ? Do not trust in the security of a past experience.

Do Not Doubt the Power of God Today

Jude says "later" the Lord destroyed, wiped out, "those who did not believe." Jude has in mind Numbers 14, when the twelve spies returned from their reconnaissance mission into the promised land. The majority report of ten said, "We can't do this. They are giants, and we are grasshoppers." The minority report of two (Joshua and Caleb) said, "No problem. After all, grasshoppers plus God can beat any giants!" However, the people, who had seen God do so much, now in unbelief said, "Well, he can't do this." The result: every person twenty years old and over died. All of them! They missed the promised land. They missed God's best. Forgetting God's grace and greatness, they dug their graves in the wilderness within sight of the land God had promised, saying, "God did it before, but I cannot trust him to do it again."

Far too many in the church believe in their hearts and say with their lives, "He saved me in the past, and he'll take me to heaven in the future, but right now I'm not so sure. I've got many issues: family, health, finances, ministry. Things are hard, and God is silent. If I don't take care of things without him, then they won't get done."

Unbelief destroyed the Hebrew people, and unbelief in the providence and goodness of God describes the apostates in Jude. Remember the danger today of unbelief.

Remember the Dishonor of Rebellion
JUDE 6

Jude 6 is one of the most difficult verses in the Bible to interpret. Who is Jude talking about? Who was Peter talking about in the parallel text in 2 Peter 2:4? Three views have been set forth:

1. An unknown fall of angels not recorded in Scripture
2. The original fall of Satan (typified in Isa 14 and Ezek 28)
3. The episode in Genesis 6 where fallen angels had sexual relations and cohabited with women and produced an evil race of men who brought God's judgment on the world through the flood

In my opinion the third option is most convincing, though for many years I resisted it. Here are the reasons I changed my mind (Schreiner, *1, 2 Peter*, 447–51):

1. It is overwhelmingly the view of Jewish tradition.
2. A parallel passage in the apocryphal book of 1 Enoch is similar, and that passage clearly sees Genesis 6 as fallen angels cohabiting with women.
3. "Sons of God" in the Old Testament consistently refers to angelic beings (cf. Job 1:6; 2:1; 38:7).
4. When angels appear in Scripture, they always appear in the male gender and can function like human persons.
5. Matthew 22:30 does not say angels do not have sexuality but that they do not marry or reproduce. Further, Jesus specifically speaks of angels "in heaven." The Sons of God in Genesis 6 came to earth as fallen angels or demons.
6. The word "likewise" in verse 7 connects the sexual immorality of Sodom and Gomorrah with the angels of verse 6.
7. This best explains why some demons are bound and some are free. The heinous nature of their sin brought a more severe judgment in terms of time on these fallen angels.

While the interpretation of this text is obviously significant, we must not lose sight of the text's plain meaning in terms of application. These fallen angels rejected at least two principles for life that we should learn to respect.

Accept God's Plan for Your Life

These angels were not satisfied with God's plan for them. They were convinced there was something better and God's way was not the best way. First, they "did not keep their own position" (NIV, "positions of authority"). Second, they "abandoned their proper dwelling." Their place and position in God's plan was not enough. They wanted something more, a different position of prominence, a better place of activity. This sounds much like many ministers of the gospel today. Through self-deception men—like these angels—rationalize their lust for position, power, prestige, and possessions. With an inflated sense of self-worth and importance, they cannot trust in the providence of God and rest in his plan.

Respect God's Power over You

Not content with heaven, these angels get hell instead. Think about what their rebellion cost them:

What They Gave Up	What They Got
Heaven	Hell
Being servants of God	Being slaves of Satan
Light	Darkness
Freedom	Chains
Joy in his presence	Condemnation in perdition
Awesome privilege	Awesome punishment
Great honor	Incredible disgrace

If revelation brings responsibility, their responsibility was greater than any. And because of God's gracious revelation in Christ Jesus through his Spirit-inspired Scriptures, our responsibility is likewise great. God is God and we are not, and we must accept his plan for and power over our lives. As the demonic prisoners show, the Lord will receive his due respect one way or another.

Remember the Destiny of the Immoral

JUDE 7

No story impacted the people of God like the destruction of Sodom and Gomorrah. It is referenced one way or another more than twenty times in the Bible. The devastation of these cities, along with Admah and Zeboiim (note "the surrounding towns"), was so horrific they stand as a perpetual reminder of God's just condemnation of sin, especially sexual sin. Sodom and Gomorrah were known for their pride and disregard for the poor (Ezek 16:49), their arrogance, injustice, and bigotry. But their sexual perversion marked them most of all. Finally a time came when God said, "Enough!" Genesis 19 records the cataclysmic judgment as "out of the sky the LORD rained on Sodom and Gomorrah burning sulfur from the LORD" (Gen 19:24). Jude is specific in his brief analysis of the judgment God brought.

Sexual Perversion Can Consume You

Sodom and Gomorrah and the surrounding cities acted in a manner similar to the fallen angels of verse 6. They committed sexual immorality (*ekporneuo*) and went after *sarkos heteras*. This reference to strange flesh is not the flesh of angels but the flesh of other men. Their sin was homosexuality. At this point I should make note of several things.

First, the Bible is clear in its treatment of homosexuality as sin. This is made plain in texts like Leviticus 18:22; 20:13; Romans 1:26-27; 1 Corinthians 6:9-10; and 1 Timothy 1:9-10. Second, the Bible is equally clear that any sexual activity, heterosexual or homosexual, outside the marriage covenant between a man and a woman is sin. Jesus himself said a man and woman in marriage become one flesh. Jesus was clear on the sex question. Third, those in slavery to sexual sin need to be loved, including those who identify as gay, lesbian, bisexual, transgender, and any others. We do not hatefully bash them; we graciously speak the truth in love and reach out to them with grace, mercy, and kindness. And finally, rampant sexual sin is not the worst sin, but it is the clearest evidence of a society that has rejected God's truth and has been given over to his judgment (Rom 1:24-28).

Eternal Punishment Can Claim You

The cities of the plains are a perpetual reminder that sin is serious to God and that God will judge it. The Bible tells us in Matthew 25:41 that hell was prepared for the devil and his angels. Jude 6 backs this up. Jude 7, however, affirms that unbelieving, rebellious, and immoral humans will also be there.

Hell is real, and hell is eternal. It is a place of suffering, sadness, and separation. It helps explain the necessity of the cross, and why, of the twelve times the word *gehenna* (hell) appears in the Bible, eleven are on the lips of Jesus. So terrible is its reality that Jesus said in Matthew 5:27-30 it would be better to enter the kingdom with only one eye or one hand than to have your whole body cast into hell.

Hell is a bad place. Eternity is a long time. The unbelieving, rebellious, and immoral will unfortunately find their destiny in this place.

Conclusion

Let me close on a positive note; it is found in 1 Corinthians 6:9-11. If any New Testament city approached the wickedness and immorality of Sodom and Gomorrah, it was Corinth. Idolatry, greed, pagan philosophy, and immorality filled the air. But Paul brought the gospel, determining "to know nothing among [them] except Jesus Christ and him crucified" (1 Cor 2:2). What was the result of his witness? Paul wrote the following later in his letter:

> *Don't you know that the unrighteous will not inherit God's kingdom?*
> *Do not be deceived: No sexually immoral people, idolaters, adulterers,*
> *or males who have sex with males, no thieves, greedy people,*
> *drunkards, verbally abusive people, or swindlers will inherit God's*
> *kingdom. And some of you used to be like this. But you were washed,*
> *you were sanctified, you were justified in the name of the Lord Jesus*
> *Christ and by the Spirit of our God.* (1 Cor 6:9-11)

Yes, God will condemn unbelievers, the rebellious, and the immoral. But he will also forgive them gladly if they are washed in the cleansing blood of the Lord Jesus.

Reflect and Discuss

1. Where do you see the increasing influence of unbelief, rebellion, and immorality in our culture? How can these attitudes creep into the church?
2. Why does Jude seem so preoccupied with judgment? How does it fit into the epistle?
3. Why do you think people tend to find assurance in past experiences? How can this be deceptive?
4. How would you help someone know what it means to examine themselves, to see if they are in the faith (cf. 2 Cor 13:5)?

5. Why do you think it's so hard to trust God in the present and so easy to look forward to what God might do in the future?
6. Explain Jude 6 and 2 Peter 2:4 in your own words. Why does Jude allude to this story?
7. Are you content with and confident that God knows what he is doing in your life? Or is your heart gripped by a spirit of rebellion, especially if you suspect what God has for you is not what you want for yourself?
8. Make a list of what Adam and Eve gave up and what they got in return for their own sin. What do you sacrifice when you go after sin?
9. How does sexual perversion consume us? How can we seek to be loving when confronting others who engage in sexual sin?
10. Why do you think Jesus spoke about hell so much? How should Christians speak about the doctrine of hell in a biblically faithful way? in a loving and compassionate way?

Are You Out of Touch with Spiritual Reality?

JUDE 8-10

Main Idea: False believers lose sight of the reality that, in his death and resurrection, Christ asserts his authority over their lives, and he desires to make them holy.

I. **Watch the Sins of Rebellion (8).**
   A. Don't become defiled.
   B. Don't become defiant.
   C. Don't become disrespectful.
II. **Watch the Sins of Arrogance (9).**
   A. Know your place in God's economy.
   B. Know your power is in God's authority.
III. **Watch the Sins of Ignorance (10).**
   A. Guard your mouth.
   B. Guard your mind.

The church has always struggled in its attempt to properly balance grace and freedom, liberty and responsibility. How can I enjoy my freedom in Christ from works as the way of salvation without crossing the line into works of the flesh? Having been set free from rules, regulations, and rituals as the means of redemption in Jesus, do I now cast off and throw away *all* rules, *every* regulation, *any* ritual observances?

I believe there is a revival of antinomianism ("antilaw attitude") in the church in our day; people don't want to observe the disciplines of the Christian faith. Our language too often parrots the language of the world. Our dress apes the dress of the world. Our morals copycat the morals of the world. Determined to fit in with the culture and to be relevant, we have lost and neglected God's call to be a holy and special people (1 Pet 1:16; 2:9).

Today we claim to be spiritual, but we are not godly. We are sporadic in church attendance and stingy in our giving. We are frequent participants in alcohol abuse, tobacco, and profanity. We dress offensively and seductively. We surf the Internet for pornography and mutilate or desecrate our bodies, which we claim are the temple of the Holy Spirit. All the while we say, "It's no big deal. I am free in Christ."

We claim to be missional but are not doing missions. We claim to be engaging the culture but are not doing evangelism. We claim to be salt and light while actually being dirt and darkness. Theology is left behind, expository preaching is lampooned, and moral integrity is laughed out of court as old-fashioned and outdated legalism.

Advocates of this "new liberty" counterpunch, asking questions like, "Why don't you address the real issues like pride, anger, lust, hatefulness, materialism, bigotry, gluttony, bitterness, selfishness, envy, and so forth?" And of course these issues do need to be addressed. In fact, they *must* be addressed, but I am convinced they are intimately intertwined with the other issues I mentioned above. They are all sins of a common core: they are sins of the heart. Sins of the heart and sins of the flesh are part and parcel of the same depraved nature. Both need the cleansing and redeeming blood of Christ; both need the cleansing and sanctifying power of the Spirit; both need the renewing work of the Word.

Allowing the Word to go to work in Jude 8-10, the half brother of Jesus again confronts head-on the false followers of Christ who were "turning the grace of our God into sensuality and denying Jesus Christ, our only Master and Lord" (v. 4). Building on this verse and making connection with his reminder in verses 5-7, Jude places three challenges before those of us who want to stay grounded in spiritual reality as those who "contend for the faith that was delivered to the saints once for all" (v. 3).

Watch the Sins of Rebellion
JUDE 8

First Corinthians 6:19-20 reminds us, "Don't you know that your body is a temple of the Holy Spirit who is in you, whom you have from God? You are not your own, for you were bought at a price." False teachers will deny, or at least de-emphasize, our ownership by God—that he purchased us out of the slave market of sin by the precious blood of his Son, "Jesus Christ, our only Master and Lord" (v. 4). Rather than accept God's spiritual authority over their lives, they prefer to live out of touch with reality, asserting their personal autonomy and living as a law unto themselves. This is a mind-set and a lifestyle Jude condemns and warns us to avoid, and he does so in his typical style with a triad of examples.

Don't Become Defiled

"In the same way" connects verse 8 with verse 7 and the sexual immorality of Sodom and Gomorrah. Jude's opponents resemble the ancient cities in their moral rebellion. Jude calls these false teachers dreamers. Rejecting the Bible as their authority, they appeal to dreams and their own imaginations as a source of *revelation* and *justification* for their immoral lifestyle.

This is the "God told me" and "I prayed about it" defense for what Jude calls "[defiling] the flesh." Claiming to have "a word from the Lord" does not legitimate what one says. False prophets in the Old Testament made such claims (cf. Deut 13:1-5; Jer 23:25-32). Claiming an extrabiblical source of authority, these false teachers attempt to justify their immoral lifestyle. The context would point to sexual sin as the primary, though not the exclusive, sin. This newfound freedom to indulge and feed the flesh was apparently credited to God.

If you choose to live loosely, immorally, lewdly, and out there on the moral edge, don't look to God to justify your foolishness and immaturity. Be honest enough to point your finger at the real enabler: yourself.

Don't Become Defiant

An immoral, unchecked lifestyle is rooted in a rebellious and unbridled spirit. Jude says false followers of Christ "reject authority." Though this could be a reference to human or even angelic authorities, I believe Jude has in mind the authority and lordship of Jesus Christ (again connecting with the description in v. 4). This is not so much a theological rejection as it is a moral and personal avoidance. The Christ who saves is denied his daily and practical sovereignty in their lives. An inappropriate and inexcusable separation is made between Jesus as Savior and Jesus as Lord. In the daily living of life, "self" is its own authority and lord. *No one is going to tell me what to do or how to live,* they think, *not even God!*

Jude rejects such unbiblical defiance, and so should we. The resurrection of Jesus Christ from the dead establishes him as the one with all authority in heaven and on earth (cf. Matt 28:18), and those who are called by his name gladly submit to this authority for their good and his glory.

Don't Become Disrespectful

False followers of Christ "blaspheme glories" (literal translation). Interestingly, some form of the word translated "slander" or "blaspheme" occurs in verses 8, 9, and 10. These false teachers "speak evil of dignitaries" (NKJV), "heap abuse on celestial beings" (NIV), or "slander glorious ones" (CSB).

Though some scholars make a good case that fallen angels or demons are in view, I believe it is better to see the text as referring to good angels (Schreiner, *1, 2 Peter*, 456–58; Moo, *2 Peter*, 245–46). These heavenly beings—who sang at God's good creation (Job 38:7) and, more importantly in our context, are the guardians and givers of God's perfect moral law (Gal 3:19; Heb 2:2)—are spoken of in evil tones by these lawless and rebellious reprobates. Casting off God's rightful authority over their lives, they blaspheme and slander these great beings who are "all ministering spirits sent out to serve those who are going to inherit salvation" (Heb 1:14).

If I don't need God's Word meddling in my moral life, they think, *I certainly don't need his angels sticking their nose in it either!* They ignore the *authority* of God, scoff at *advice* from angels, and eventually reject *accountability* from their brothers and sisters in the community of believers. Self-centered and self-focused, "my will, my way, and my wants" become preeminent above all other things.

Here is the lifestyle of the immoral. Here is the lifestyle of the fool. Proverbs says it well: "When people do not accept divine guidance, they run wild. But whoever obeys the law is joyful" (Prov 29:18 NLT).

Watch the Sins of Arrogance
JUDE 9

This is one of the most mysterious and difficult verses in the Bible to interpret. Its application is easier to grasp, but the exact meaning Jude intended is elusive and even troubling to some.

The actors in this spiritual drama are pretty clear. Michael is the archangel, the chief angel in terms of position and authority. The term *archangel* only occurs one other time in Scripture (1 Thess 4:16). No name is associated there with the title, though most believe Michael is in view. In Daniel 10:13 he is called "one of the chief princes" who came to help Daniel ("your prince" in v. 21). In Daniel 12:1 he is called "the great prince" who watches over Israel. In Revelation 12:7 Michael fights against the dragon (Satan) and defeats him, driving him out of heaven.

The devil is Satan, Lucifer, the greatest of all God's creatures (Isa 14:12-15; Ezek 28:11-19) who fell from heaven due to his pride.

Apparently he carried one-third of the angelic host with him (cf. Rev 12:4). These are the demons who do his bidding.

Moses is the great leader of Israel. The record of his death is found in Deuteronomy 34. We are told the Lord buried him and that no one knows where his grave is (Deut 34:6).

This verse then describes an event not recorded in biblical revelation. Scholars believe the story may have been found in a noncanonical book called The Assumption of Moses or The Testament of Moses, though the account has not been preserved in any writing in our possession today (Moo, *2 Peter*, 246). Our best guess is that the story shows Satan wanting the body of Moses as a potential relic for idolatry, or perhaps he challenged Moses's right to be buried by God because he had murdered an Egyptian.

Before we move to apply the text, it will be helpful to raise the important question of how we should respond when biblical authors cite nonbiblical sources. The first response we must have is to recognize that this actually occurs. Here in Jude 9 The Assumption of Moses is cited, and later in verse 14 Jude alludes to the book of Enoch. The most famous example is that of Paul in Acts 17:28, where the apostle cites pagan poets and philosophers. So it is clear that some extrabiblical material and even non-Christian material is informing the biblical author's writings as the Holy Spirit guides him.

We must also recognize that all truth is God's truth, wherever it is found. Whether it is found on the lips of a pagan or a saint, truth belongs to the Lord. Next we must recognize that the sixty-six books of the Bible, though true, do not contain *all* the truth there is in the world. For example, 2+2=4 is true, but it is not in the Bible.

Moreover, we believe that the Holy Spirit may have and likely did direct the biblical writers to a variety of sources in writing their books (cf. Luke 1:1-4). We must also keep in mind that to cite or quote a part of a nonbiblical source does not require one to believe that all of that source is correct or that it is inspired by God. Speaking truth is not the only requirement to qualify someone as divinely inspired. With the guidance of the Holy Spirit, the early church came to recognize and compile the books of the Bible that truly belong. This means books not recognized as inspired were excluded. The sixty-six books of the Bible belong not because the early church *declared* that they belonged, but rather they in fact belong (i.e., were divinely inspired) and the early church *recognized* this to be the case.

Since we can trust the Holy Spirit's inspiration as Jude wrote, what did he want us to learn from this fascinating account?

Know Your Place in God's Economy

Michael is an archangel, a warrior angel, the greatest angel, but he is still just an angel. He is a creature, not the Creator; a servant, not the sovereign Lord; a minister, not the Master. As great as he is, he knows his proper place in God's plan—something false teachers have failed to grasp. He is not his own authority, master, or lord. He does not set policy and make up the rules as he wishes. No arrogance, haughtiness, rebellion, or pride runs through his angelic veins. If this is how Michael sees himself, we would do well to follow his example and accept our place in the Lord's economy.

Know Your Power Is in God's Authority

Michael, as you would expect, is an excellent student of the Word of God. Knowing the Word, he is ready for war. He engages the devil in battle; and following the model of Jesus shown in Matthew 4 and Luke 4 when he was tempted by Satan, Michael quotes the Word of God.

"The Lord rebuke you" comes from Zechariah 3:2, another occasion when Satan made accusation against one of God's servants—a man by the name of Joshua who was at that time the high priest. Just as the Lord rebuked Satan and vindicated Joshua, he also rebuked Satan and vindicated Moses and gave victory to Michael.

Our authority for spiritual warfare is in God, not in ourselves. In our own strength the devil will defeat us every time. Perhaps Michael could have taken on the devil, given who he is, but he did not because he knew the true source of his authority. In our case, to battle Satan without help is sheer folly. If we want to have victory over the evil one, we must know that our power is in God's authority and nowhere else. We can overcome him, as Revelation 12:11 says, "by the blood of the Lamb and by the word of [our] testimony," a testimony that says our confidence is in Christ, even in the face of death.

Watch the Sins of Ignorance
JUDE 10

At the heart of false teaching is wrong thinking. Human depravity does not prevent us from using our minds, but it does prevent us from using

them correctly. Animals think, but they think like animals. False followers of Christ think, but they too think like animals, and eventually they
live like animals. In what they say and what they do, they plummet to the
level of "brute beasts" (KJV) or "irrational animals." If we want to avoid
the seductive and enticing traps that would enslave us and bring us to
the level of an animal, what must our spiritual strategy be?

Guard Your Mouth

Jude addresses first the fruit rather than the root of wrong thinking and
living on the level of an animal. They "blaspheme" whatever they do
not understand. Arrogant and ignorant, they slander what they do not
even know or understand—a reference to the angels of verse 8. Talking
without thinking, without all the facts, and from emotion, pride, and
selfish desires, they make themselves *look* like fools as they *talk* like fools.

Their example is a good reminder to us all that just because you
think something does not mean it is smart to say it. If you don't say it, you
won't have to apologize for it. The tongue is an organ of the body that
is vitally connected to another organ of the body: the heart. It betrays
what is inside of us, which is most truly who we are. As Proverbs 23:7 so
importantly reminds us, "For as [a person] thinks in his heart, so is he"
(NKJV). So when it comes to guarding our mouths, we must be diligent
not to speak from evil intent or ignorance.

Not only do we guard our mouths; we must also guard what controls
the mouth.

Guard Your Mind

False followers of Christ do not think *biblically*; they think *naturally* (cf.
1 Cor 2:14–3:3). They do not think in moral categories but live by their
emotional impulses, just like an animal.

Whatever they "understand" naturally, like an unreasoning (*aloga*)
animal, they use to corrupt and destroy themselves. Jude's irony is
striking. Claiming a higher spiritual understanding, their knowledge
does not rise even above that of the animals. Claiming liberty and freedom, they are slaves and prisoners of their own lust and basic instincts.
Claiming to be right, they could not be more wrong. Claiming to live for
God, they live for themselves. Claiming to rise higher, they actually sink
lower. Saying, "We are free in Christ," they become chained and shack-
led by their own selfish desires, wants, and passions. Professing to exalt
Christ, by their lives they embarrass him and bring shame to his name.

Thankfully, God's Son did not die for us to express ourselves in such a debased way. God's Son did not die so we could live for ourselves. God's Son died so that you and I would exalt him. He died to make us look like him. He died so that you and I would live for him (Phil 1:21), and this will require that we are transformed by the constant renewal of our minds (Rom 12:2). Thanks be to God that he did not leave us in our ignorance!

Conclusion

Do you want to get in touch with spiritual reality—with true, genuine reality? Then you must be zealous and passionate for high moral standards, personal purity, and biblical holiness. You must run from the works of the flesh, which, Paul says,

> *are obvious: sexual immorality, moral impurity, promiscuity, idolatry, sorcery, hatreds, strife, jealousy, outbursts of anger, selfish ambitions, dissensions, factions, envy, drunkenness, carousing, and anything similar.* (Gal 5:19-21)

Yes, let's run from these, and let's then run after love, joy, peace, patience, kindness, goodness, faithfulness, gentleness, self-control, humility, and Spirit control (cf. Gal 5:22-26). Let us say with the great apostle, "I will never boast about anything except the cross of our Lord Jesus Christ. The world has been crucified to me through the cross, and I to the world" (Gal 6:14). For the true reality of God's saving work in this world is that Christ himself died to make for himself a people who would die to sin and live to righteousness in him (1 Pet 2:24). This is the privilege and responsibility of all who are called by his name into his reality.

Reflect and Discuss

1. How would you explain the error of antinomianism? Why is it dangerous in the church?
2. How do we know when the church is becoming too much like the world? How do we know where to draw boundaries?
3. What is wrong with a "God told me" defense for defiling the flesh? How do we know whether to trust our subjective "dreams" and experiences?
4. Do you think it is easy or difficult to submit to spiritual authority? Why? In what areas of your life do you tend to reject any outside authority?

5. How would you explain the scene in verse 9 to a new student of the Bible?

6. What should Christians make of extrabiblical sources that the biblical authors reference? Are they also inspired?

7. Where else in Scripture do we see people failing to grasp their place in God's economy? What are the consequences of this sin?

8. What does Michael's dispute show us about how to contend with the devil? Where else in Scripture can we see this strategy?

9. What does Jude mean by comparing the false believers to animals? Is he simply insulting them?

10. Read Luke 6:43-45 and see what Jesus says about the connection between our words and our hearts. What do your words reveal about your heart?

When God Condemns the Ungodly

JUDE 11-16

Main Idea: Because Christ came to redeem a people for himself, false teachers who lead people away from God will be condemned.

I. **God Condemns the Ungodly Because of Their Decisions (11).**
   A. They are hateful.
   B. They are greedy.
   C. They are rebellious.
II. **God Condemns the Ungodly Because of Their Deception (12-13).**
   A. They are destructive (12).
   B. They disappoint (12).
   C. They are destitute (12).
   D. They defile (13).
   E. They disappear (13).
III. **God Condemns the Ungodly Because It Is Their Destiny (14-15).**
   A. Their condemnation is predicted (14).
   B. Their condemnation is proper (15).
IV. **God Condemns the Ungodly Because of Their Deeds (16).**
   A. They complain without shame.
   B. They cater to the sensual.
   C. They charm the simple.

In 1962 Ralph Elliott was dismissed from his seminary faculty over his book *The Message of Genesis*. The book was infected with skeptical conclusions drawn from the historical-critical method. Elliott was not dismissed for heresy. He was fired for insubordination when he refused to not have the book republished. Thirty years later, in 1992, Elliott reflected on his dismissal in *The Genesis Controversy*. In this book Elliott makes a startling and breathtaking confession. He plainly acknowledged the dishonesty and deception of many professors. Their crime: the sin of "doublespeak." Elliott wrote,

> "Doublespeak" has become an insidious disease within
> Southern Baptist life. . . . Professors and students learn to
> couch their beliefs in acceptable terminology and in holy

jargon so that although thinking one thing, the speaker
calculated so as to cause the hearer to affirm something else.

Elliott would go on to rightly state the issue was "a basic question of
integrity" (Elliott, *Genesis Controversy*, 33–34).

On this latter point he is right, and on this latter point false teachers receive a failing grade. Dishonest and duplicitous, they deceive
the church of God and, in so doing, invite his swift and sure condemnation of their lives. Ungodly in character and ungodly in conduct,
God exposes them for their hypocrisy and condemns them for their
actions. Note the four reasons God condemns the ungodly according
to Jude.

God Condemns the Ungodly Because of Their Decisions
JUDE 11

Those who forget the past, we are told, are certain to repeat its mistakes.
Jude recalls from the Old Testament three examples of the bad decision
making that characterizes false teachers of any generation.

They Are Hateful

"Woe to them!" recalls the words of Jesus in Matthew 23 and his condemnation of the scribes and Pharisees (Matt 23:13-31). In these three
pronouncements Jude uses a verb form that affirms the certainty of the
future judgment and destruction of these spiritual terrorists.

The "way of Cain" is the way of murder and hate, jealousy and anger,
rebellion and disobedience (Gen 4). Self-centered in character and
consumed by self-love, he chose his way over God's and in the process
killed his brother. Guilty of fostering a man-made religion, he turned
from God and turned *on* others.

They Are Greedy

The prophet Balaam appears in Numbers 22–24. Through duplicitous
means (Num 24:1; 31:16) he led Israel into sexual sin because of the
financial enticement (Num 22:7,17,37; 24:11) offered by King Balak of
Moab (Num 22:4). He was a prophet for pay, a hireling, a profiteer-
ing preacher. Gold was his god and money his master. Ministry was for

making money, not caring for God's people. People were a means to an end, and God killed him for it (Num 31:8).

They Are Rebellious

Numbers 16 is the record of a Levite who rejected the God-ordained spiritual authority of Moses and Aaron. As a result, God destroyed him, his household, and his followers. Like Korah, these men in Jude's day were a law unto themselves, rebellious in heart and nonsubmissive in attitude. Like Korah, they would perish. Arrogance and pride are always on the radar screen for God's certain condemnation.

God Condemns the Ungodly Because of Their Deception
JUDE 12-13

Jude next provides five illustrations from the realm of nature to expose the vacuous and empty promises of false teachers. Because of their deception, they disappoint. They do not deliver what they promise.

They Are Destructive (12)

"These people are dangerous reefs at your love feasts," without fear, serving only themselves. They are hypocrites, dishonest. Pretending to be full of love and concern for others, they are egocentric and selfish. Stepping into positions of leadership, they are like destructive reefs hidden just below the surface. They are slow to reveal their true colors and commitments; and when they do, the body of Christ can be damaged or destroyed. A church, a college, a seminary, even a denomination is vulnerable if it is not vigilant in keeping its eyes open and its guard up.

They Disappoint (12)

"They are waterless clouds carried along by winds." They promise much but deliver little. Proverbs 25:14 reminds us, "The one who boasts about a gift that does not exist is like clouds and wind without rain." Appearing to bring the refreshing water of the Word, they blow past once they have taken what they want, preying on others as they move on. These false teachers promise liberty but enslave; they promise prosperity but impoverish; they promise refreshment and leave their followers parched; and they promise life but bring death.

They Are Destitute (12)

Late into harvest season, when fruit should be present, these false teachers are barren, destitute, "fruitless." Indeed, they are dead on the surface and dead at the source—"twice dead." Death runs throughout what they teach and the way they live. They project a false understanding of godliness and the spiritual life, and those who buy into their deception eventually discover they produce no good thing. Fruitless and rootless, dead top to bottom, they are uprooted and destroyed. They show no fruit of regeneration, no fruit of character, no fruit for King Jesus.

They Defile (13)

Immorality is a close companion of virtually all false teaching. Our creed and conduct are inseparable. Belief and behavior are twins that are virtually impossible to separate. These teachers are raging waves of the sea, foaming up the filth and shame of their false teachings and immoral living. Ligon Duncan says, "They crash like waves and all they do is stir up moral filth" ("Contradiction"). They make a lot of noise with great swelling words, but they do not have a life to back it up. They may tour and fill arenas, get on television and write books, blog and gain a following, but none of this proves their genuine faith. Jude says, "Watch their lives. Time will tell. They are filthy."

They Disappear (13)

False teachers are shooting stars, here today and gone tomorrow. They burn bright for a night and then vanish into the midnight darkness, never to be seen or heard from again. Their history is short lived, leaving a legacy of no real significance.

Because they wander about, these teachers show no consistency or reliability. They promise spiritual light; but they are aimless, erratic, and destined for God's condemnation, which is described here as "the blackness of darkness" reserved forever. They may fool men, but they do not fool God.

With such terrible character and such a horrible destiny, why would anyone attach themselves to teachers like this? Why would anyone follow such deceivers, such masters of deception? They may sound good, but they show little. Jude instructs us to remember that one's life reveals one's heart. False prophets have a heart only for themselves, not for our Savior. This shows in their life and ministry.

God Condemns the Ungodly Because It Is Their Destiny
JUDE 14-15

In verse 4 Jude says the condemnation of these men was marked out, written about long ago. Verse 14 shows that this marking out goes back to Enoch, the seventh from Adam counting inclusively, who "walked with God; then he was not there because God took him" (Gen 5:24). Hebrews 11:5 informs us, "He did not experience death. . . . For before he was taken away, he was approved as one who pleased God."

Some Bible teachers have tried to tie Enoch's prophecy in Jude 14-15 to the birth of his son Methuselah and the timing of the flood. However, it seems clear that Jude quotes the nonbiblical book of 1 Enoch 1:9, affirming the truth of this statement without endorsing the whole of the book as divine or special revelation. Whether the quotation came from the historical Enoch is unclear, though the possibility of the oral transmission of such a prediction is certainly possible. What does Enoch say concerning these false and deceiving teachers?

Their Condemnation Is Predicted (14)

Prior even to the flood, God made known his verdict concerning false teachers as well as the certainty of his coming at the end of time. Enoch declared, "Look!" Behold! Take notice! "The Lord [Jesus Christ] comes." It is as if condemnation has already commenced, so sure is its coming. Schreiner says the verb functions as a "prophetic perfect," meaning it is a certain and settled reality (*1, 2 Peter*, 472).

The "tens of thousands of his holy ones" refers to the angels. Numerous times in both the Old Testament and the New Testament God is pictured as coming with his angels (cf. Zech 14:5; Matt 16:27; 25:31; 1 Thess 3:13; 2 Thess 1:7).

At this coming, things will be radically different from his first visit to earth. Here he comes to a crown, not a cross. He comes to a throne, not a cradle. He comes to reign, not to die. He comes to judge, not to be judged. The next time he comes will be the last time he comes, and angels will be both his escort and his agents of judgment (v. 15).

Their Condemnation Is Proper (15)

Jude is fond of the word "ungodly," using it four times in this verse. It refers to those who live without reverence and respect for God. They *walk* in an ungodly manner, with evil deeds, they *think* in ungodly ways, and they *talk* with ungodly and harsh words. In works, wisdom (cf. Jas 3:14-16), and words they condemn themselves. No evil action, thought, or word will go unpunished, nor will it be erased from the divine memory (Prov 11:21; Nah 1:3). These men and those like them will have no defense, no retrial, no appeal. As Romans 3:19 says, every mouth will be silenced.

God Condemns the Ungodly Because of Their Deeds
JUDE 16

The lifestyle and dispositions of those Enoch prophesied God would condemn is further explored in verse 16. Emphasis falls on their mouths and the evil desires that direct what flows from their tongues. Again we are reminded the tongue is that organ of the body intimately connected to the heart and its desires.

They Complain without Shame

Speaking harshly against God, his will, and his ways, they grumble and complain (cf. v. 15). Like the Hebrew children in the wilderness, they find fault with God, griping and complaining, accusing him of withholding his best and what they believe they deserve. They are critical and negative, possessing a cloudy disposition with thunderstorms on the horizon. This disposition is like a cancer and is deadly to an effective ministry and a healthy church life. It leaves them always judgmental and without joy.

They Cater to the Sensual

The source of this negative disposition and attitude was their lust ("their own evil desires," NIV). Living by the "personal pleasure principle," they were consumed with what they wanted. Their desires trumped all others', including God's.

I read this description and think how different these men are from a simple woman named Emma Lou, who was my mother. As my brother-in-law said at her funeral, I never heard Emma say, "I want . . ." Like the Lord she loves and now sees, she was always putting others ahead of herself, her wants, and her desires—though it may be that her desire was to always put others first! You may know someone like Emma Lou. If you do, these men were the polar opposite!

They Charm the Simple

False teachers mouth great, swelling, "arrogant words." "They boast about themselves" (NIV). They are big talkers who say more about themselves than about the Word of God. They portray themselves as the hero of every story, giving the appearance of a spiritual superiority. Such teachers find an easy target in the biblically illiterate and theologically immature. They are experts in flattery in order to take financial advantage of the gullible and unsuspecting. In other words, they are good at locating itching ears (2 Tim 4:3-4) and telling people what they want to hear and what makes them feel good. Masters of manipulation, they empty the pockets of others and fill their own. The suffering servant named Jesus is banished to the sidelines.

Some do so on TV. Some do it on the radio or in podcasts. Some do it in a local church. Some do it in a college or seminary. Anywhere and everywhere, any place they can gain a hearing and get an audience, you can be sure these "smooth operators" will show up.

Conclusion

Some liberal theologians and spiritual advisors talk of a "softer" view of God, a God whose vengeance and condemnation have slowly evaporated and disappeared, a God of love but no wrath. Such theologians obviously have not read Jude. Let us not follow in their footsteps. To do so is to walk the path of deception and destruction. It is to come face-to-face with the God who condemns the ungodly—every single one of them.

Reflect and Discuss

1. Is God justified in condeming the ungodly? Why or why not?
2. How have you seen hate, greed, and rebellion lead people into poor decisions?
3. In what ways were these false teachers being deceptive? How have you seen such deception in our day?
4. Why can't false teachers deliver on their promises?
5. Jude seems to be reacting pretty strongly against false teaching. What's so dangerous about what they are saying?
6. How does Jude use the idea of fruitlessness to accuse the false teachers? Where else does Scripture connect the fruit of one's life to one's true character?

7. Since Jude cites 1 Enoch, should we consider that book to be authoritative Scripture? Why or why not?
8. How does Enoch describe the coming judgment?
9. What can we learn about a teacher from his or her audience? Is there always a direct connection between the messenger, the message, and the hearers?
10. In what ways is Jesus the opposite of these false teachers? How can we see this in Scripture?

Godly Wisdom for a Healthy Christian

JUDE 17-23

Main Idea: Since there will always be false teachings, Christians should diligently watch for false teachers and seek to rescue all from their destructive message, even as they eagerly await the return of Christ.

I.   **Remember the Words of Our Lord (17-19).**
  A. The presence of false teachers is certain (17-18).
  B. The portrait of false teachers is clear (18-19).
    1. They are scoffers (18).
    2. They are sensual (18-19).
    3. They are schismatic (19).
    4. They are Spiritless (19).
II. **Remain in the Watch Care of God's Love (20-21).**
  A. Grow in the Scriptures (20).
  B. Pray in the Spirit (20).
  C. Wait for the Savior (21).
III. **Rescue the Wandering Who Are Lost (22-23).**
  A. Deal gently with those who doubt (22).
  B. Deal quickly with those who are in danger (23).
  C. Deal carefully with those who are defiled (23).

False teaching and heresy can be painful, but they can also be helpful. They may be a nuisance, but they are also inevitable. In the New Testament and the early church period, the emergence of false teaching helped Christians clarify several key doctrines, in particular the doctrines of Christ (Christology), the Holy Spirit (pneumatology), salvation (soteriology), and the end times (eschatology). Despite the challenge it caused Christians, heresy forced the church to think more clearly about Christ, to focus on the central Christian message, the gospel, and eventually to identify the canon of Scripture.

Today heresy continues to orbit about us, shooting forth from every conceivable direction its meteors of deception and error. Sometimes the heresy comes from the culture in the form of "lost" gospels or political reinterpretations of Jesus's message or psychoanalytic theories of Jesus's death and resurrection. We've been hearing for years that Jesus wasn't the founder of Christianity; Paul was. And we've been informed countless times that a virgin birth is scientifically impossible and Christians should "get with the program," as if the writers of the New Testament were completely ignorant of how basic human reproduction works. The theories come and they go, but they always come back again.

Sometimes, however, heresy may emerge within our own ranks. It may come from theological liberals who discard elements of the faith once for all delivered to the saints as they acquiesce to the whims of the culture. Consider Kirby Godsey, former president of Mercer University, who in his book *Centering Our Souls* writes,

> Jesus' death was not some cosmic drama by which Jesus was trying to appease God's wrath. Jesus did not have to die for God's grace to be released upon a torn and crippled world.
> . . .
>   We do not have to repent, or to confess. We don't have to do anything to win God's forgiveness. . . . When the light breaks, we begin to see people, friends and enemies, as children of God's grace. (Godsey, *Centering Our Souls*, 12, 46–47)

Or consider the bizarre event that took place several years ago in Austin, Texas, when avowed atheist and journalism professor Robert Jensen joined St. Andrew's Presbyterian Church. Jensen said of himself, "So, I am a Christian, sort of. A secular Christian. A Christian atheist perhaps. But, in a deep sense, I would argue, a real Christian." Rather than rejecting the membership application of this admitted unbeliever, Jim Rigby stated, "Neither the church nor Jensen views his membership as surrendering anything. . . . If God wanted us to simply recite creeds, Jesus would have come as a parrot" (cited in Mohler, "Why He Is Not a Christian"). We could go on, reciting endless versions of "Christianity" that promise health, wealth, and happiness in this life if we would only have enough faith. Or we could consider open theists who attempt to save God from the predicament of evil's existence by arguing that God either cannot or will not know the future. All of this one way or another is spiritually sick and theologically wrongheaded. But the questions remain, What do we do? What is the answer? Jude would respond, "We need godly wisdom to be a healthy Christian," and that is exactly what he gives us in verses 17-23. His prescription for what spiritually ails us will revolve around three ideas: remember, remain, and rescue.

Remember the Words of Our Lord
JUDE 17-19

Jude's letter shifts gears in verse 17, signaled by the words "dear friends." Jude moves from the "these people," the false teachers (v. 16), to the "you" of the believing community. The "you" is emphatic, and what follows is the first imperative in the letter, though four more will follow in rapid-fire succession. Jude says, "Remember!" Remember two important truths.

The Presence of False Teachers Is Certain (17-18)

By means of his apostles, our Lord (deity) Jesus (humanity) Christ (God's Messiah, the Anointed One) had warned that false teachers would come. Indeed, they warned us that scoffers would appear specifically in the last times. Jesus warned us in Matthew 7:15-23; 24:11,14. Paul warned us in Acts 20:29-30; 1 Timothy 4:1-3; and 2 Timothy 3:1-9. Peter warned us in 2 Peter 2:1-3,12-22. John also warned us in 1 John 2:18-23; 4:1-3. And Jude warns us through his whole letter. In effect, the false teachers' presence is a confirmation of Scripture's truth.

The Portrait of False Teachers Is Clear (18-19)

Jude provides a fourfold picture of these wolves in sheeps' clothing, these diabolical masqueraders who manipulate and worm their way into our community of faith. The portrait is not pretty.

They are scoffers (v. 18). Jude calls them mockers or scoffers. The NEB says they are "men who pour scorn on religion." Peter says they scoffed at the reality of Jesus's return (2 Pet 3:4). Jude says they laugh at, sneer at, and make light of God's holiness and moral perfection. They joke about God's righteous character and have no reverence for his purity.

They are sensual (vv. 18-19). Mocking God's law and moral precepts, these men walk according to their own ungodly lust. Echoing verse 16, Jude adds that following after and being controlled by their lust, they pursue anything that pleases their selfish desires. They live on the earthly plane, not the heavenly. They are not spiritual but carnal. For them lust is lord. Passion is their sovereign dictator.

They are schismatic (v. 19). Satan loves to divide, rip, and tear apart. These evil emissaries follow their master and cause divisions. Like Diotrephes in 3 John, they promote and foster strife instead of unity. Lacking respect for spiritual leaders, making sport of moral conviction, and lampooning theological distinctives, they can demolish in a day what took a decade to build. The application for the church regarding such divisive teachers is clear: When you see them coming, don't let them in! When you see them within, get them out!

They are Spiritless (v. 19). The last characteristic is the most telling and tragic. These persons are lost, unregenerate, "not having the Spirit." Romans 8:9 says, "If anyone does not have the Spirit of Christ, he does not belong to him." They claim Christ but do not know him. They boast of the Spirit, but their lives betray their confession. They are spiritual frauds, religious shams. As Titus 1:16 says, "They claim to know God, but they deny him by their works."

The presence of false teachers is certain. Jude helpfully provides this portrait of false teachers so that we may confidently identify them.

Remain in the Watch Care of God's Love
JUDE 20-21

Jude now lays down a game plan, a spiritual strategy for the nurturing of a healthy Christian. His formula is basic, but it is certain to work if carefully followed and put into practice.

The grammar of these verses is fascinating: Jude anchors his instruction with the imperative "keep" and then sets in place three participles that explain how we keep ourselves in the love of God. Schreiner is most certainly correct in spotting an implicit Trinitarianism in the text (*1, 2 Peter*, 481). Yes, perseverance is a Trinitarian work, but what is our role? How do we keep our love for him grounded in his love for us and his work on our behalf?

Grow in the Scriptures (20)

The participles *building, praying,* and *waiting* have an imperatival force because they are linked to the main command. First, Jude admonishes his readers to "build yourselves up in your most holy faith." The faith "that was delivered to the saints once for all" (v. 3) has become *their* faith, and it alone is the foundation on which to build. Ephesians 2:20 affirms that our foundation is "the apostles and prophets, with Christ

Jesus himself as the cornerstone." Christ and his gospel, found in the Scriptures, is our foundation. God and his Word are the sure rock on which we stand. From here we grow and mature as the Word permeates our minds and fills our hearts. As we learn the Bible and understand its truth, we are strengthened, we grow, we mature, we are built up. Without the Scriptures there is no growth. Without the Word there is no maturity. Without the gospel nothing of eternal good will last. Like the air we breathe, the water we drink, and the food we eat, it is vital that we daily ingest and digest God's Word and its truth.

Pray in the Spirit (20)

"Praying in the Holy Spirit" is the second plank of our spiritual strategy for spiritual health. This is not speaking of "praying in tongues." A good connection is found in Ephesians 6:18, where the apostle Paul says, "Pray at all times in the Spirit with every prayer and request." Praying in the Spirit means we will pray for God's will to be done, not our will. This practice will keep us close to God, and it will keep us in the sphere and presence of his love. Jude contrasts false teachers who do not have the Spirit with those who can pray in the Spirit. Because we are the temple of the Holy Spirit (1 Cor 6:19-20), the presence of God resides and lives in us, guiding us, convicting us, even praying for us (Rom 8:26).

Building up is our *edification*. Praying in the Spirit is our *communion*. Looking for the Savior, which comes next, is our *anticipation*.

Wait for the Savior (21)

"Waiting" has the idea of watching—looking expectantly and with certainty. As Christians we do not have to wonder if Jesus is coming again; we *know* he is coming again. As 1 Thessalonians 4:16 says, "For the Lord himself will descend from heaven with a shout, with the archangel's voice, and with the trumpet of God." Titus 2:13 calls this "the blessed hope." Jude says it is a coming of mercy unto eternal life through our Lord Jesus Christ (cf. vv. 14,17). The mercy Jude prayed in verse 2 would be multiplied at that time will be realized as the eastern sky is split wide open and the King of glory comes in; the Lord, strong and mighty, the Lord, mighty in battle (Ps 24:7-8).

The Christian's heart and eyes are fixed heavenward, looking for a rider on a white horse whose name is Faithful and True, whose eyes are like a fiery flame, and on his head are many crowns. We are looking for one whose robe is dipped in blood, and on his thigh he has a name written: King of kings and Lord of lords (cf. Rev 19:11-16). Until then we will grow in his Word, pray by his Spirit, and watch for his coming.

Rescue the Wandering Who Are Lost
JUDE 22-23

According to the North American Mission Board, 95 percent of Southern Baptists—my own people—*never* verbally share the gospel with a lost person. Never! They never tell someone how to be saved. They never share the gospel even once in their lifetime. In 1950 the ratio of members to baptisms was 19 to 1; in 2004 it was 42 to 1 ("ACP Analyst," 44). George Barna has said American Christians have "commitment issues." He sees us "lowering the bar on Church commitment" and the emergence of a "soft Christianity." He writes,

> Americans are willing to expend some energy in religious
> activities such as attending church and reading the Bible,
> and they are willing to throw some money in the offering
> basket. Because of such activities, they convince themselves
> that they are people of genuine faith. But when it comes time
> to truly establishing their priorities and making a tangible
> commitment to knowing and loving God, and to allowing
> Him to change their character and lifestyle, most people stop
> short. We want to be "spiritual" and we want to have God's
> favor, but we're not sure we want Him taking control of our
> lives and messing with the image and outcomes we've worked
> so hard to produce. (Barna, "Americans Have Commitment
> Issues")

Did you notice no mention of soul winning, sharing the gospel, or doing the work of an evangelist? In light of such an analysis, we would do well to remind ourselves that the Son of Man came on a rescue mission for lost, dying, wandering souls, to seek and save the lost (Luke 19:10). If we do not care if people are saved, we might also well consider whether *we* are saved.

A love for Christ will compel us to have a love for the lost—those who come in all kinds of national, ethnic, racial, and social groups. Jude notes in particular three classes of people we must seek to rescue and the strategy by which we carry out our mission.

Deal Gently with Those Who Doubt (22)

Verses 22-23 are a land mine of textual issues. The basic meaning is clear, but the details are a challenge. Both the ESV and CSB see three groups in view (whereas some translations identify two), and they also capture best, in my judgment, the sense of the author's meaning.

Jude calls us to have mercy (NKJV, "compassion") on those who doubt. Those who have mercy multiplied in Christ (v. 2) and receive that mercy in its fullness at his coming (v. 21) are to extend that same mercy to those who doubt, waver, or struggle with the truth of the gospel and Holy Scripture because of the influence of false teaching. Such persons should not be rejected or ignored, ridiculed or harassed. With compassion and conviction, kindness and firmness, mercy and concern, we encourage them in the truth, patiently pointing them to Jesus and his all-sufficiency.

Deal Quickly with Those Who Are in Danger (23)

A second group faces an even more serious and precarious situation, so close are they to the fires of hell and eternal condemnation. Jude quickly interjects, "Save others by snatching them from the fire." Sounding the alarm, Jude calls for quick and decisive action. It is almost too late; they are almost too far gone. However, there is still time to rescue them, but we must act now. There is urgency in Jude's voice. There is a heightened concern in his heart. I suspect there is a tear in his eye.

Hell is not a popular subject. People don't want to talk or even think about it. Many, even in the church, act as if it is not real. They think if we ignore it, it will just go away. We, however, must never forget as long as we live: given enough time, every person will one day believe in hell. Sometimes confrontational evangelism is necessary. Sometimes it is our only hope!

Deal Carefully with Those Who Are Defiled (23)

This third group is in the most desperate condition of all. Having bought into the lies of false teaching, their lives are now corrupted as well. Both in how they think and how they live, they are corrupt, defiled, and depraved. They are a danger to themselves, but they are also a danger to others. Jude, therefore, sounds a wise word of warning: "Have mercy on others but with fear, hating even the garment defiled by the flesh."

The word picture is vivid and striking. Sin has stained and contaminated these persons. Love them, show mercy, but don't get too close, for even their clothes can defile you if you are not careful. They are carriers of a spiritual disease; sin has broken out all over them. We may still be able to reach them and rescue them, but we cannot get too close, nor can we become like them.

It is a lie of Satan that says we have to live like the lost to reach the lost—I have to drink like them, curse like them, party like them, be like them. The opposite was true in my own life. My friends opened up to my witness when Jesus changed me at the age of nineteen. They saw the difference Jesus made in my life, and then and only then were they willing to let me tell them about the Christ who changed me and could change them. A number of areas in my life came to a screeching halt, never to appear again. This did not terminate our friendship. It did cause them to wonder, *What happened to him?* In mercy and love, maintaining a distance of wisdom, I told them about my Jesus.

So we deal with some gently, with some quickly, and with some carefully. But, dear brothers and sisters, we must deal with all we can in one way or another before it is too late.

Conclusion

William Booth was the founder of the Salvation Army. Booth is often credited with saying,

> If I had my way, I would not send my workers to four years
> of college. If I had my way, I would not put them through
> three years of seminary. If I had my way, I would put all
> of my workers in hell for five minutes! That would be the
> best theological training they would ever receive. (Source
> unknown)

Lost people matter to God; lost people must matter to us. Healthy Christians remember the words of our Lord, and they remain in his love. And they rescue the perishing and care for the dying. They understand life is short, time is limited, and heaven and hell are real.

Reflect and Discuss

1. How can false teaching be a blessing to the church? How can we see such blessings in church history?

2. What attacks on orthodox Christianity have you seen come from the culture around us?

3. What attacks on orthodox Christianity have you seen come from those who claim to be believers?

4. Discuss the portrait of a false teacher as described in this text. What might each of the four characteristics look like in today's context?

5. If God ultimately preserves the Christian, how can believers keep themselves in the love of God?

6. What role do the Scriptures play in the believer's perseverance? What role do they play in your life?

7. What does it mean to pray in the Holy Spirit?

8. How can the church be a merciful place for those who struggle with doubts about their faith? What doubts have you had, and how has the Lord responded?

9. Who should be "snatched from the fire"? Why does Jude use such urgent language?

10. What does it look like to have mercy on someone, even while being careful not to be defiled by them? Does this mean Christians should withdraw from the world?

The Doxology of God and the Security of the Believer

JUDE 24-25

Main Idea: Christians are saved by the grace of God in Christ, and they are preserved for all eternity because God in Christ saves them eternally.

I. Believers Are Secure in the Power of God (24).
   A. God will preserve us.
   B. God will protect us.
II. Believers Are Secure in the Promise of God (24).
   A. We will see his glory.
   B. We will share his joy.
III. Believers Are Secure in the Person of God (25).
   A. He is our Sovereign.
   B. He is our Savior.
IV. Believers Are Secure in the Praise of God (25).
   A. Praise him for his glory forever.
   B. Praise him for his majesty forever.
   C. Praise him for his power forever.
   D. Praise him for his authority forever.

Few doctrines of Scripture are more precious and comforting than the doctrine of eternal security. Spurgeon said, "If there is one doctrine I have preached more than another, it is the doctrine of the perseverance of the saints even to the end" ("Perseverance without Presumption"). *The Abstract of Principles,* penned by Basil Manly Jr. in 1858, addresses this wonderful doctrine in article XIII, titled "Perseverance of the Saints":

> Those whom God hath accepted in the Beloved, and sanctified by His Spirit, will never totally nor finally fall away from the state of grace, but shall certainly persevere to the end; and though they may fall, through neglect and temptation, into sin, whereby they grieve the Spirit, impair their graces and comforts, bring reproach on the Church, and temporal

judgments on themselves, yet they shall be renewed again unto repentance, and be kept by the power of God through faith unto salvation. (See Works Cited.)

The Baptist Faith and Message 2000 also speaks to this issue in article V on "God's Purpose of Grace." It repeats much of the language of *The Abstract of Principles*. It states in paragraph 2,

All true believers endure to the end. Those whom God has accepted in Christ, and sanctified by His Spirit, will never fall away from the state of grace, but shall persevere to the end. Believers may fall into sin through neglect and temptation, whereby they grieve the Spirit, impair their graces and comforts, and bring reproach on the cause of Christ and temporal judgments on themselves; yet they shall be kept by the power of God through faith unto salvation. (See Works Cited.)

I believe the doctrine of eternal security is absolutely necessary to a correct understanding of the gospel and the truth of the Bible's concept of eternal or everlasting life. The bottom line is this: If it can be lost, it is not eternal; if I can lose it, it is not everlasting; if I can work my way out of salvation, my salvation is ultimately dependent on me and not God. If I can lose it, my confidence, comfort, and hope are pulled out from beneath me, and I am suspended in uncertainty as to my final destiny.

Fortunately the Bible addresses the doctrine of our security clearly and repeatedly. In John 10:27-30 Jesus says,

My sheep hear my voice, I know them, and they follow me. I give them eternal life, and they will never perish. No one will snatch them out of my hand. My Father, who has given them to me, is greater than all. No one is able to snatch them out of the Father's hand. I and the Father are one.

In Romans 8:38-39 Paul writes,

For I am persuaded that neither death nor life, nor angels nor rulers, nor things present nor things to come, nor powers, nor height nor depth, nor any other created thing will be able to separate us from the love of God that is in Christ Jesus our Lord.

In Ephesians 1:13-14 Paul adds,

In him you also were sealed with the promised Holy Spirit when you heard the word of truth, the gospel of your salvation, and when you believed. The Holy Spirit is the down payment of our inheritance, until the redemption of the possession, to the praise of his glory.

The author of Hebrews writes,

Therefore, he is able to save completely those who come to God through him, since he always lives to intercede for them. (Heb 7:25)

In Hebrews 13:5 he states further,

Keep your life free from the love of money. Be satisfied with what you have, for he himself has said, I will never leave you or abandon you.

In 1 John 2:19 the beloved disciple writes,

They went out from us, but they did not belong to us; for if they had belonged to us, they would have remained with us. However, they went out so that it might be made clear that none of them belongs to us.

And in 1 John 5:13 he affirms,

I have written these things to you who believe in the name of the Son of God so that you may know that you have eternal life.

Now to all of this Jude adds, in a glorious doxology of worship, praise, and adoration, that our God "is able to protect [us] from stumbling," and that our God will "make [us] stand in the presence of his glory, without blemish and with great joy." Thus the praise of God and the perseverance of the believer are joined in a tightly woven piece of spiritual cloth never to be torn or separated.

Limiting ourselves to just these two verses, we can see at least four biblical reasons to believe in the eternal security of the believer.

Believers Are Secure in the Power of God
JUDE 24

Every theology of salvation will either start with God or with man; it will be either theocentric or anthropocentric. The author of Hebrews reminds us that Jesus is the author and finisher of faith (Heb 12:2). Jude began his epistles telling us we are "kept for Jesus Christ" (v. 1). Now he closes by telling us we are kept from stumbling and falling prey to false teaching by "him who is able."

God Will Preserve Us

God has power to keep us from stumbling. "Protect" has the idea of "guard" or "preserve." Yes, we are to keep ourselves in the sphere of God's love (v. 21), but our Lord keeps us from "stumbling" or falling. The Greek philosopher Xenophon used the word for a sure-footed horse who does not stumble, and the Stoic Epictetus used it to speak of a good man who does not lapse morally (Vaughan and Lea, *1, 2 Peter*, 234). God watches over us and by his omnipotent power keeps us from falling into the error and the sin of false teachers. He preserves us in Christ.

God Will Protect Us

He will keep "you" from stumbling. The promise is personal and individual, corporate and all-encompassing for every child of God. The one who preserves us is God. The one who protects us from stumbling is our Father. We are related to him who has the sovereign power to keep us. We are under his Fatherly care, which protects us from falling away. Hebrews 12:5-13 is so helpful here. There the author of Hebrews explains that even God's discipline shows his vested interest in preserving those he loves. Discipline is a sign of our security.

Believers Are Secure in the Promise of God
JUDE 24

My eternal security as a Christian is grounded in God's power, not mine. Likewise, my eternal security is grounded in God's promise, not mine. In the latter part of verse 24, there is a truly magnificent promise of hope and assurance. We will be kept from stumbling by "him who is able"—God. Kept where? Kept for what? These are great questions with equally great answers.

We Will See His Glory

Because he keeps us from stumbling, he will present us "without blemish." Being unblemished means we are faultless, irreproachable. The same idea is applied to Jesus in 1 Peter 1:19, where he is said to be "an unblemished and spotless lamb." In the same way that God looked on his sinless Son, whom he placed on the cross as our sacrifice, so he will look on you and me. He will see us as sinless, faultless, and clothed in the imputed righteousness of Christ. But now note the place of this presentation: "in the presence of his glory." We will not simply stand faultless; we will stand faultless before the presence of the glory of God. Because of his promise to bring our salvation to completion, we will see his glory. We will know his glory. We will enjoy his glory forever. This will be our joy.

We Will Share His Joy

Jude says in his presence, as we see and experience his glory, there will be great, exceeding joy. There will be a celebration with rejoicing and exulting. In Revelation 19 we catch a glimpse of this joy in the marriage supper of the Lamb. Four times there is the shout, "Hallelujah," and verse 7 tells us why: "Let us be glad, rejoice, and give him glory, because the marriage of the Lamb has come, and his bride has prepared herself." What a promise of security!

Believers Are Secure in the Person of God
JUDE 25

Eternal security has its source in the person and character of God. An intimate, personal, and biblical understanding of God will aid our assurance and confirm our confidence in the Lord who saves and saves completely.

He Is Our Sovereign

He is the only God, the *monō theō*. Paul tells us in 1 Timothy 1:17 he is "the King eternal, immortal, invisible, the only God." Jude is quick and concise. He is the only God, the only Lord, the only Sovereign to whom and with whom we must reckon and give an account. All will stand before him. None will escape. He is our sovereign. But, for those who know him, he is more still.

He Is Our Savior

Jude tells us this God is "our Savior." Our God is a saving God. He is a saving Father, saving Son, and saving Spirit. The Father saves us, the Son secures us, and the Spirit seals us. God did not save me to lose me. He saved me to keep me. That is the kind of God he is.

Believers Are Secure in the Praise of God
JUDE 25

Jude brings this short but powerful letter to a close with a doxology, a word of praise to the only God who is our Savior through Jesus Christ our Lord. A fourfold acknowledgment of the greatness and awesomeness of God is made. A quick look at each is instructive, especially since Jude charges us to recognize these truths about our God "before all time, now and forever."

Praise Him for His Glory Forever

"Glory" is *doxa* in Greek, from which we get our word *doxology*. Glory is the honor rightly ascribed to God for who he is and what he has done. It is the outshining of his character and nature. In one sense glory is not what God has but what God is. James Merritt well says,

> Glory is an attribute that is inherent and intrinsic to God. Glory is as essential to God as light is to the sun, as blue is to the sky, as wet is to water. You do not make the sun light, it is light. You do not make the sky blue, it is blue. You do not make the water wet, it is wet. Likewise, you do not make God glorious, God is glorious. You do not really give God glory; you acknowledge the glory that God already has. (Unpublished sermon notes for "No Doubt about It: Jude 24-25")

Glory is indeed the outward manifestation of the inner essence and character of our God. It is what he is, and we will spend eternity extolling him because of his glorious goodness.

Praise Him for His Majesty Forever

"Majesty" is *megalosunē* in Greek. It speaks of our Lord's greatness, his awesome and marvelous transcendence, his status as the King and Sovereign over all. It is his greatness being loosed and spread throughout all of his creation.

Praise Him for His Power Forever

"Power" or dominion is *kratos* in Greek. It speaks of his control over all creation. Our God is omnipotent, capable of doing anything consistent with his character and attributes. He is not limited by might, space, or time. The past is his, the future is his, and the present is his.

Praise Him for His Authority Forever

"Authority" is the Greek word *exousia*. Moo says it is God's "intrinsic right to rule all things" (*2 Peter*, 301). It informs us that all things are in his hands. It is humbling to think that the same truth that children learn in Sunday school—"He's got the whole world in his hands"—will inspire us to worship for eternity.

God's authority means the world is not running willy-nilly out of control, in a course with no direction, with no one at the helm. Human extinction is not a possibility because he has all things in his hands. Nuclear annihilation is not a possibility because he has all things in his hands. Evangelistic defect is not a possibility because he has all things in his hands. Missionary failure is not a possibility because he has all things in his hands. Losing my salvation is not a possibility because he has all things (including me) in his hands.

In the end our God wins! He is glorious and majestic. He has dominion and power. *For his glory* he will keep me. *In his majesty* he will keep me. *Through his power* he will keep me. *By his authority* he will keep me. Hallelujah! What a Savior!

Conclusion

I conclude with a word of practical application. It's worth considering why people lack assurance, doubting their eternal security. I believe there are at least five possible reasons this is such a troubling issue for many Christians today. There may be

1. faulty understanding of the fact that it is God who does the saving;
2. faulty methods of assurance at the time of salvation (works, tongues, etc.);
3. doubt of God's faithfulness to keep his word;
4. lack of proper teaching on the Christian life; or
5. presence of sin in one's life.

What can we do to help people settle the issue and gain the security they should experience in Christ? First, we must look to the cross and use God's Word, remembering two crucial truths: by his work on the cross Jesus *obtained* my salvation, and by his work in heaven Jesus *maintains* my salvation. Second, we can ask questions about their experience of the Christian life. These questions are not complicated theological tests but the basics of the normal Christian life:

1. Do you believe the gospel and trust Christ?
2. Do you experience remorse over sin and have a desire to please God?
3. Do you see any evidence of fruit in your life?
4. Does the Holy Spirit witness to your spirit that you are a child of God?
5. When you sin, do you experience the discipline of the Father?

Someone who is walking with Christ and trusting in his gospel has good reason to rest in the preserving grace of God. Augustus Montague Toplady said it beautifully:

> My name from the palms of His hands eternity will not erase;
> Impressed on His heart it remains, in marks of indelible grace.
> Yes, I to the end shall endure, as sure as the earnest is giv'n;
> More happy, but not more secure, the glorified spirits in
>   heav'n. ("A Debtor to Mercy Alone," 1771)

Psalm 37:23-24 provides a fitting final and encouraging word:

> *A person's steps are established by the LORD,*
>   *and he takes pleasure in his way.*
> *Though he falls, he will not be overwhelmed,*
>   *because the LORD supports him with his hand.*

Secure in him. Secure forever.

Reflect and Discuss

1. How does the idea that you can lose your salvation relate to works-based righteousness?
2. Can eternal life be lost? Why or why not?
3. How does God's power ensure the believer's security? Does it matter if we are weak and sinful?
4. What promises of God guarantee the perseverance of God's people? Where do you find them in Scripture?
5. What other characteristics of God speak to the believer's security in salvation?

6. What is the connection between God's preserving work and the praise he receives from his people?

7. What might be misleading about the oft-used phrase, "once saved, always saved"?

8. Consider the five possible reasons someone might doubt their security in Christ. Have you struggled with any of these?

9. How does the presence of sin in the Christian's life affect his or her eternal security? How does it affect assurance of security?

10. Write your own psalm, expressing praise to God for his saving and preserving work.

WORKS CITED

"ACP Analyst Reflects on SBC Trends." *Facts & Trends*, May/June 2006, 43–47.

The Baptist Faith and Message. Accessed January 30, 2015, at http://www.sbc.net/bfm2000/bfm2000.asp

Barna, George. "Americans Have Commitment Issues, New Survey Shows." November 30, 1999. Accessed January 30, 2015, at https://www.barna.org/culture-articles/155-americans-have-commitment-issues-new-survey-shows.

———. "One-Quarter of Self-Described Born Again Adults Rely on Means Other Than Grace to Get to Heaven." November 29, 2005. Accessed January 29, 2015, at http://www.barna.org/FlexPage.aspx?Page=BarnaUpdate&BarnaUpdateID=204.

Bauckham, Richard J. *2 Peter and Jude*. Word Biblical Commentary. Waco: Word, 1983.

Beck, Hartmut, and Colin Brown. "Peace." In *The New International Dictionary of New Testament Theology*, edited by Colin Brown, 2:776–83. Grand Rapids, MI: Zondervan, 1975.

Carson, D. A. *The Difficult Doctrine of the Love of God*. Wheaton, IL: Crossway, 1999.

———. *Love in Hard Places*. Wheaton, IL: Crossway, 2002.

Davids, Peter H. *The Letters of 2 Peter and Jude*. Pillar New Testament Commentary. Grand Rapids: Eerdmans, 2006.

Dodd, C. H. *The Johannine Epistles*. Moffatt New Testament Commentary. New York: Harper & Brothers, 1946.

Duncan, J. Ligon. "The Contradiction of Ungodliness." Sermon preached at First Presbyterian Church of Jackson, TN, on May 23, 2004. Accessed January 29, 2015, at http://www.fpcjackson.org/resource-library/sermons/the-contradiction-of-ungodliness.

Elliott, Ralph H. *The Genesis Controversy and Continuity in Southern Baptist Chaos: A Eulogy for a Great Tradition.* Macon, GA: Mercer University Press, 1992.

Gaebelein, Frank E. *The Meaning of Inspiration.* Downers Grove, IL: InterVarsity, 1950.

George, Timothy. *Amazing Grace: God's Pursuit, Our Response.* Wheaton, IL: Crossway, 2011.

Godsey, R. Kirby. *Centering Our Souls: Devotional Reflections of a University President.* Macon, GA: Mercer University Press, 2005.

Green, Gene L. *Jude and 2 Peter.* The Baker Exegetical Commentary. Grand Rapids: Baker, 2008.

Green, Michael. *2 Peter and Jude.* Tyndale New Testament Commentary. Downers Grove, IL: InterVarsity, 1987.

Helm, David. *1 & 2 Peter and Jude.* Preaching the Word Commentary. Wheaton, IL: Crossway, 2008.

Hernando, James D. *Dictionary of Hermeneutics.* Springfield, MO: Gospel Publishing House, 2005.

Hewitt, Hugh. "Reality TV." *WORLD,* January 28, 2006. Accessed March 15, 2018, at http://www.worldmag.com/2006/01/reality_tv.

Hick, John. *Death and Eternal Life.* Louisville: Westminster/John Knox, 1994.

Hoder, Randye. "Sex Education for Parents Too." *Los Angeles Times,* February 13, 2006. Accessed March 15, 2018, at http://articles .latimes.com/2006/feb/13/opinion/oe-hoder13.

Luther, Martin. *Commentary on Peter & Jude.* Grand Rapids: Kregel, 1990.

MacArthur, John, Jr. *2 Peter and Jude.* The MacArthur New Testament Commentary. Chicago: Moody, 2005.

Manly, Basil, Jr. "Abstract of Principles." Accessed March 15, 2017, at http://www.theopedia.com/abstract-of-principles-baptist.

Mohler, R. Albert, Jr. "Why He Is Not a Christian—an Atheist Joins a Church." *AlbertMohler.com.* Accessed January 30, 2015, at http:// www.albertmohler.com/2006/05/01/why-he-is-not-a-christian -an-atheist-joins-a-church.

Moo, Douglas J. *2 Peter, Jude.* NIV Application Commentary. Grand Rapids, MI: Zondervan, 1996.

Pinnock, Clark. "The Destruction of the Finally Impenitent." *Criswell Theological Review,* No. 4 (Spring 1990): 243–59.

Plowman, Edward E. "Beginnings and Ends." *WORLD*, December 3, 2005. Accessed March 15, 2018, at http://www.worldmag.com/2005/12 /beginnings_and_ends.

Rogers, Adrian. "Battle for the Bible: A Fight for the Faith." A sermon preached at Bellevue Baptist Church on May 6, 1998. Accessed March 15, 2017, at https://adrianrogerslibrary.com/wp-content /uploads/2016/08/Jude-2016.pdf.

————. "Snakes in the Garden." A sermon preached at Bellevue Baptist Church on March 10, 1985. Accessed March 15, 2017, at https:// adrianrogerslibrary.com/wp-content/uploads/2016/08/Jude -2016.pdf.

Russell, Bertrand. *Why I Am Not a Christian.* New York: Simon and Schuster, 1964.

Schreiner, Thomas R. *1 and 2 Peter, Jude.* New American Commentary. Nashville: B&H, 2003.

Shimron, Yonat. "Evangelist Stirs Hope at RBC Revival." *News & Observer.* Accessed January 29, 2015, at http://www.newsobserver. com/2006/01/28/83608/evangelist-stirs-hope-at-rbc-revival.html.

Spurgeon, Charles Haddon. "Perseverance without Presumption." A sermon preached at the Metropolitan Tabernacle on March 7, 1872. Accessed January 29, 2015, at http://www.spurgeongems. org/vols16-18/chs1056.pdf.

Starr, J. M. *Sharers in Divine Nature: 2 Peter 1:4 in Its Hellenistic Context.* Coniectanea Neotestamentica or Coniectanea Biblica: New Testament Series 33. Stockholm: Almqvist & Wiksell, 2000.

Vaughan, Curtis, and Thomas D. Lea. *1, 2 Peter, Jude.* The Bible Study Commentary. Grand Rapids: Zondervan, 1988.

SCRIPTURE INDEX